THE FUSE™

VOL 4 · CONSTANT ORBITAL REVOLUTIONS

WRITER · ANTONY JOHNSTON

ARTIST · JUSTIN GREENWOOD

COLORIST · SHARI CHANKHAMMA

LETTERER · RYAN FERRIER

image

fusecomic.com

FUSE CREATED BY JOHNSTON & GREENWOOD

IMAGE COMICS, INC.
Robert Kirkman—Chief Operating Officer
Erik Larsen—Chief Financial Officer
Todd McFarlane—President
Marc Silvestri—Chief Executive Officer
Jim Valentino—Vice-President

Eric Stephenson—Publisher
Corey Murphy—Director of Sales
Jeff Boison—Director of Publishing Planning & Book Trade Sales
Chris Ross—Director of Digital Sales
Kat Salazar—Director of PR & Marketing
Branwyn Bigglestone—Controller
Susan Korpela—Accounts Manager
Drew Gill—Art Director
Brett Warnock—Production Manager
Meredith Wallace—Print Manager
Briah Skelly—Publicist
Aly Hoffman—Conventions & Events Coordinator
Sasha Head—Sales & Marketing Production Designer
David Brothers—Branding Manager
Melissa Gifford—Content Manager
Erika Schnatz—Production Artist
Ryan Brewer—Production Artist
Shanna Matuszak—Production Artist
Tricia Ramos—Production Artist
Vincent Kukua—Production Artist
Jeff Stang—Direct Market Sales Representative
Emilio Bautista—Digital Sales Associate
Leanna Caunter—Accounting Assistant
Chloe Ramos-Peterson—Library Market Sales Representative
IMAGECOMICS.COM

THE FUSE VOL 4: CONSTANT ORBITAL REVOLUTIONS. First printing. Feb 2017.

ISBN: 978-1-5343-0040-8. Contains material originally published in magazine form as THE FUSE #19-24. Published by Image Comics, Inc. Office of publication: 2701 NW Vaughn St., Suite 780, Portland, OR 97210.

Printed in the U.S.A. For information regarding the CPSIA on this printed material call: 203-595-3636 and provide reference # RICH–720405. For international rights, contact: foreignlicensing@imagecomics.com

THE FUSE™

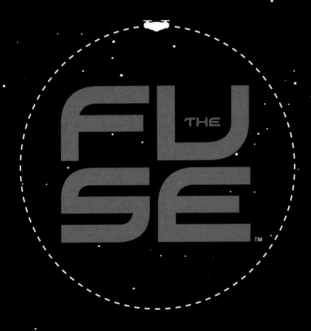

REQUEST FOR RETIREMENT

P A R T   1

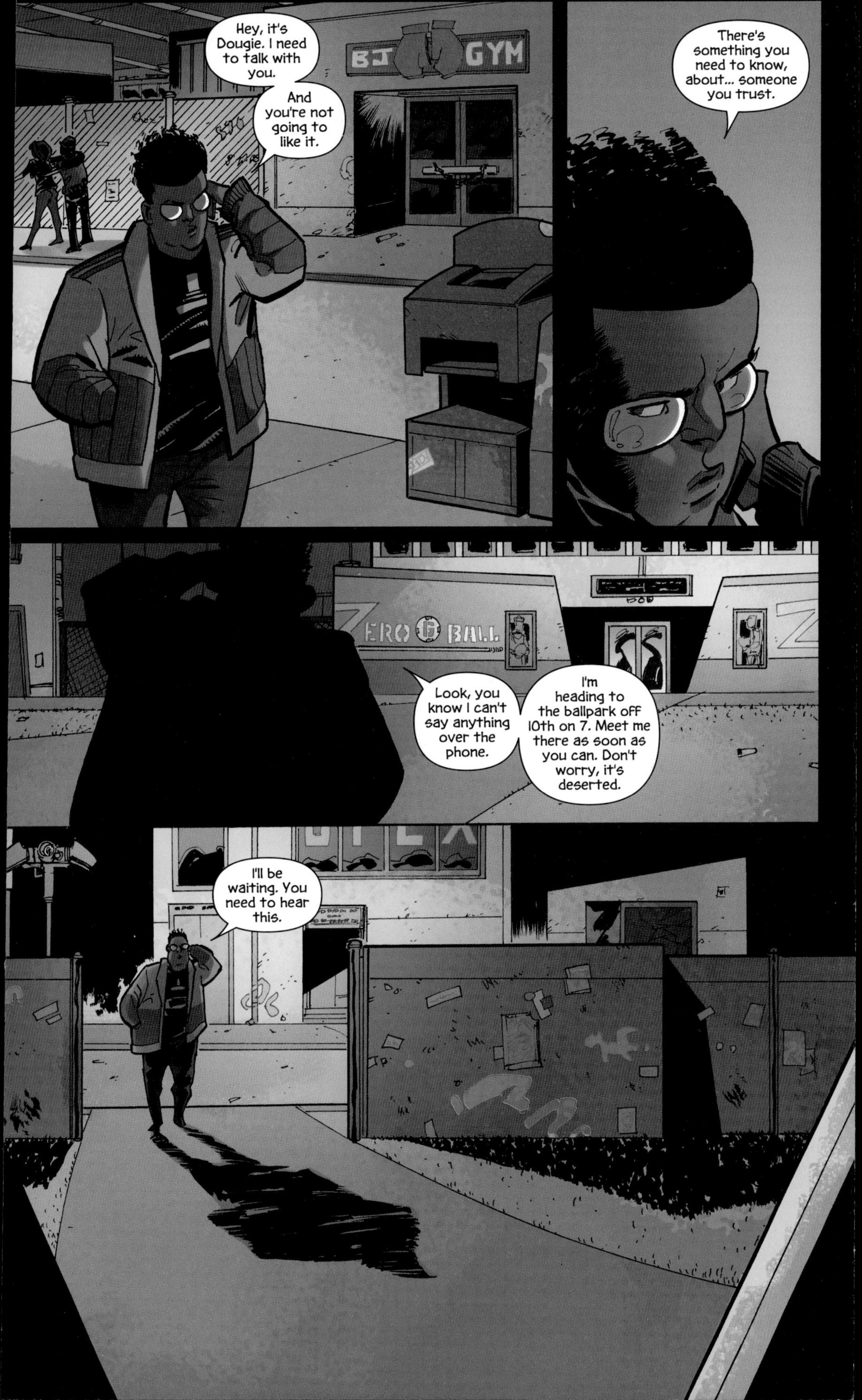
BJ GYM
Hey, it's Dougie. I need to talk with you.
And you're not going to like it.
There's something you need to know, about... someone you trust.
ZERO G BALL
Look, you know I can't say anything over the phone.
I'm heading to the ballpark off 10th on 7. Meet me there as soon as you can. Don't worry, it's deserted.
I'll be waiting. You need to hear this.

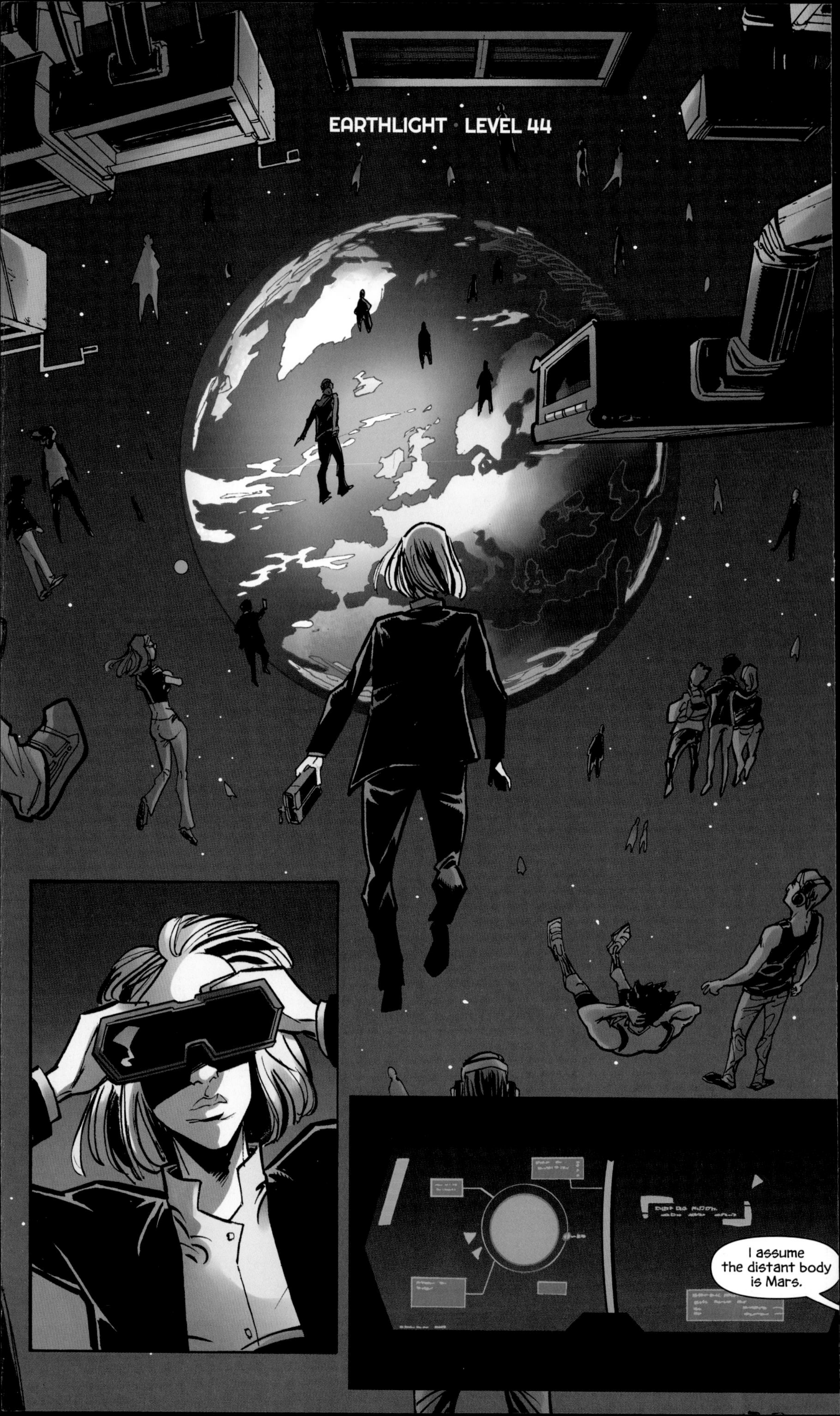
EARTHLIGHT · LEVEL 44
I assume the distant body is Mars.

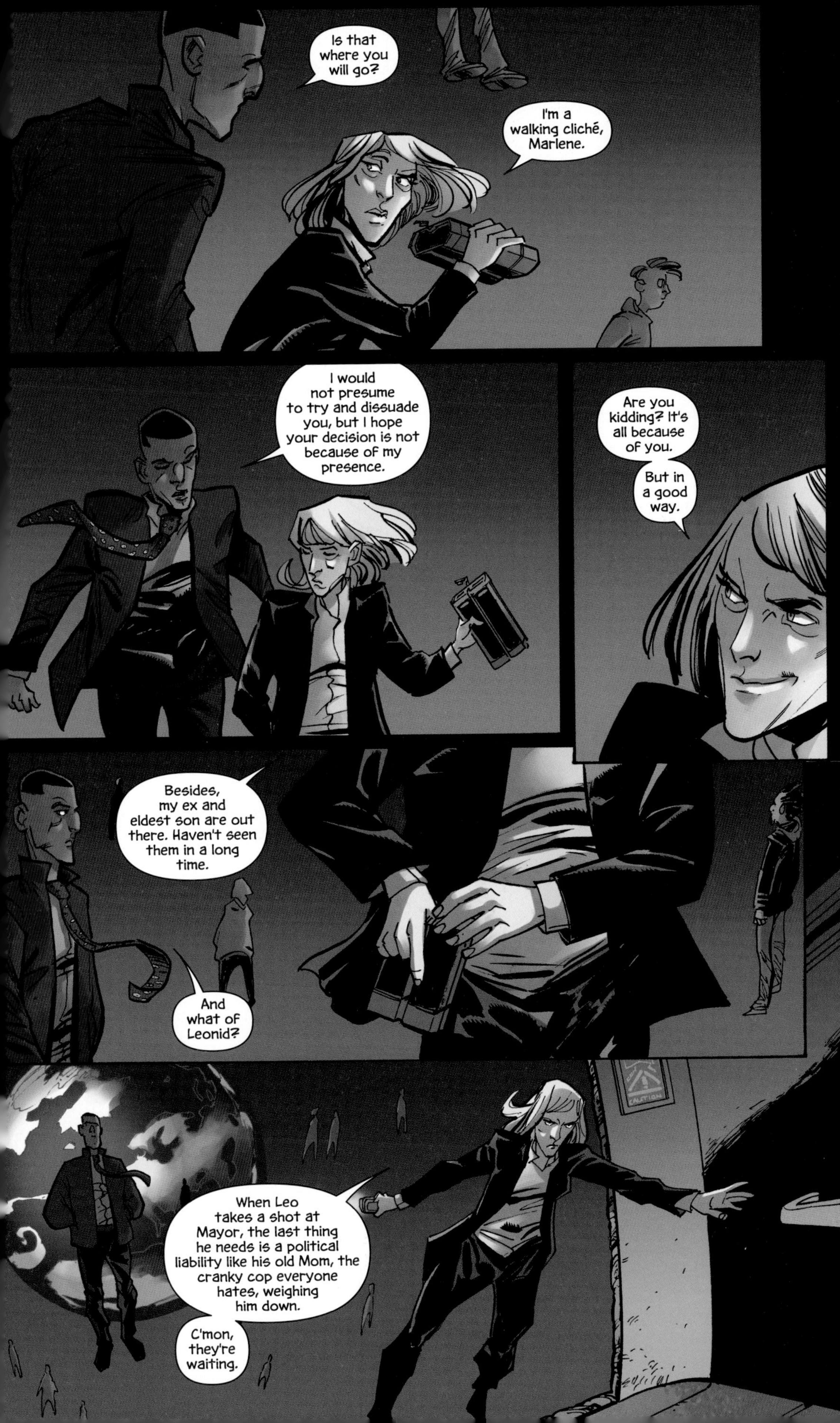

Is that where you will go?
I'm a walking cliché, Marlene.
I would not presume to try and dissuade you, but I hope your decision is not because of my presence.
Are you kidding? It's all because of you.
But in a good way.
Besides, my ex and eldest son are out there. Haven't seen them in a long time.
And what of Leonid?
When Leo takes a shot at Mayor, the last thing he needs is a political liability like his old Mom, the cranky cop everyone hates, weighing him down.
C'mon, they're waiting.
CAUTION

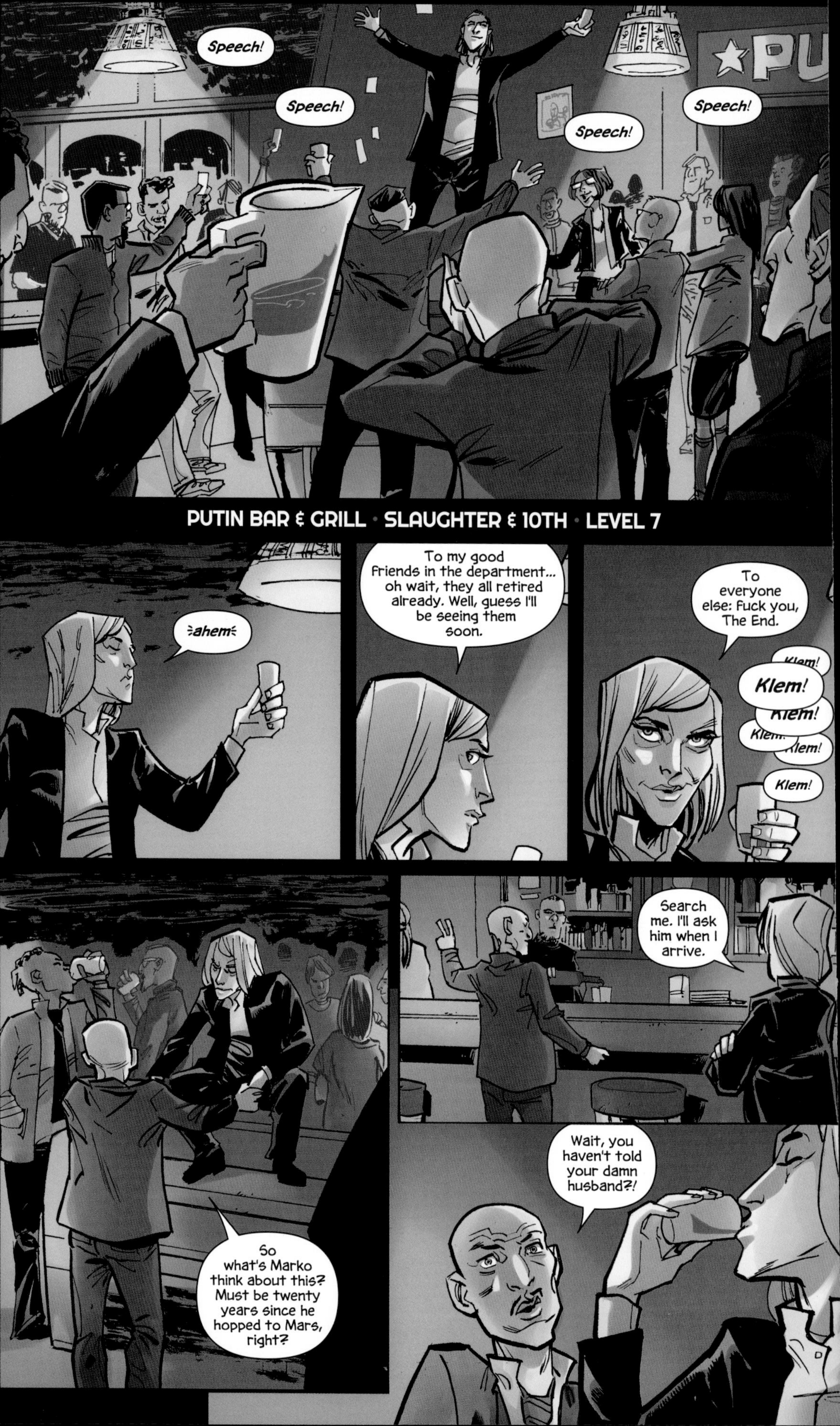
Speech!
Speech!
Speech!
Speech!
PU
PUTIN BAR & GRILL · SLAUGHTER & 10TH · LEVEL 7
ahem
To my good friends in the department... oh wait, they all retired already. Well, guess I'll be seeing them soon.
To everyone else: Fuck you, The End.
Klem!
Klem!
Klem!
Klem!
Klem!
Klem!
So what's Marko think about this? Must be twenty years since he hopped to Mars, right?
Search me. I'll ask him when I arrive.
Wait, you haven't told your damn husband?!

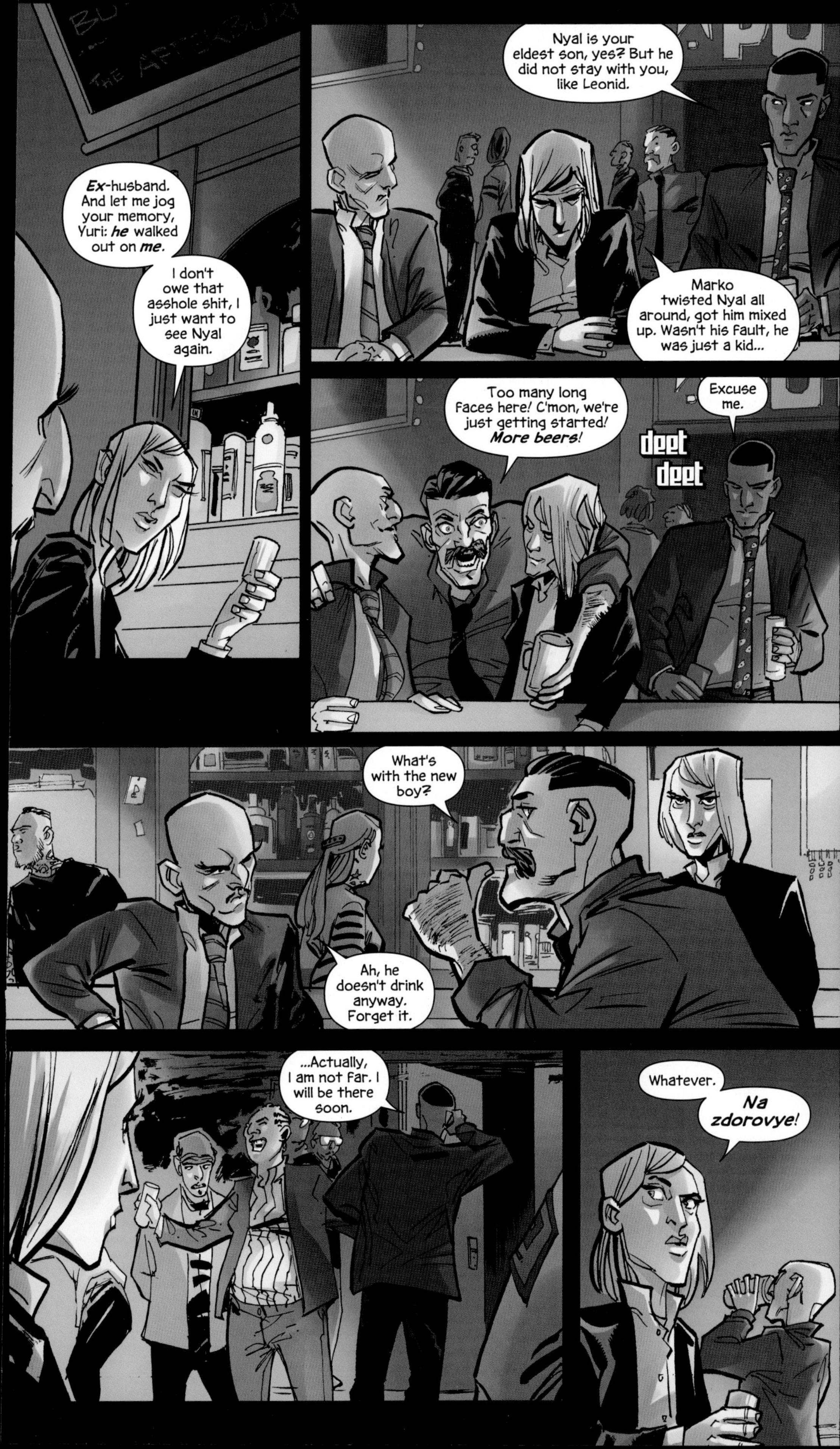
Ex-husband. And let me jog your memory, Yuri: he walked out on me.
I don't owe that asshole shit, I just want to see Nyal again.
Nyal is your eldest son, yes? But he did not stay with you, like Leonid.
Marko twisted Nyal all around, got him mixed up. Wasn't his fault, he was just a kid...
Too many long faces here! C'mon, we're just getting started! More beers!
Excuse me.
deet deet
What's with the new boy?
Ah, he doesn't drink anyway. Forget it.
...Actually, I am not far. I will be there soon.
Whatever.
Na zdorovye!

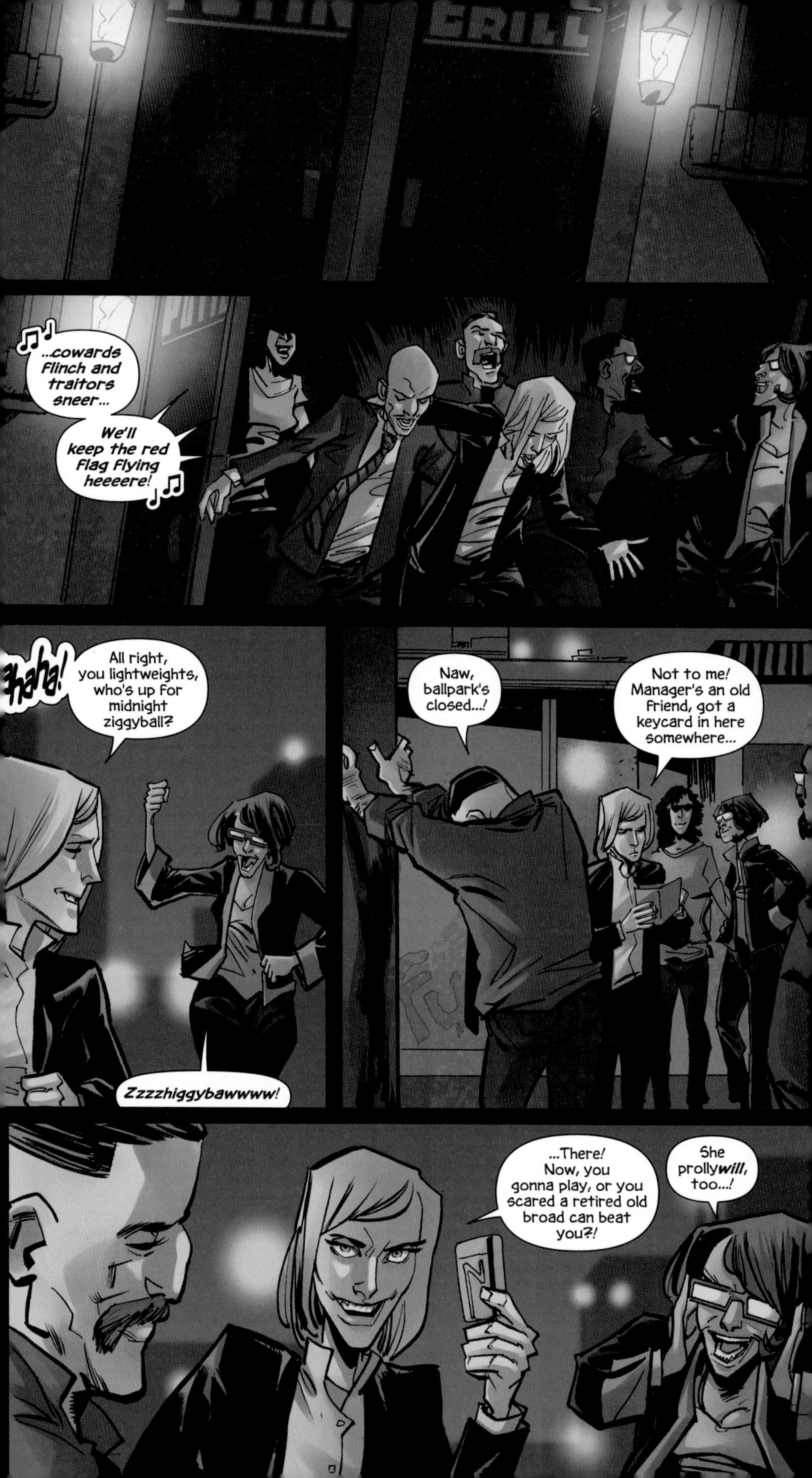

GRILL
...cowards Flinch and traitors sneer...
We'll keep the red flag flying heeeere!
haha!
All right, you lightweights, who's up for midnight ziggyball?
Zzzzhiggybawwww!
Naw, ballpark's closed...!
Not to me! Manager's an old friend, got a keycard in here somewhere...
...There! Now, you gonna play, or you scared a retired old broad can beat you?!
She prolly *will*, too...!

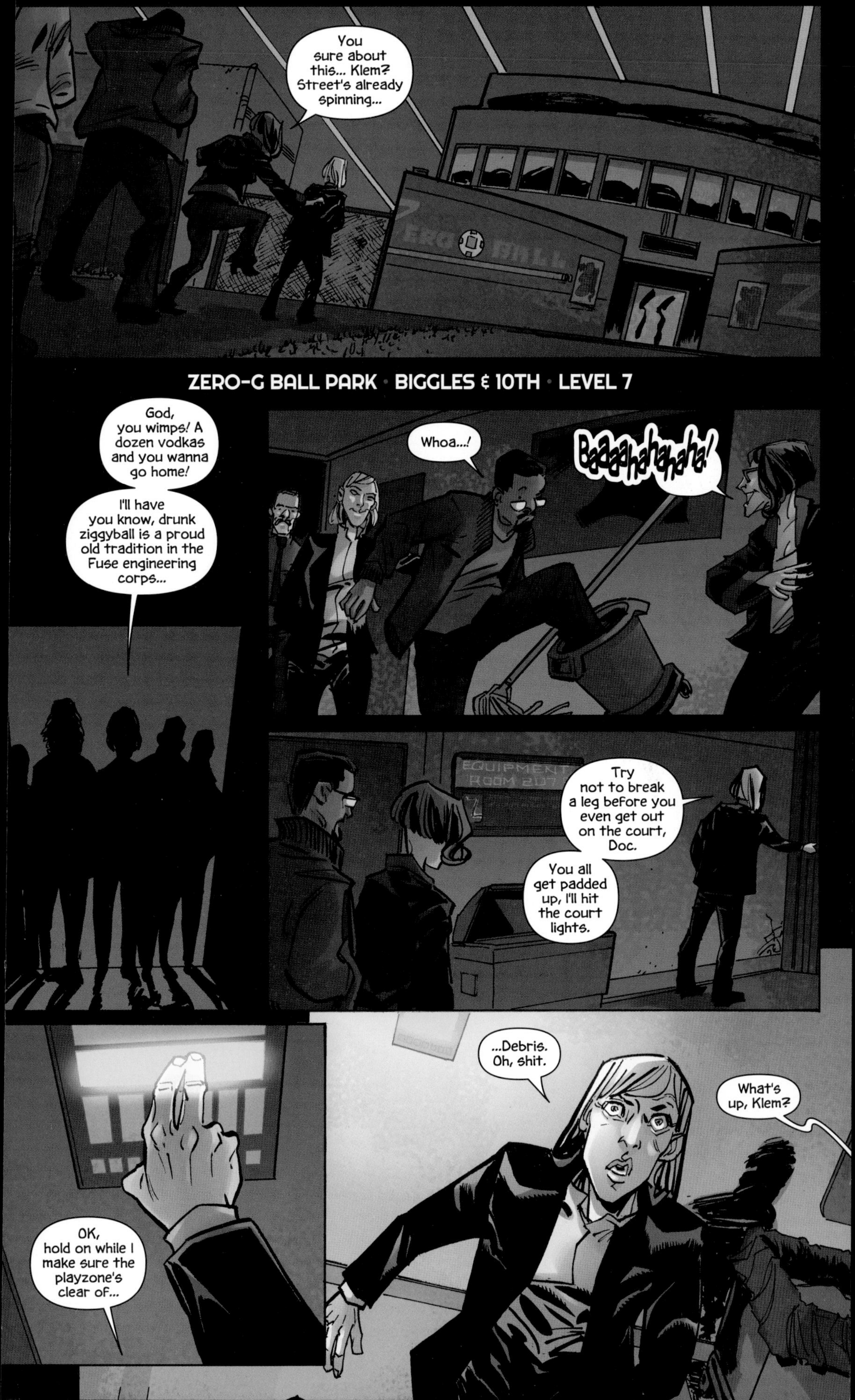

You sure about this... Klem? Street's already spinning...
ZERO-G BALL PARK • BIGGLES & 10TH • LEVEL 7
God, you wimps! A dozen vodkas and you wanna go home!
I'll have you know, drunk ziggyball is a proud old tradition in the Fuse engineering corps...
Whoa...!
Baaaahahahaha!
EQUIPMENT ROOM 207
Try not to break a leg before you even get out on the court, Doc.
You all get padded up, I'll hit the court lights.
OK, hold on while I make sure the playzone's clear of...
...Debris. Oh, shit.
What's up, Klem?

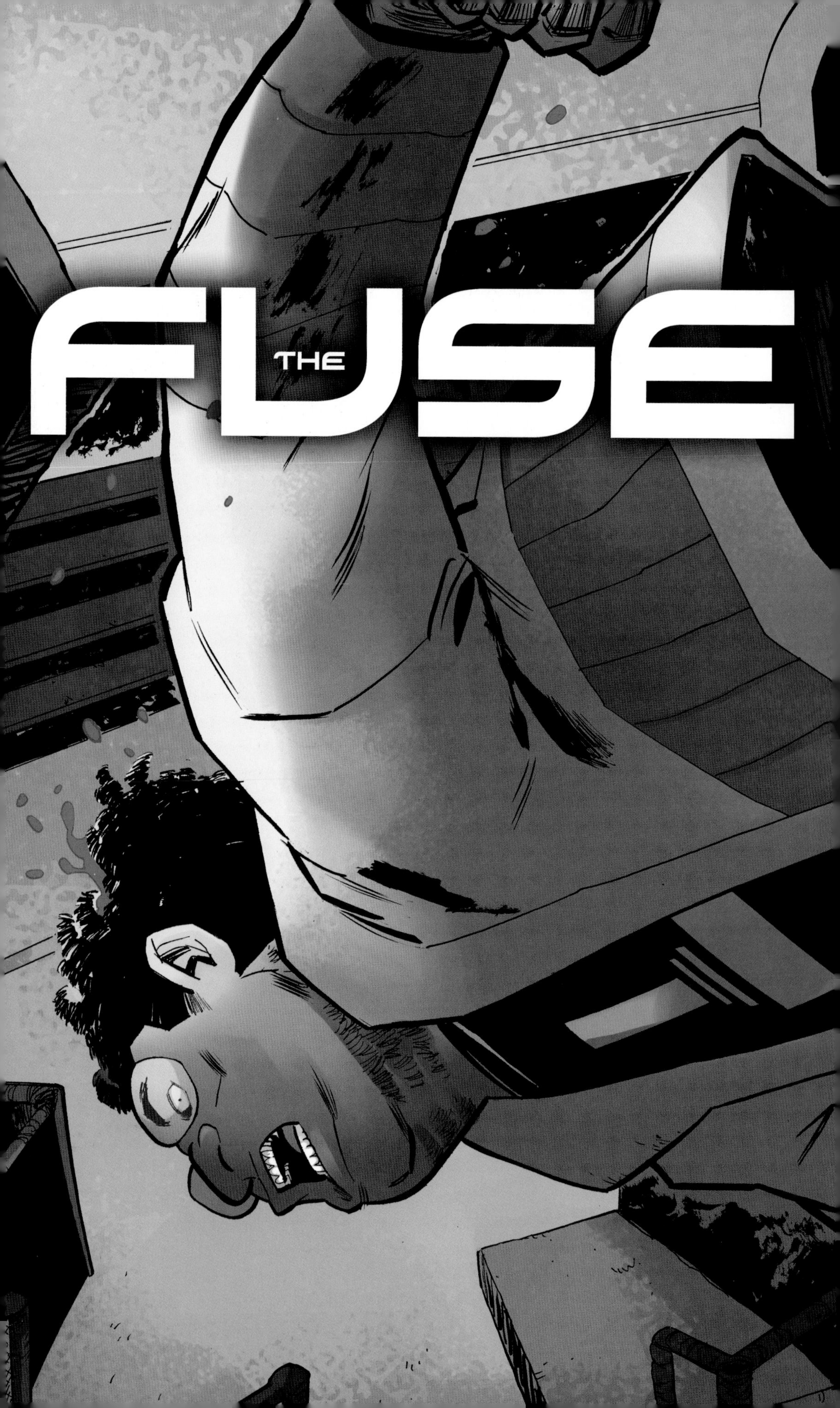
THE FUSE

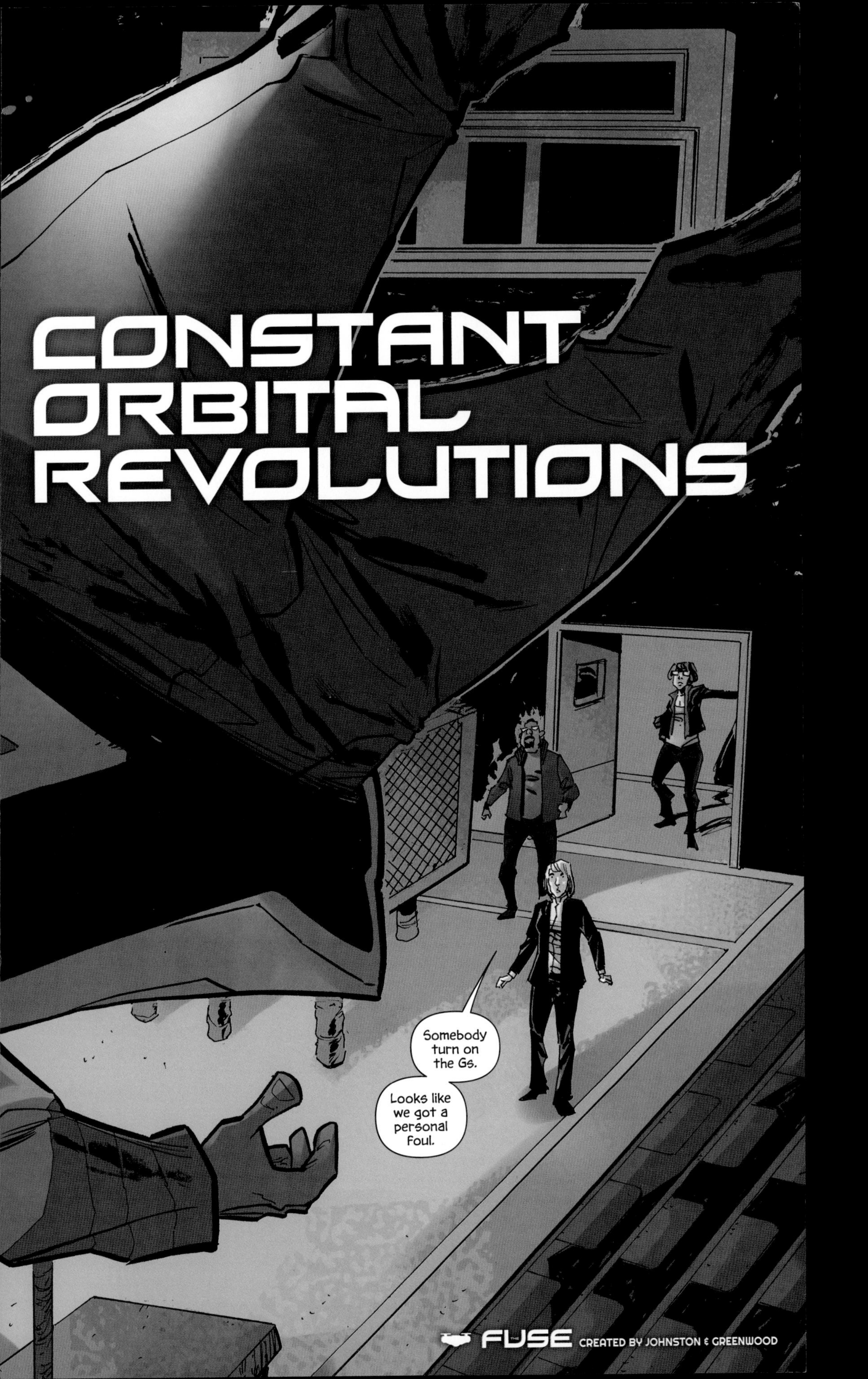
CONSTANT ORBITAL REVOLUTIONS
Somebody turn on the Gs.
Looks like we got a personal foul.
FUSE CREATED BY JOHNSTON & GREENWOOD

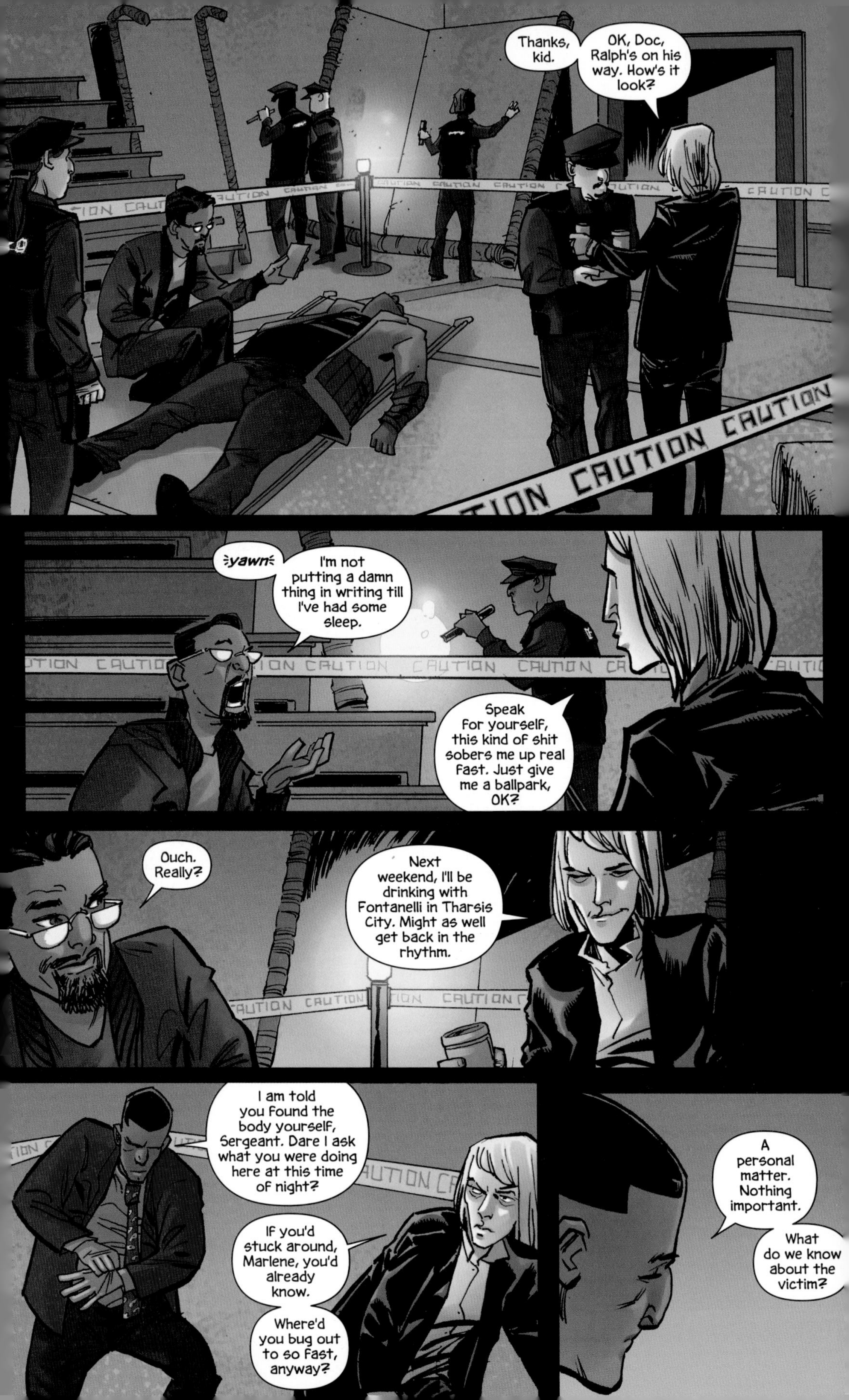
Thanks, kid.
OK, Doc, Ralph's on his way. How's it look?
CAUTION
yawn
I'm not putting a damn thing in writing till I've had some sleep.
Speak for yourself, this kind of shit sobers me up real fast. Just give me a ballpark, OK?
Ouch. Really?
Next weekend, I'll be drinking with Fontanelli in Tharsis City. Might as well get back in the rhythm.
I am told you found the body yourself, Sergeant. Dare I ask what you were doing here at this time of night?
If you'd stuck around, Marlene, you'd already know.
Where'd you bug out to so fast, anyway?
A personal matter. Nothing important.
What do we know about the victim?

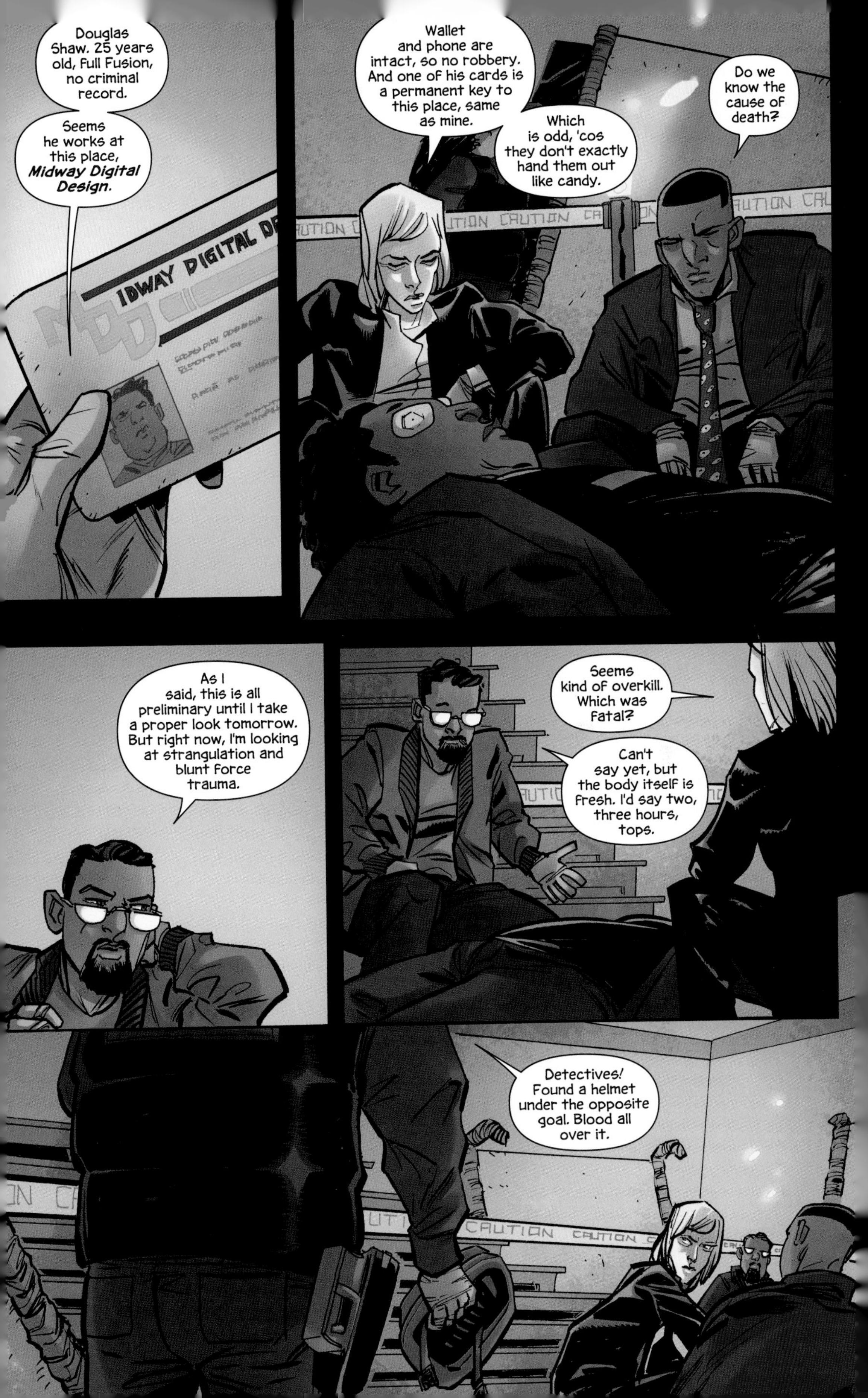
Douglas Shaw. 25 years old, full Fusion, no criminal record.
Seems he works at this place, ***Midway Digital Design***.
Wallet and phone are intact, so no robbery. And one of his cards is a permanent key to this place, same as mine.
Which is odd, 'cos they don't exactly hand them out like candy.
Do we know the cause of death?
As I said, this is all preliminary until I take a proper look tomorrow. But right now, I'm looking at strangulation and blunt force trauma.
Seems kind of overkill. Which was fatal?
Can't say yet, but the body itself is fresh. I'd say two, three hours, tops.
Detectives! Found a helmet under the opposite goal. Blood all over it.

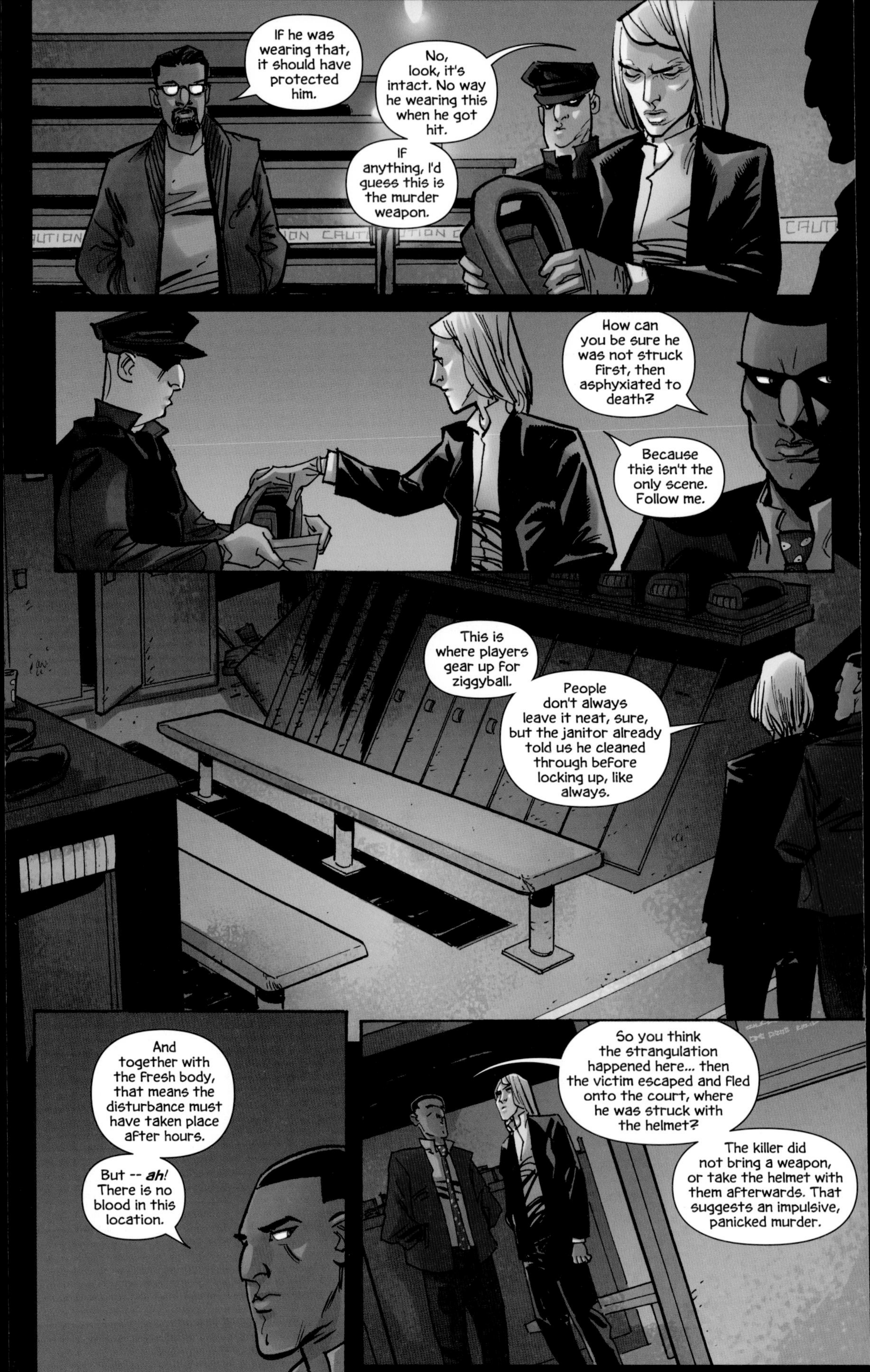

If he was wearing that, it should have protected him.
No, look, it's intact. No way he wearing this when he got hit.
If anything, I'd guess this is the murder weapon.
CAUTION CAUTION CAUTION
How can you be sure he was not struck first, then asphyxiated to death?
Because this isn't the only scene. Follow me.
This is where players gear up for ziggyball.
People don't always leave it neat, sure, but the janitor already told us he cleaned through before locking up, like always.
And together with the fresh body, that means the disturbance must have taken place after hours.
But -- *ah!* There is no blood in this location.
So you think the strangulation happened here... then the victim escaped and fled onto the court, where he was struck with the helmet?
The killer did not bring a weapon, or take the helmet with them afterwards. That suggests an impulsive, panicked murder.

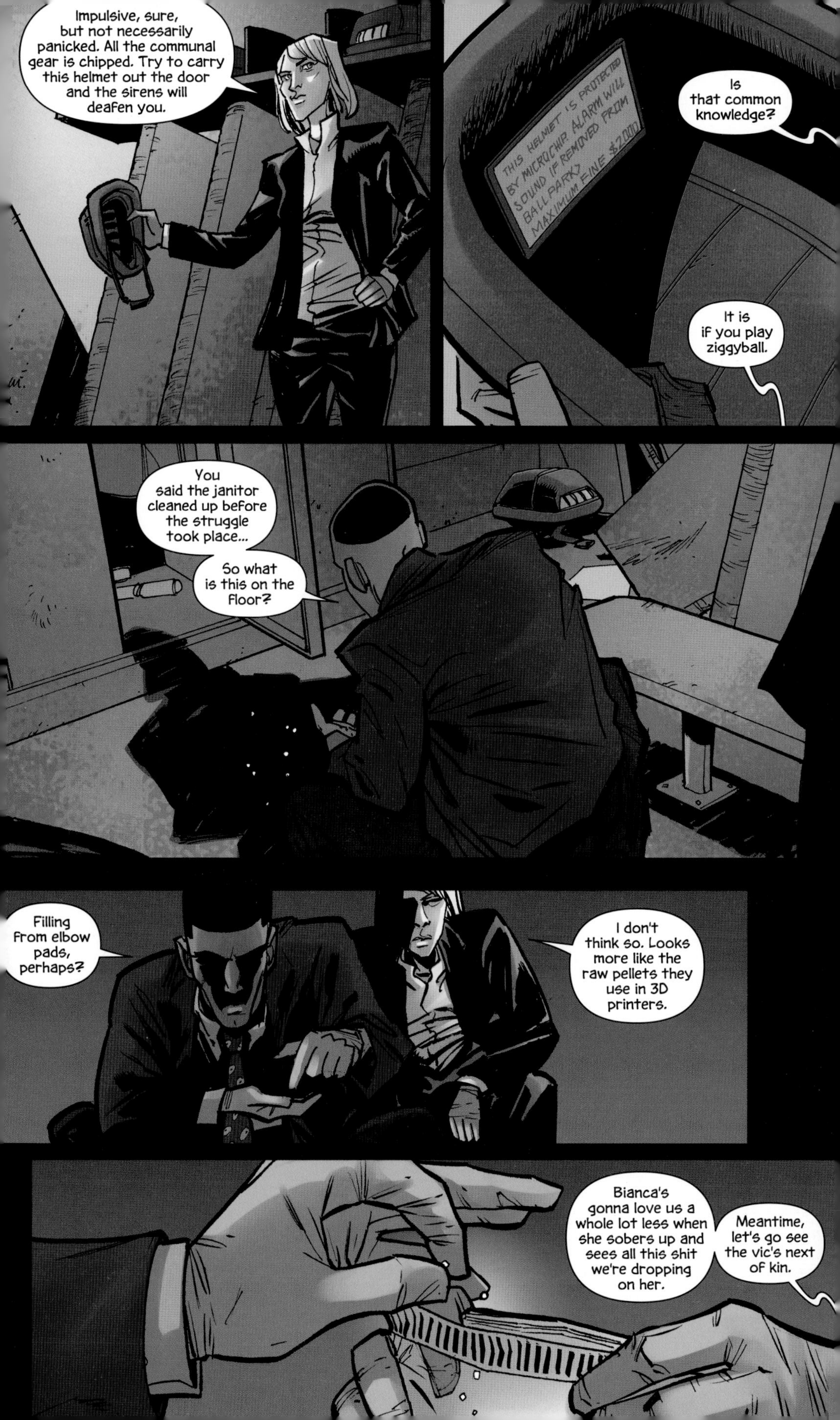
Impulsive, sure, but not necessarily panicked. All the communal gear is chipped. Try to carry this helmet out the door and the sirens will deafen you.
THIS HELMET IS PROTECTED BY MICROCHIP. ALARM WILL SOUND IF REMOVED FROM BALLPARK. MAXIMUM FINE $2,000
Is that common knowledge?
It is if you play ziggyball.
You said the janitor cleaned up before the struggle took place...
So what is this on the floor?
Filling from elbow pads, perhaps?
I don't think so. Looks more like the raw pellets they use in 3D printers.
Bianca's gonna love us a whole lot less when she sobers up and sees all this shit we're dropping on her.
Meantime, let's go see the vic's next of kin.

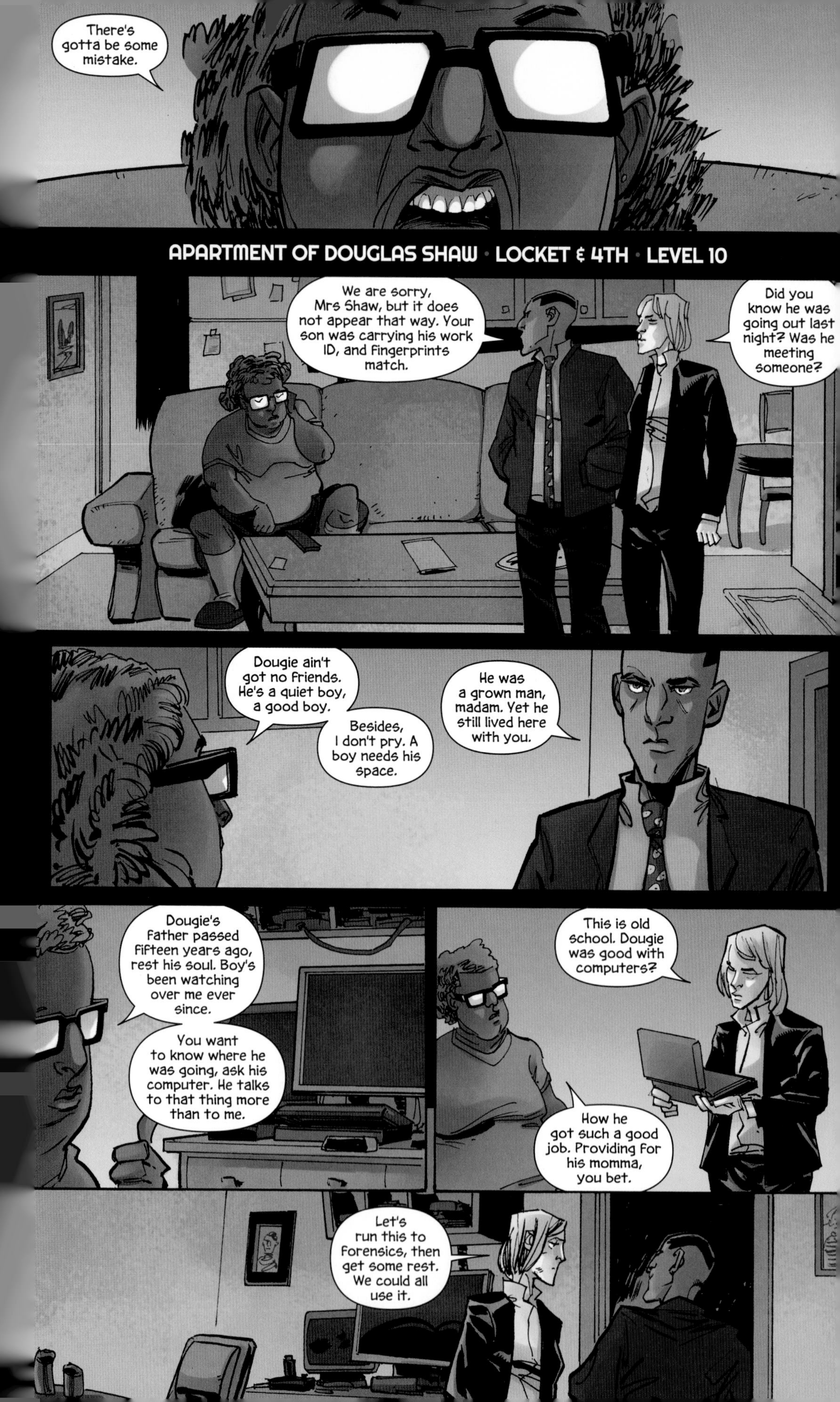

There's gotta be some mistake.
APARTMENT OF DOUGLAS SHAW · LOCKET & 4TH · LEVEL 10
We are sorry, Mrs Shaw, but it does not appear that way. Your son was carrying his work ID, and fingerprints match.
Did you know he was going out last night? Was he meeting someone?
Dougie ain't got no friends. He's a quiet boy, a good boy.
Besides, I don't pry. A boy needs his space.
He was a grown man, madam. Yet he still lived here with you.
Dougie's father passed fifteen years ago, rest his soul. Boy's been watching over me ever since.
You want to know where he was going, ask his computer. He talks to that thing more than to me.
This is old school. Dougie was good with computers?
How he got such a good job. Providing for his momma, you bet.
Let's run this to forensics, then get some rest. We could all use it.

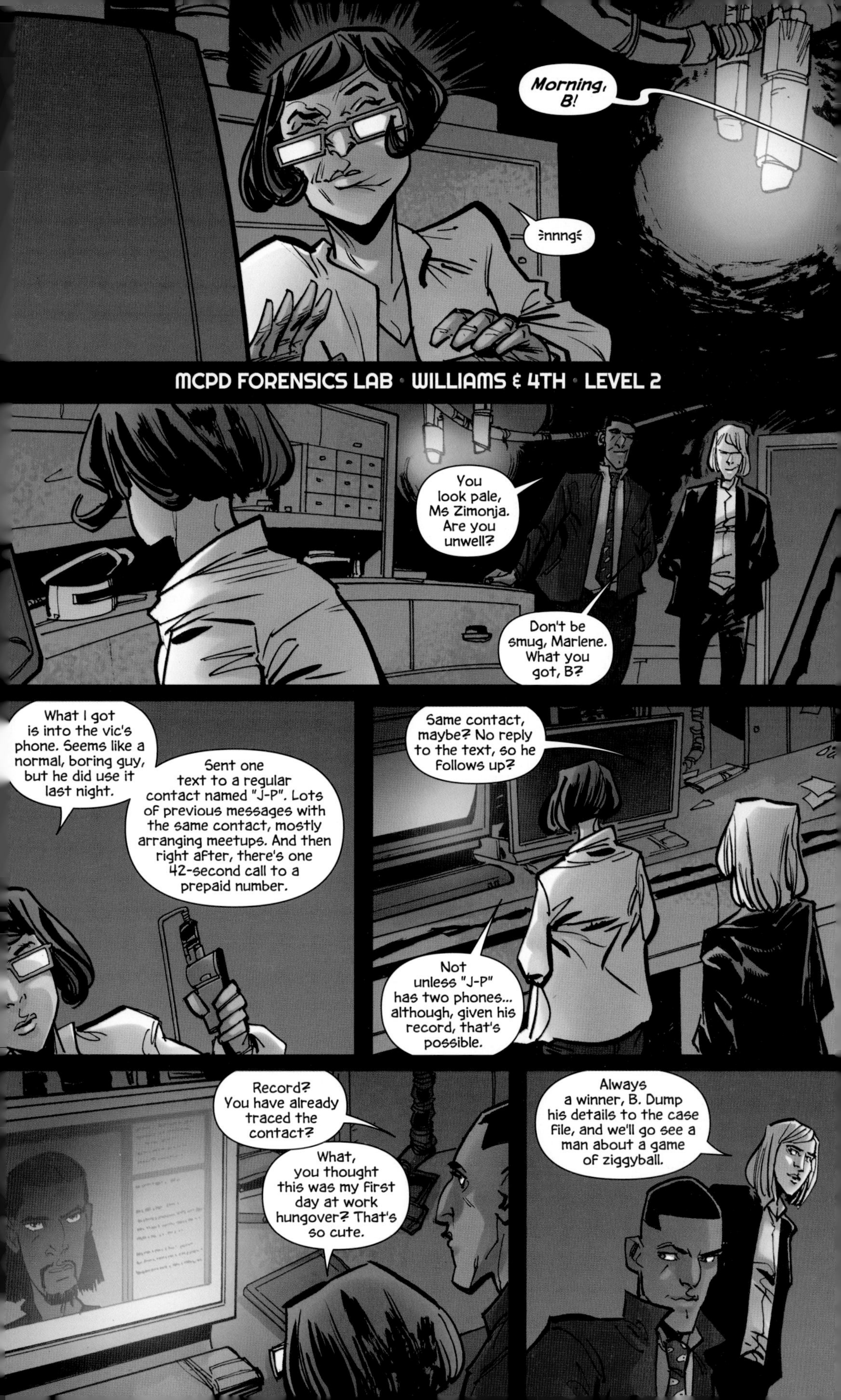
Morning, B!
=nnng=
MCPD FORENSICS LAB · WILLIAMS & 4TH · LEVEL 2
You look pale, Ms Zimonja. Are you unwell?
Don't be smug, Marlene. What you got, B?
What I got is into the vic's phone. Seems like a normal, boring guy, but he did use it last night.
Sent one text to a regular contact named "J-P". Lots of previous messages with the same contact, mostly arranging meetups. And then right after, there's one 42-second call to a prepaid number.
Same contact, maybe? No reply to the text, so he follows up?
Not unless "J-P" has two phones... although, given his record, that's possible.
Record? You have already traced the contact?
What, you thought this was my first day at work hungover? That's so cute.
Always a winner, B. Dump his details to the case file, and we'll go see a man about a game of ziggyball.

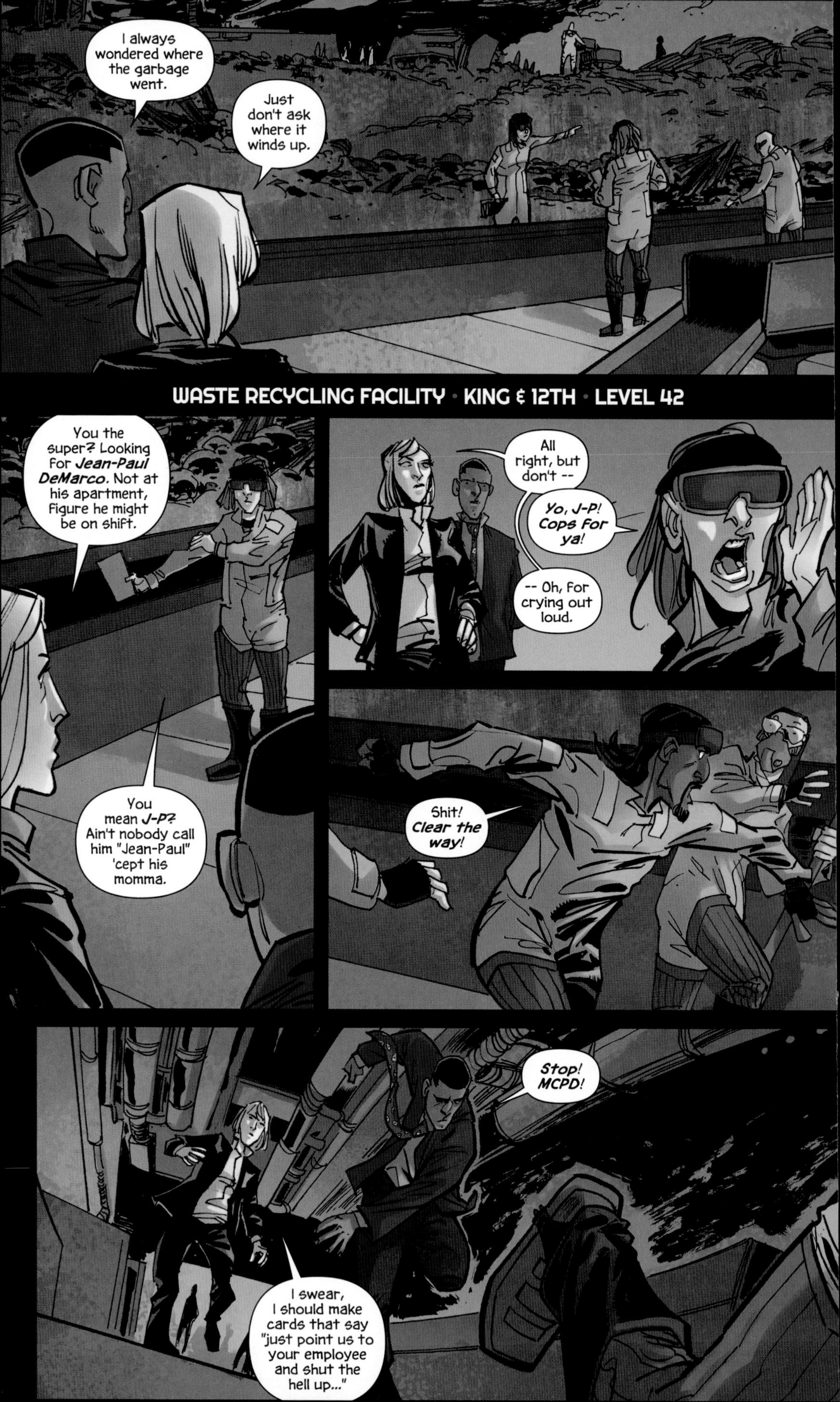
I always wondered where the garbage went.
Just don't ask where it winds up.
WASTE RECYCLING FACILITY • KING & 12TH • LEVEL 42
You the super? Looking for Jean-Paul DeMarco. Not at his apartment, figure he might be on shift.
You mean J-P? Ain't nobody call him "Jean-Paul" 'cept his momma.
All right, but don't --
Yo, J-P! Cops for ya!
-- Oh, for crying out loud.
Shit! Clear the way!
Stop! MCPD!
I swear, I should make cards that say "just point us to your employee and shut the hell up..."

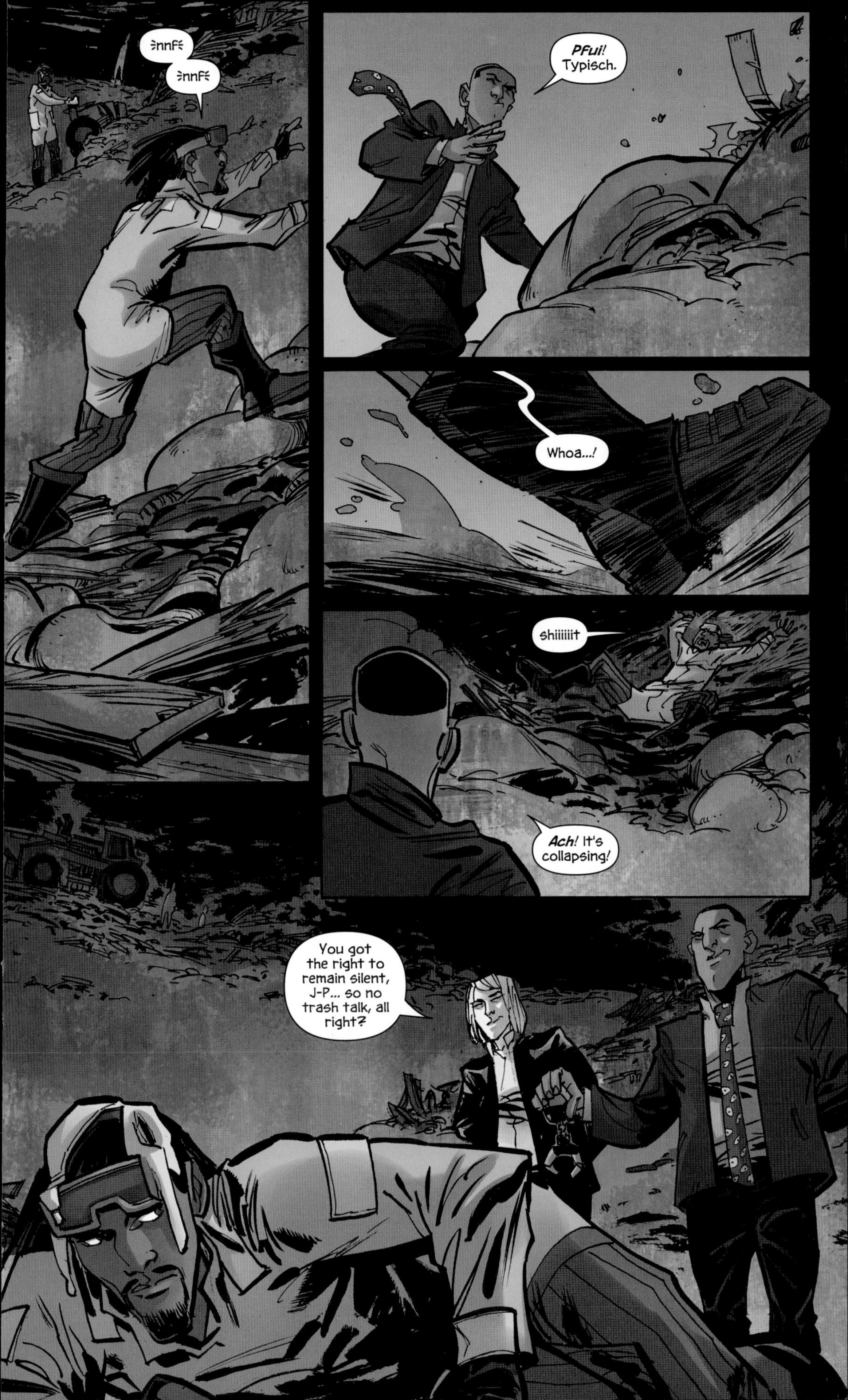

nnf
nnf
Pfui! Typisch.
Whoa...!
shiiiiiit
Ach! It's collapsing!
You got the right to remain silent, J-P... so no trash talk, all right?

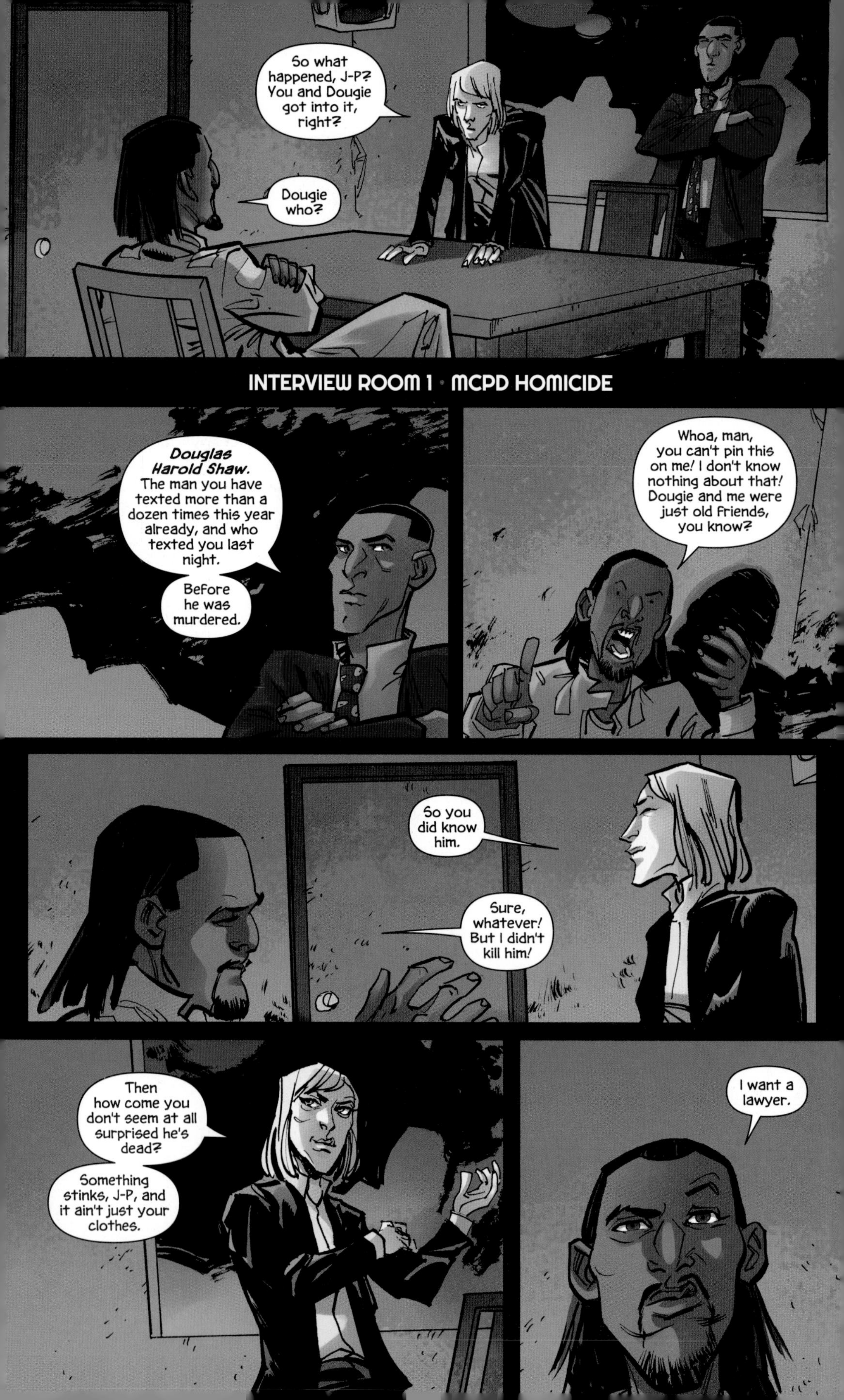
So what happened, J-P? You and Dougie got into it, right?
Dougie who?
INTERVIEW ROOM 1 · MCPD HOMICIDE
Douglas Harold Shaw. The man you have texted more than a dozen times this year already, and who texted you last night.
Before he was murdered.
Whoa, man, you can't pin this on me! I don't know nothing about that! Dougie and me were just old friends, you know?
So you did know him.
Sure, whatever! But I didn't kill him!
Then how come you don't seem at all surprised he's dead?
Something stinks, J-P, and it ain't just your clothes.
I want a lawyer.

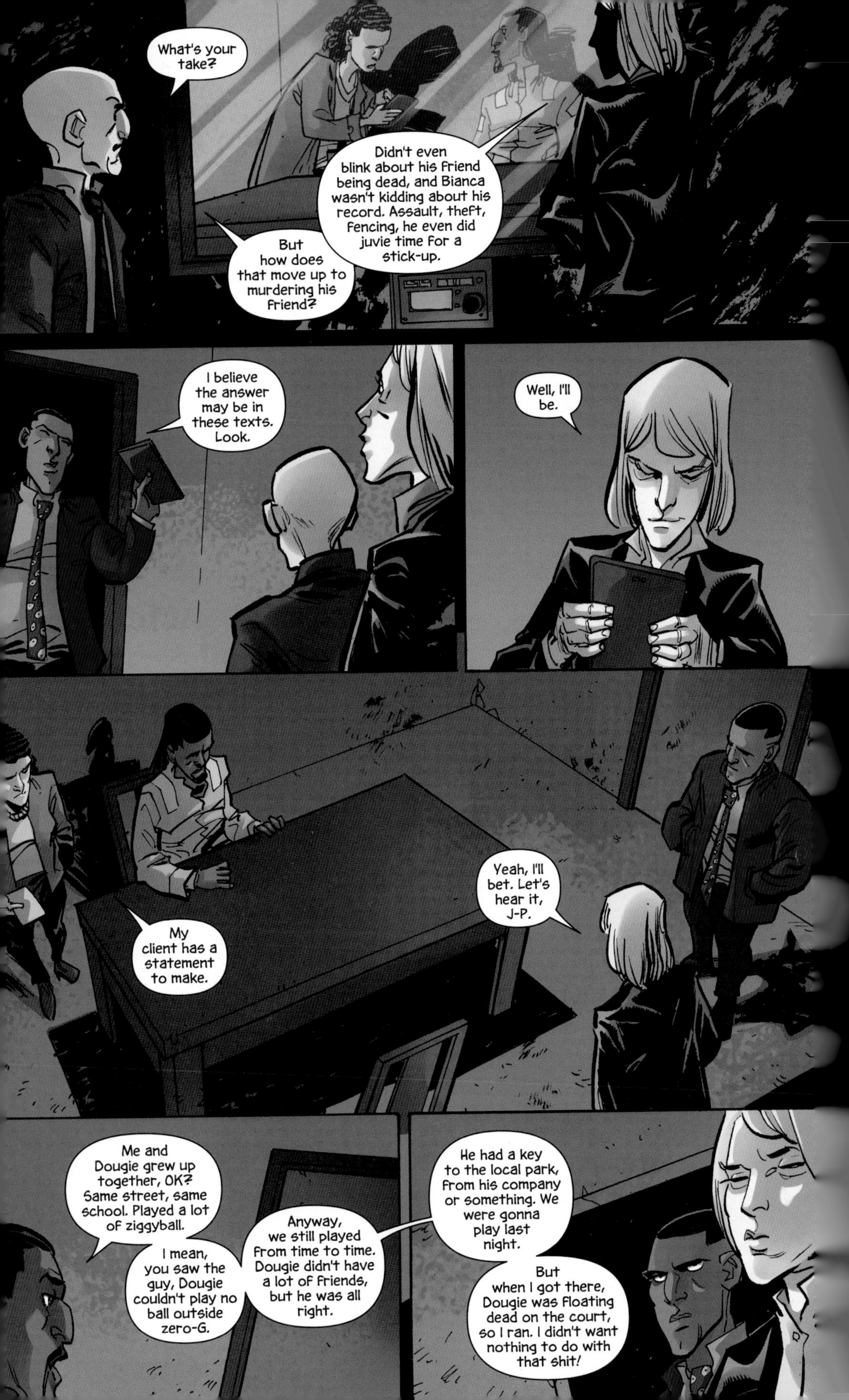
What's your take?
Didn't even blink about his friend being dead, and Bianca wasn't kidding about his record. Assault, theft, fencing, he even did juvie time for a stick-up.
But how does that move up to murdering his friend?
I believe the answer may be in these texts. Look.
Well, I'll be.
My client has a statement to make.
Yeah, I'll bet. Let's hear it, J-P.
Me and Dougie grew up together, OK? Same street, same school. Played a lot of ziggyball.
I mean, you saw the guy, Dougie couldn't play no ball outside zero-G.
Anyway, we still played from time to time. Dougie didn't have a lot of friends, but he was all right.
He had a key to the local park, from his company or something. We were gonna play last night.
But when I got there, Dougie was floating dead on the court, so I ran. I didn't want nothing to do with that shit!

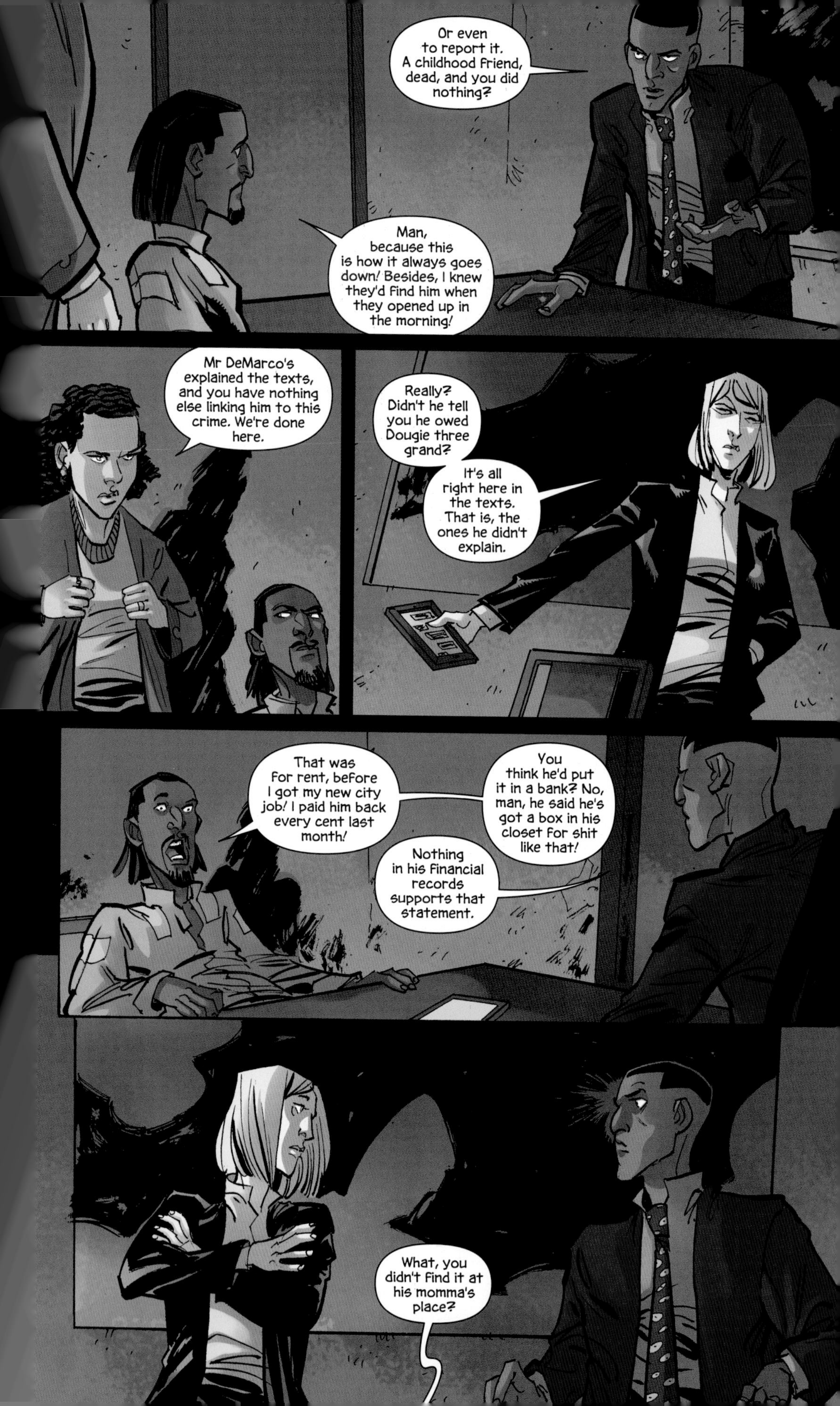
Or even to report it. A childhood friend, dead, and you did nothing?
Man, because this is how it always goes down! Besides, I knew they'd find him when they opened up in the morning!
Mr DeMarco's explained the texts, and you have nothing else linking him to this crime. We're done here.
Really? Didn't he tell you he owed Dougie three grand?
It's all right here in the texts. That is, the ones he didn't explain.
That was for rent, before I got my new city job! I paid him back every cent last month!
Nothing in his financial records supports that statement.
You think he'd put it in a bank? No, man, he said he's got a box in his closet for shit like that!
What, you didn't find it at his momma's place?

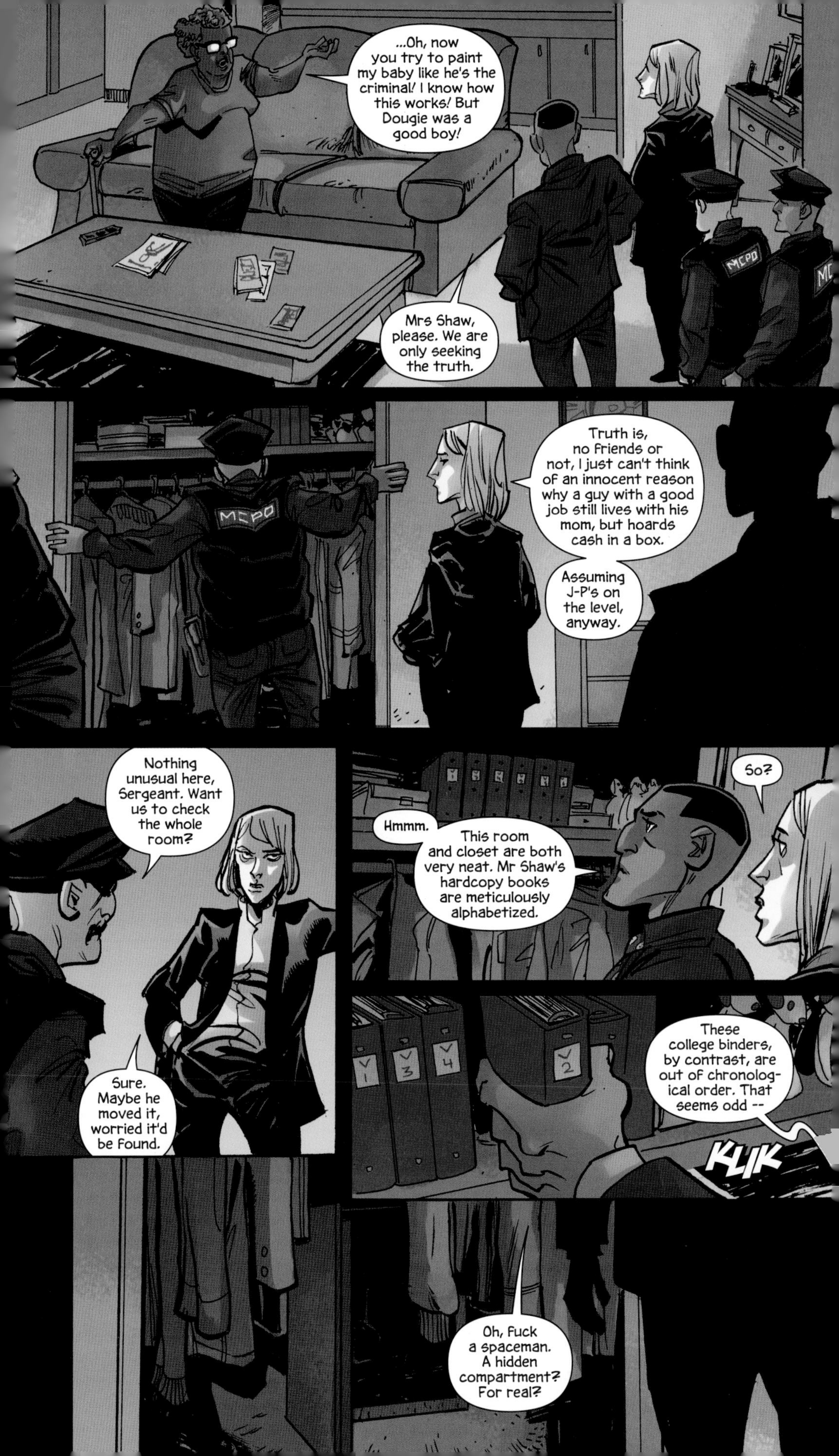
...Oh, now you try to paint my baby like he's the criminal! I know how this works! But Dougie was a good boy!
Mrs Shaw, please. We are only seeking the truth.
MCPD
Truth is, no friends or not, I just can't think of an innocent reason why a guy with a good job still lives with his mom, but hoards cash in a box.
Assuming J-P's on the level, anyway.
Nothing unusual here, Sergeant. Want us to check the whole room?
Sure. Maybe he moved it, worried it'd be found.
So?
Hmmm.
This room and closet are both very neat. Mr Shaw's hardcopy books are meticulously alphabetized.
These college binders, by contrast, are out of chronological order. That seems odd --
KLIK
Oh, fuck a spaceman. A hidden compartment? For real?

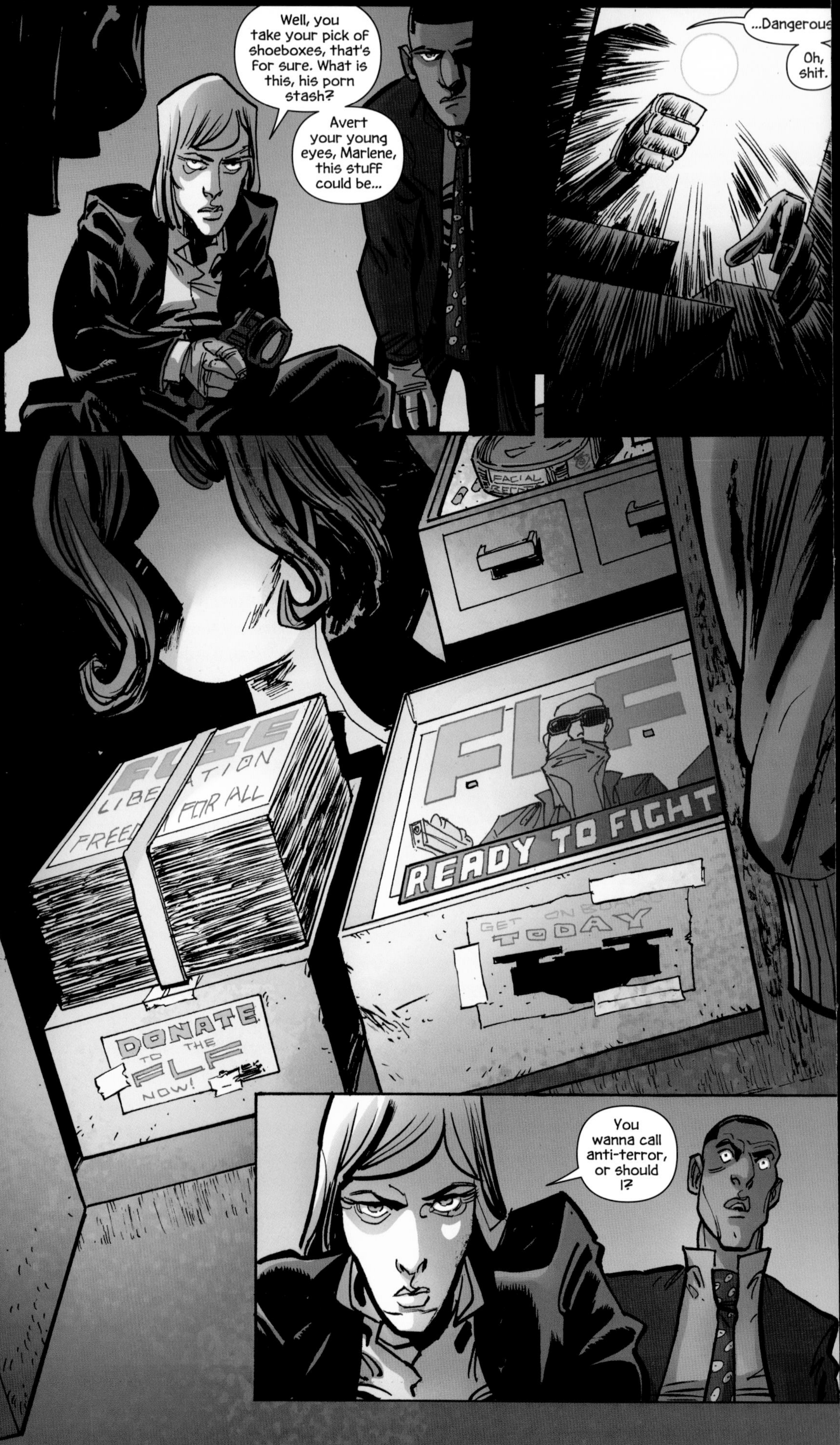
Well, you take your pick of shoeboxes, that's for sure. What is this, his porn stash?
Avert your young eyes, Marlene, this stuff could be...
...Dangerous
Oh, shit.
READY TO FIGHT
GET ON BOARD TODAY
DONATE TO THE FLF NOW!
FOR ALL
You wanna call anti-terror, or should I?

PART 2

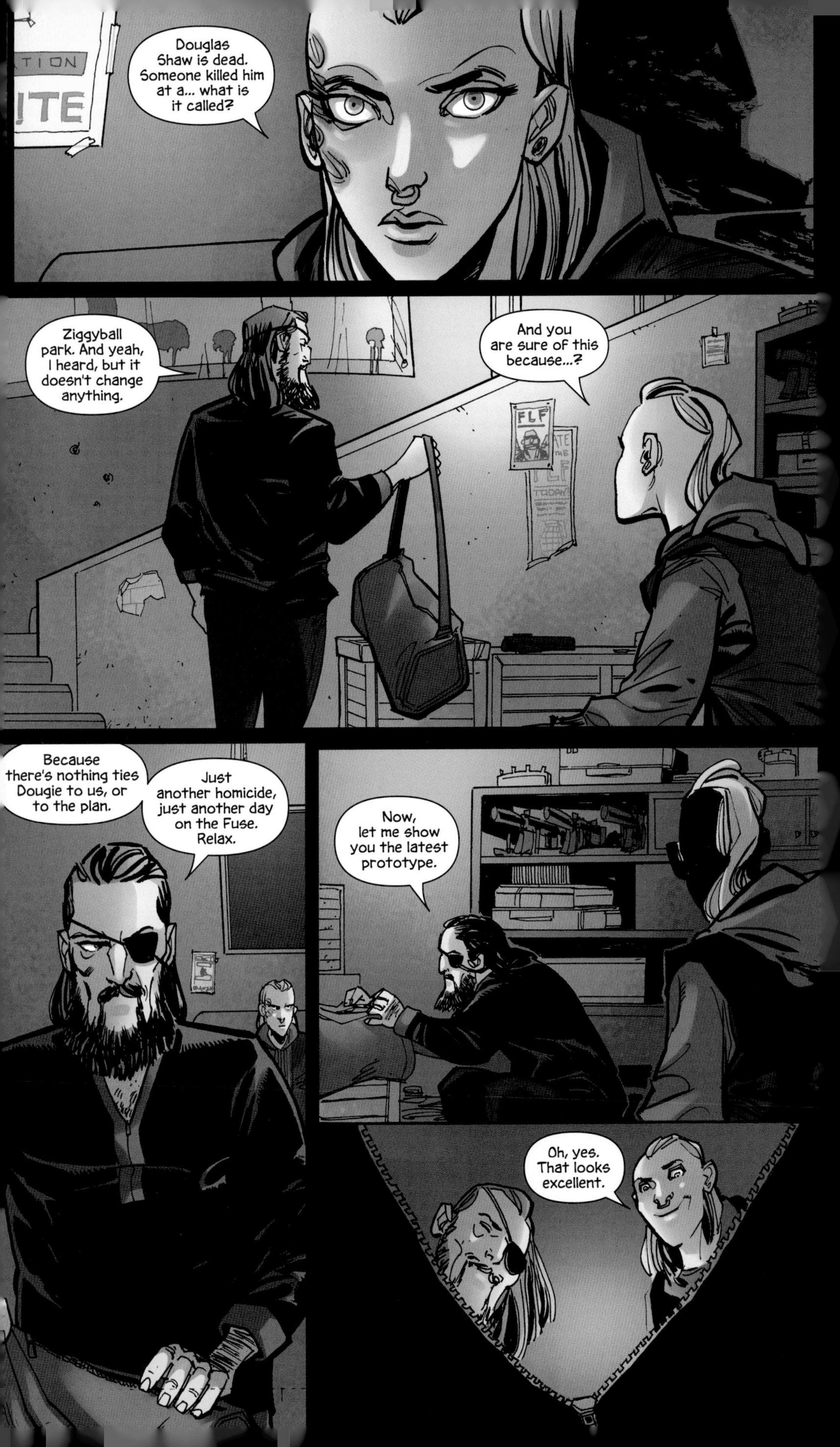

ATION
ITE
Douglas Shaw is dead. Someone killed him at a... what is it called?
Ziggyball park. And yeah, I heard, but it doesn't change anything.
And you are sure of this because...?
FLF
Because there's nothing ties Dougie to us, or to the plan.
Just another homicide, just another day on the Fuse. Relax.
Now, let me show you the latest prototype.
Oh, yes. That looks excellent.

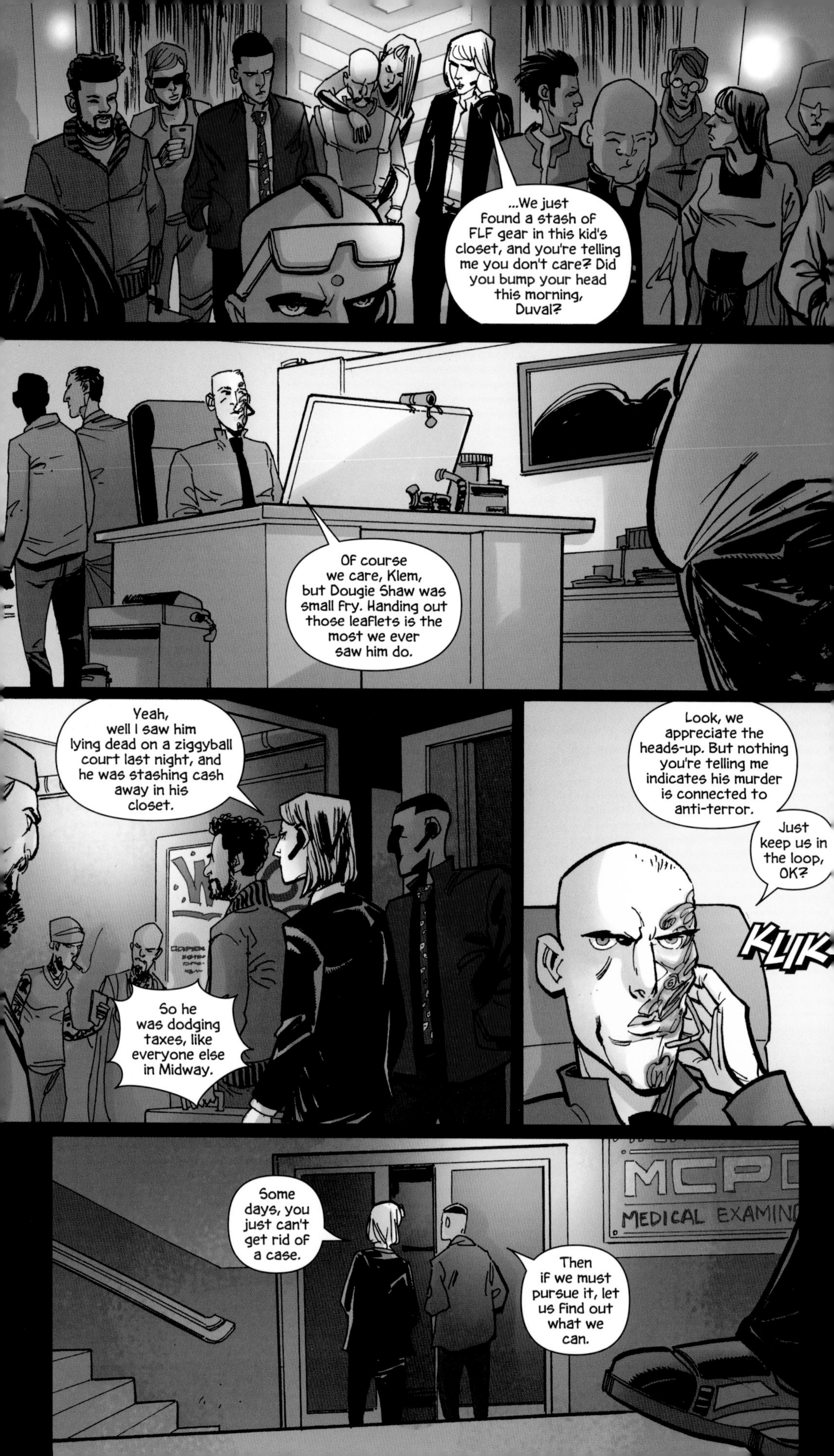

...We just found a stash of FLF gear in this kid's closet, and you're telling me you don't care? Did you bump your head this morning, Duval?
Of course we care, Klem, but Dougie Shaw was small fry. Handing out those leaflets is the most we ever saw him do.
Yeah, well I saw him lying dead on a ziggyball court last night, and he was stashing cash away in his closet.
So he was dodging taxes, like everyone else in Midway.
Look, we appreciate the heads-up. But nothing you're telling me indicates his murder is connected to anti-terror.
Just keep us in the loop, OK?
KLIK
MCPD
MEDICAL EXAMIN
Some days, you just can't get rid of a case.
Then if we must pursue it, let us find out what we can.

OFFICE OF THE MEDICAL EXAMINER · HAGENS & 1ST · LEVEL 2

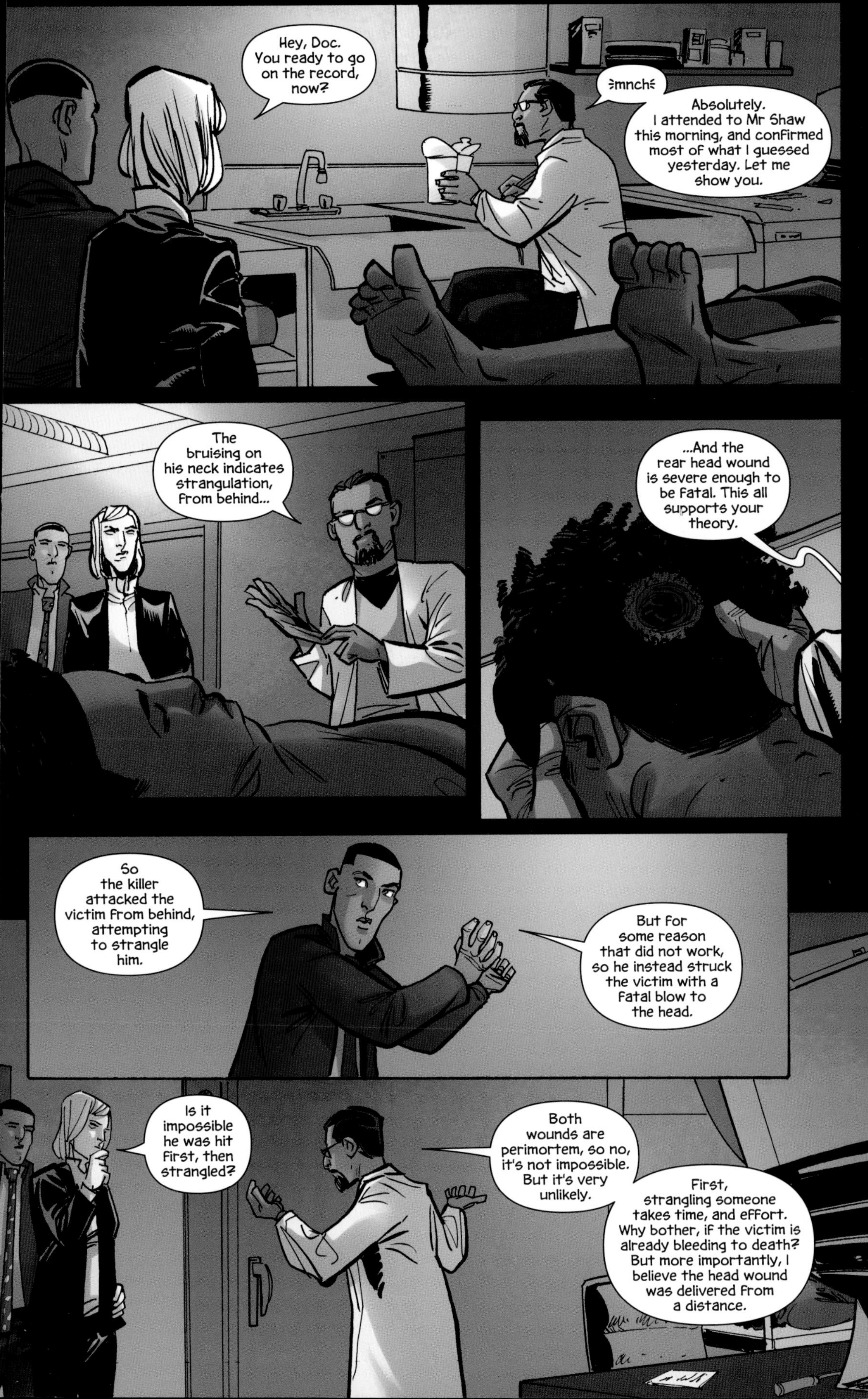
Hey, Doc. You ready to go on the record, now?
mnch
Absolutely. I attended to Mr Shaw this morning, and confirmed most of what I guessed yesterday. Let me show you.
The bruising on his neck indicates strangulation, from behind...
...And the rear head wound is severe enough to be fatal. This all supports your theory.
So the killer attacked the victim from behind, attempting to strangle him.
But for some reason that did not work, so he instead struck the victim with a fatal blow to the head.
Is it impossible he was hit first, then strangled?
Both wounds are perimortem, so no, it's not impossible. But it's very unlikely.
First, strangling someone takes time, and effort. Why bother, if the victim is already bleeding to death? But more importantly, I believe the head wound was delivered from a distance.

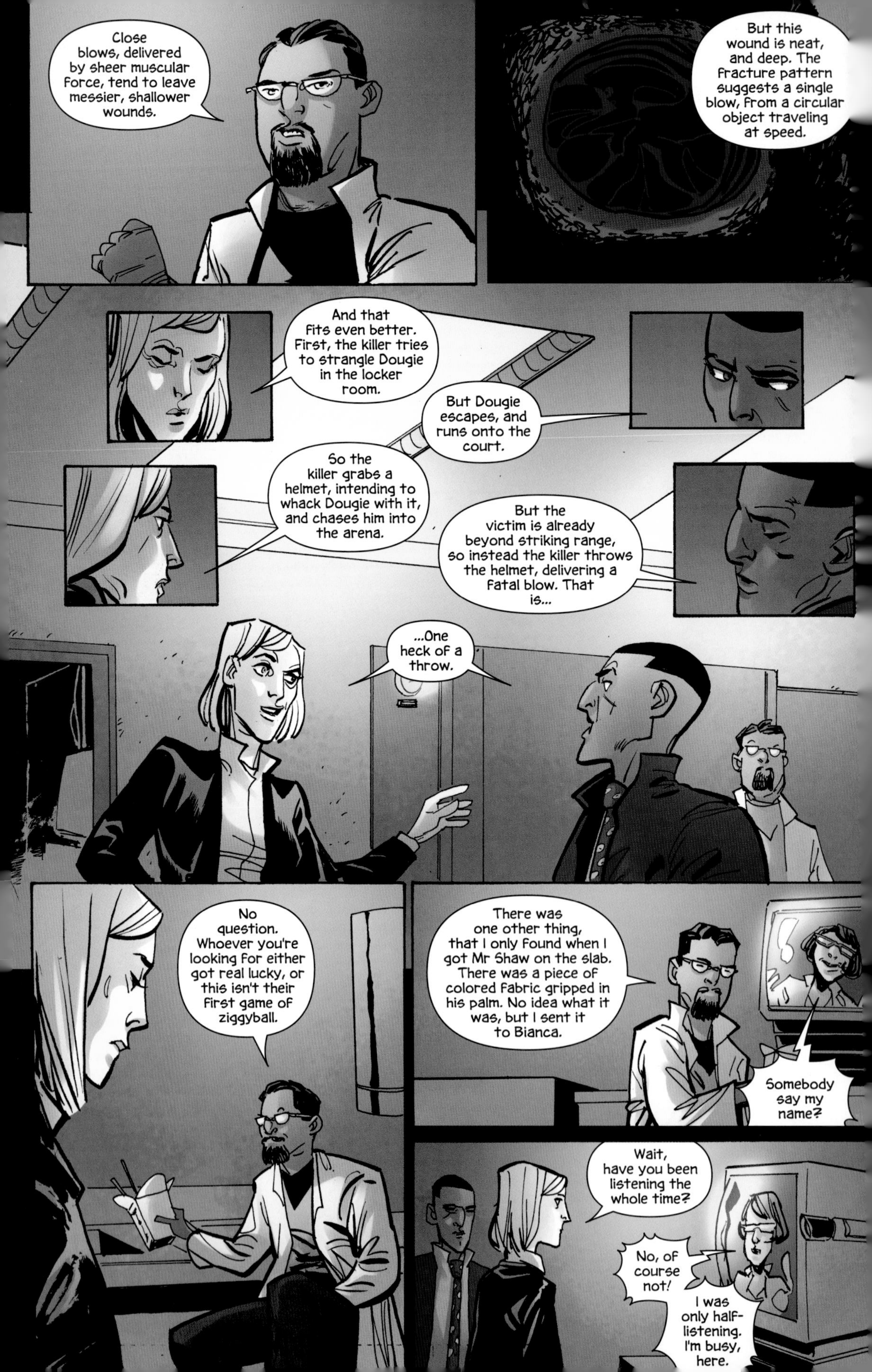
Close blows, delivered by sheer muscular force, tend to leave messier, shallower wounds.
But this wound is neat, and deep. The fracture pattern suggests a single blow, from a circular object traveling at speed.
And that fits even better. First, the killer tries to strangle Dougie in the locker room.
But Dougie escapes, and runs onto the court.
So the killer grabs a helmet, intending to whack Dougie with it, and chases him into the arena.
But the victim is already beyond striking range, so instead the killer throws the helmet, delivering a fatal blow. That is...
...One heck of a throw.
No question. Whoever you're looking for either got real lucky, or this isn't their first game of ziggyball.
There was one other thing, that I only found when I got Mr Shaw on the slab. There was a piece of colored fabric gripped in his palm. No idea what it was, but I sent it to Bianca.
Somebody say my name?
Wait, have you been listening the whole time?
No, of course not!
I was only half-listening. I'm busy, here.

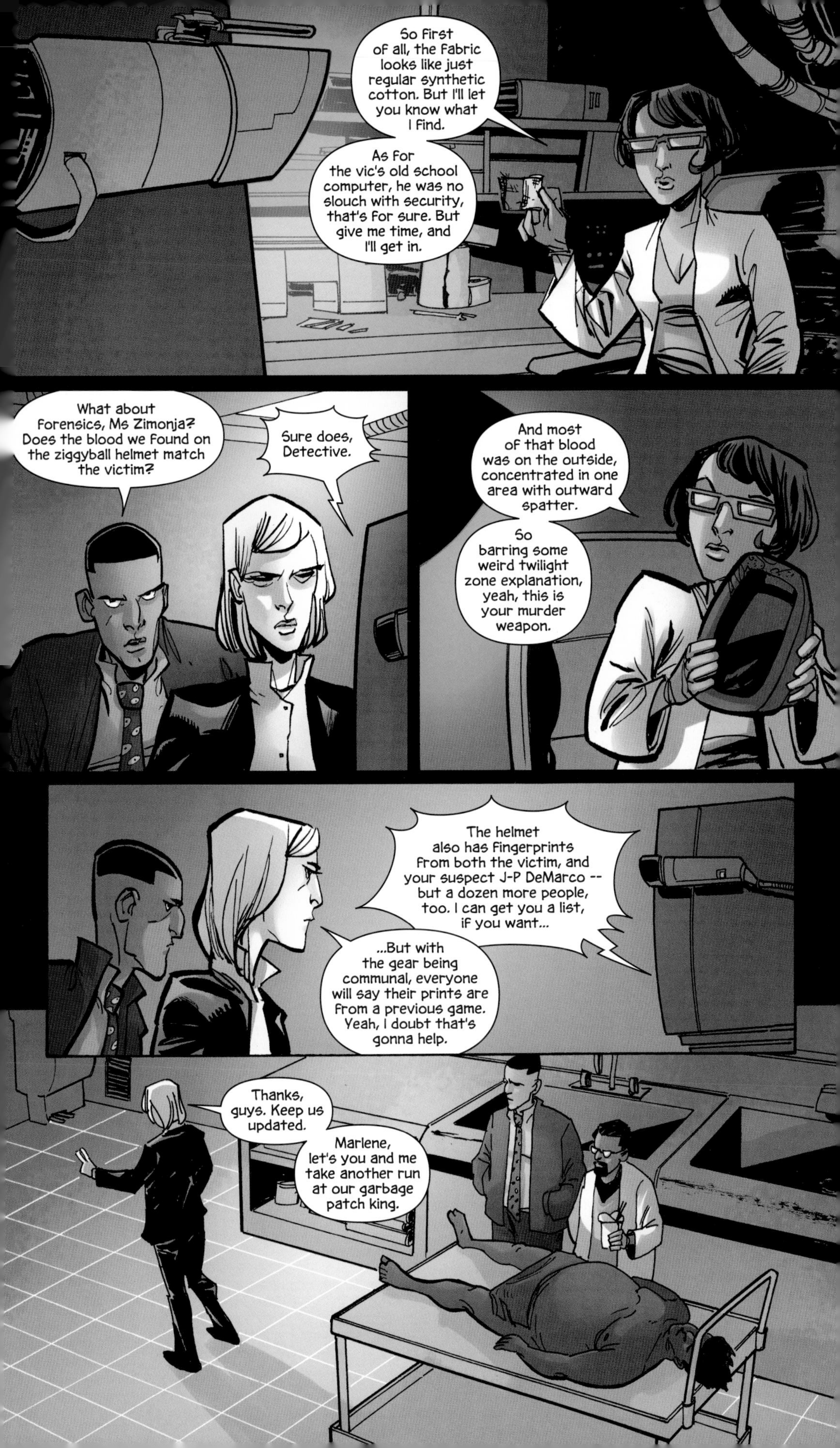
So first of all, the fabric looks like just regular synthetic cotton. But I'll let you know what I find.
As for the vic's old school computer, he was no slouch with security, that's for sure. But give me time, and I'll get in.
What about forensics, Ms Zimonja? Does the blood we found on the ziggyball helmet match the victim?
Sure does, Detective.
And most of that blood was on the outside, concentrated in one area with outward spatter.
So barring some weird twilight zone explanation, yeah, this is your murder weapon.
The helmet also has fingerprints from both the victim, and your suspect J-P DeMarco -- but a dozen more people, too. I can get you a list, if you want...
...But with the gear being communal, everyone will say their prints are from a previous game. Yeah, I doubt that's gonna help.
Thanks, guys. Keep us updated.
Marlene, let's you and me take another run at our garbage patch king.

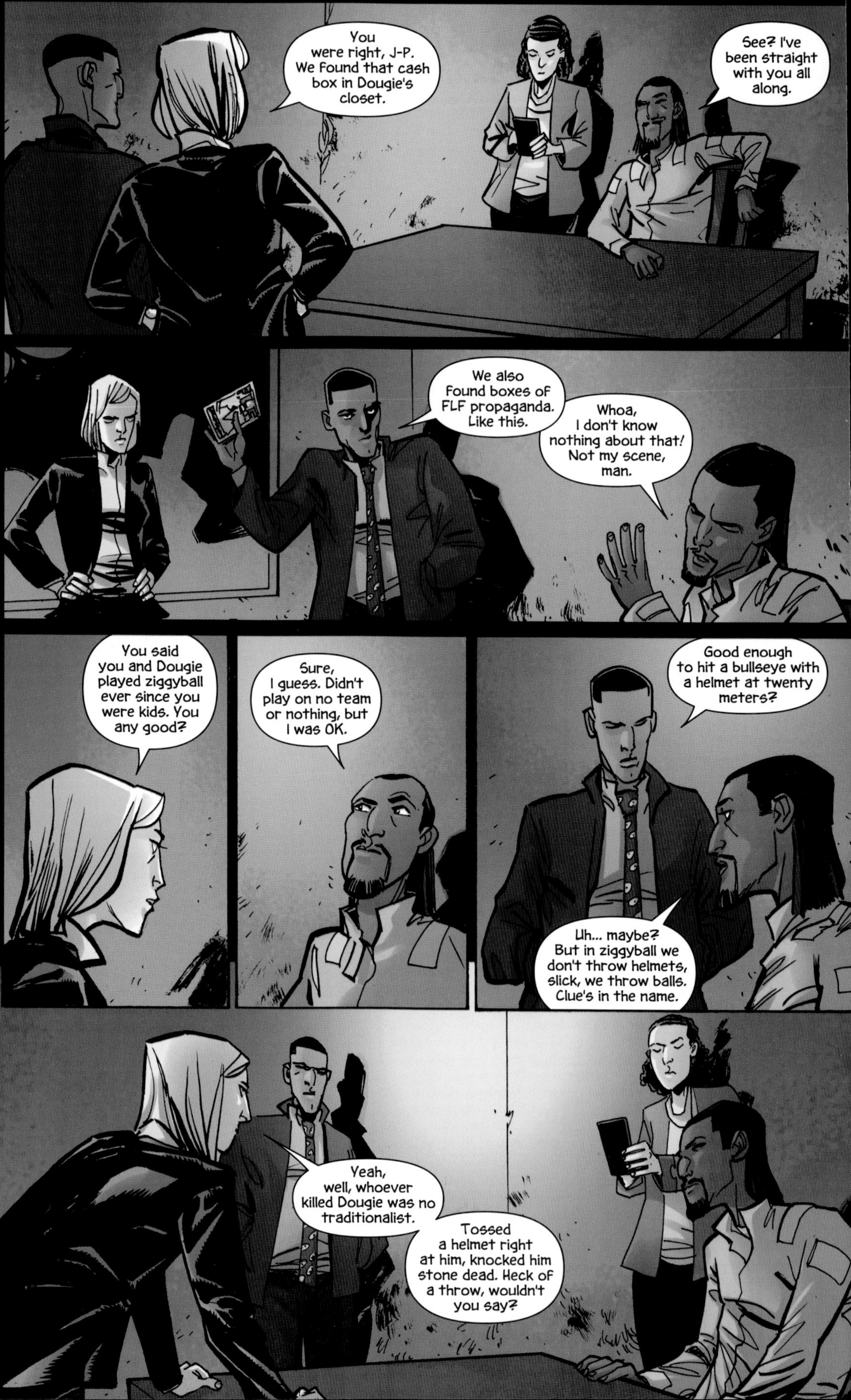
You were right, J-P. We found that cash box in Dougie's closet.
See? I've been straight with you all along.
We also found boxes of FLF propaganda. Like this.
Whoa, I don't know nothing about that! Not my scene, man.
You said you and Dougie played ziggyball ever since you were kids. You any good?
Sure, I guess. Didn't play on no team or nothing, but I was OK.
Good enough to hit a bullseye with a helmet at twenty meters?
Uh... maybe? But in ziggyball we don't throw helmets, slick, we throw balls. Clue's in the name.
Yeah, well, whoever killed Dougie was no traditionalist.
Tossed a helmet right at him, knocked him stone dead. Heck of a throw, wouldn't you say?

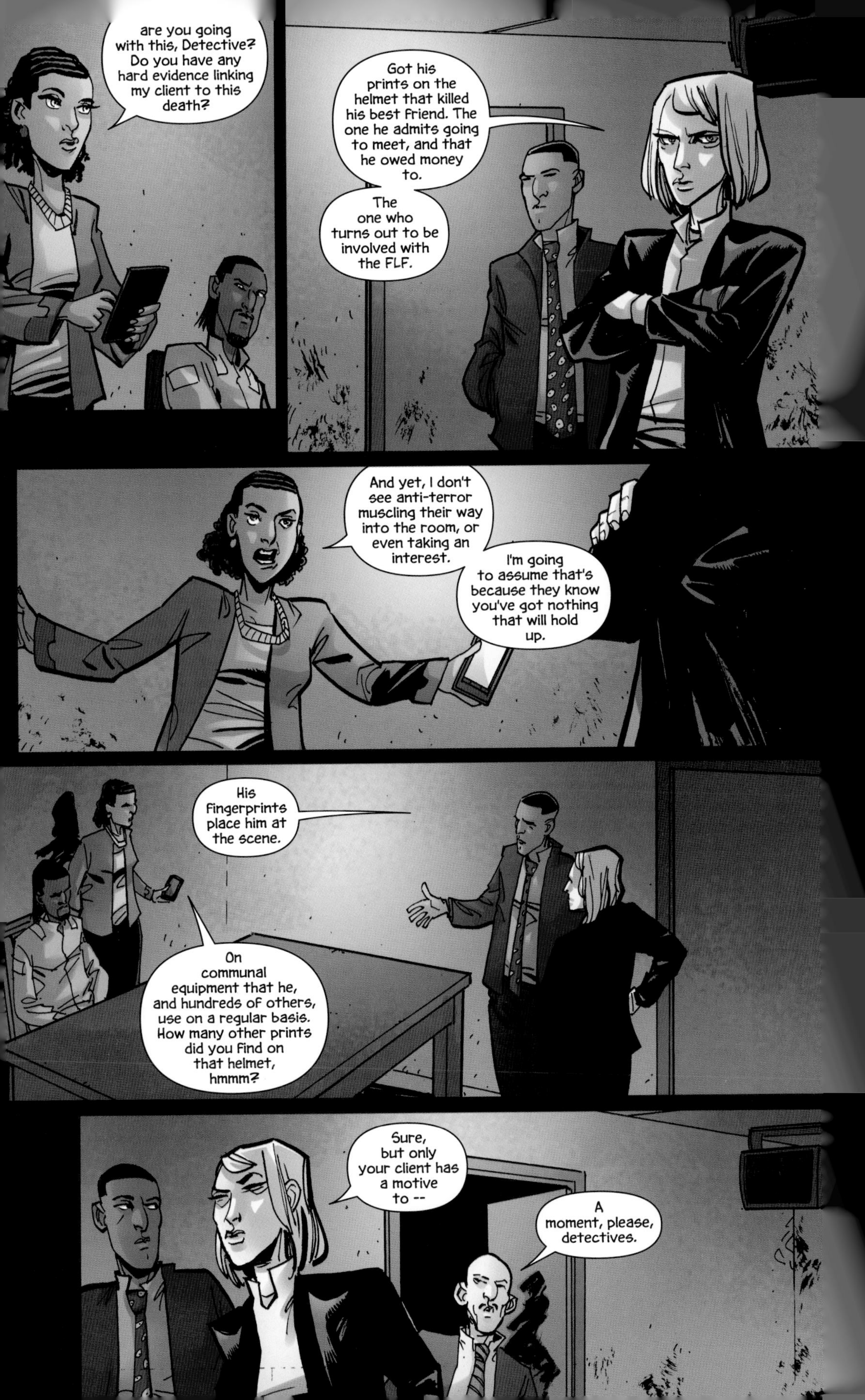

are you going with this, Detective? Do you have any hard evidence linking my client to this death?
Got his prints on the helmet that killed his best friend. The one he admits going to meet, and that he owed money to.
The one who turns out to be involved with the FLF.
And yet, I don't see anti-terror muscling their way into the room, or even taking an interest.
I'm going to assume that's because they know you've got nothing that will hold up.
His fingerprints place him at the scene.
On communal equipment that he, and hundreds of others, use on a regular basis. How many other prints did you find on that helmet, hmmm?
Sure, but only your client has a motive to --
A moment, please, detectives.

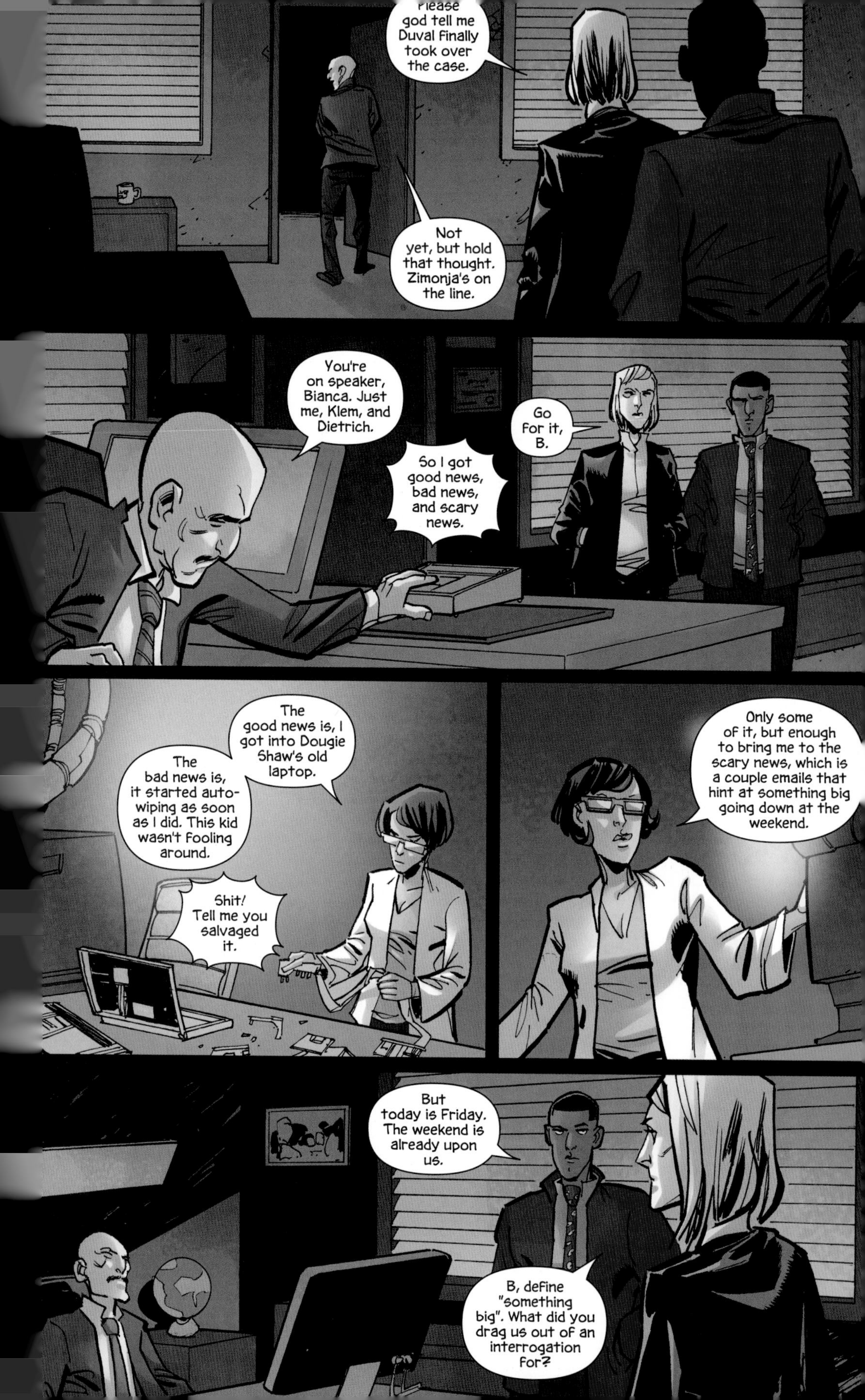
Please god tell me Duval finally took over the case.
Not yet, but hold that thought. Zimonja's on the line.
You're on speaker, Bianca. Just me, Klem, and Dietrich.
Go for it, B.
So I got good news, bad news, and scary news.
The good news is, I got into Dougie Shaw's old laptop.
The bad news is, it started auto-wiping as soon as I did. This kid wasn't fooling around.
Shit! Tell me you salvaged it.
Only some of it, but enough to bring me to the scary news, which is a couple emails that hint at something big going down at the weekend.
But today is Friday. The weekend is already upon us.
B, define "something big". What did you drag us out of an interrogation for?

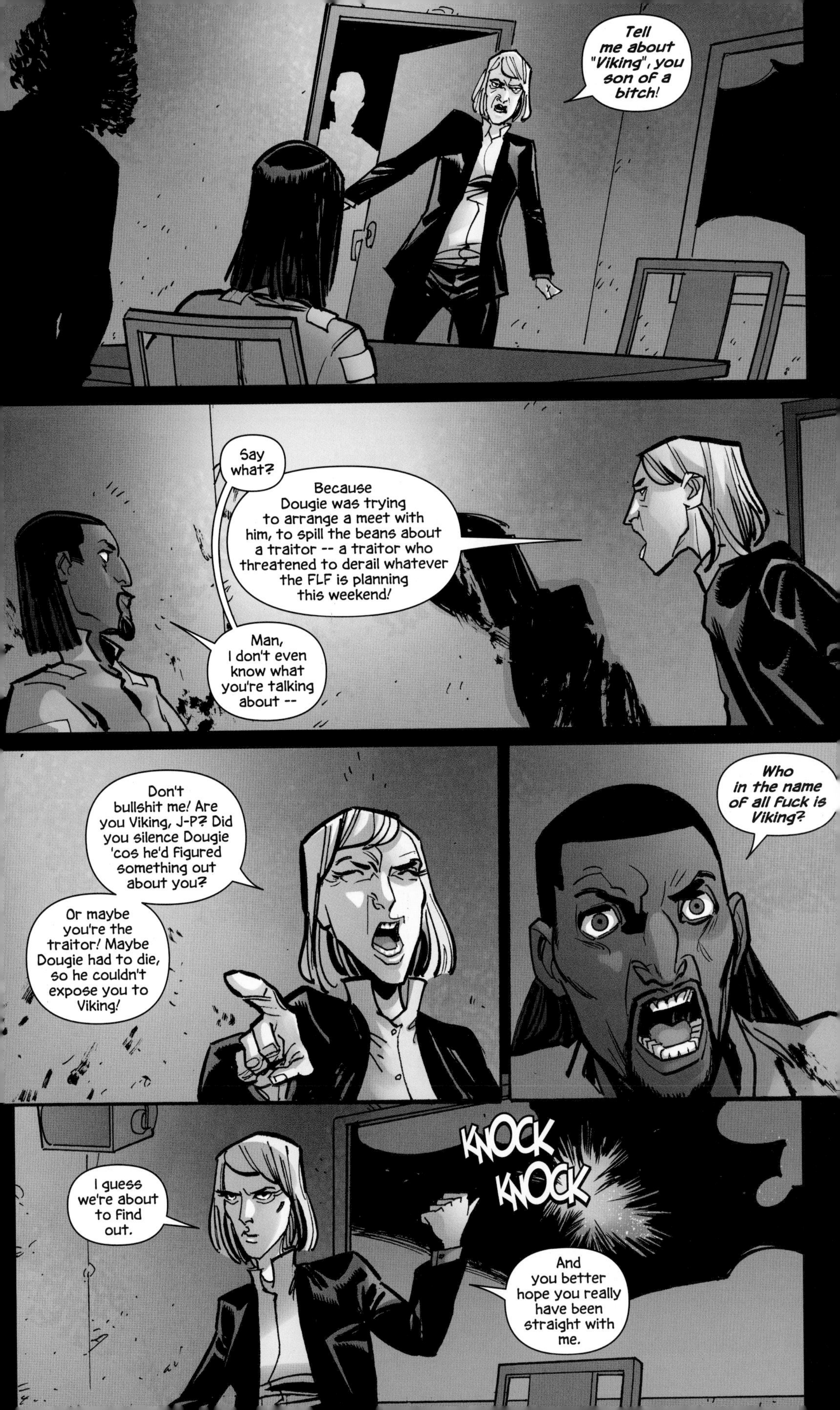

Tell me about "Viking", you son of a bitch!
Say what?
Because Dougie was trying to arrange a meet with him, to spill the beans about a traitor -- a traitor who threatened to derail whatever the FLF is planning this weekend!
Man, I don't even know what you're talking about --
Don't bullshit me! Are you Viking, J-P? Did you silence Dougie 'cos he'd figured something out about you?
Or maybe you're the traitor! Maybe Dougie had to die, so he couldn't expose you to Viking!
Who in the name of all fuck is Viking?
KNOCK
KNOCK
I guess we're about to find out.
And you better hope you really have been straight with me.

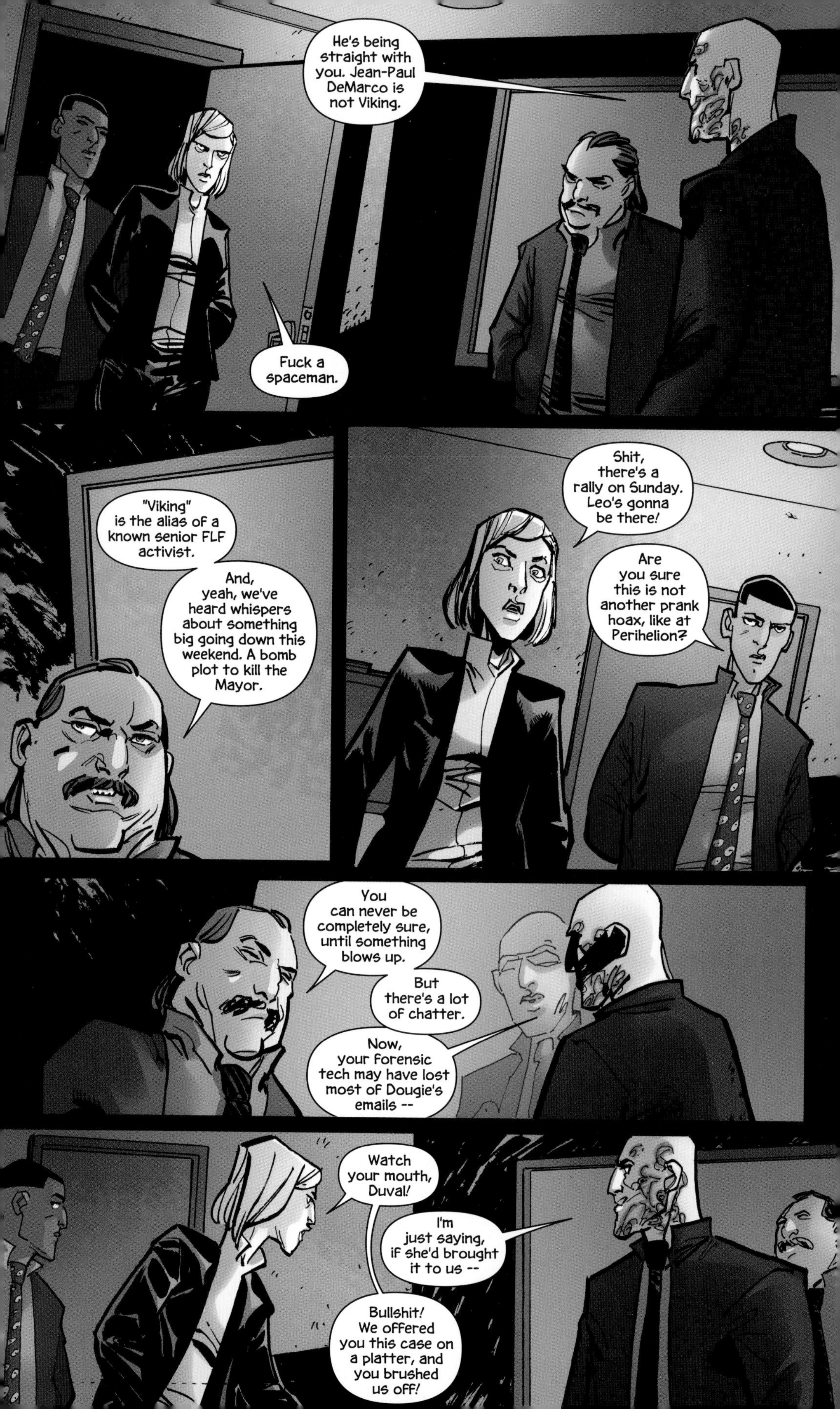

He's being straight with you. Jean-Paul DeMarco is not Viking.
Fuck a spaceman.
"Viking" is the alias of a known senior FLF activist.
And, yeah, we've heard whispers about something big going down this weekend. A bomb plot to kill the Mayor.
Shit, there's a rally on Sunday. Leo's gonna be there!
Are you sure this is not another prank hoax, like at Perihelion?
You can never be completely sure, until something blows up.
But there's a lot of chatter.
Now, your forensic tech may have lost most of Dougie's emails --
Watch your mouth, Duval!
I'm just saying, if she'd brought it to us --
Bullshit! We offered you this case on a platter, and you brushed us off!

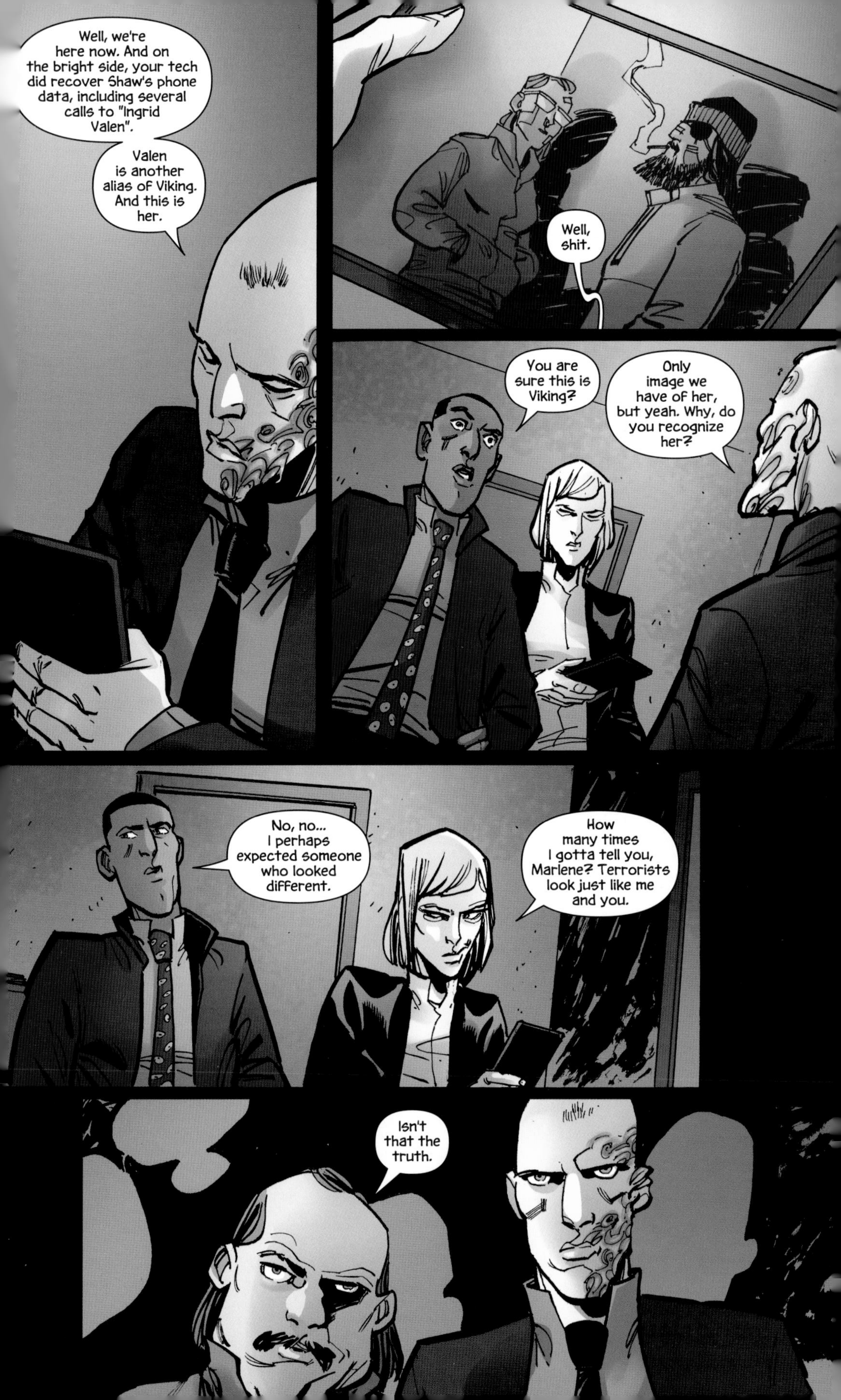
Well, we're here now. And on the bright side, your tech did recover Shaw's phone data, including several calls to "Ingrid Valen".
Valen is another alias of Viking. And this is her.
Well, shit.
You are sure this is Viking?
Only image we have of her, but yeah. Why, do you recognize her?
No, no... I perhaps expected someone who looked different.
How many times I gotta tell you, Marlene? Terrorists look just like me and you.
Isn't that the truth.

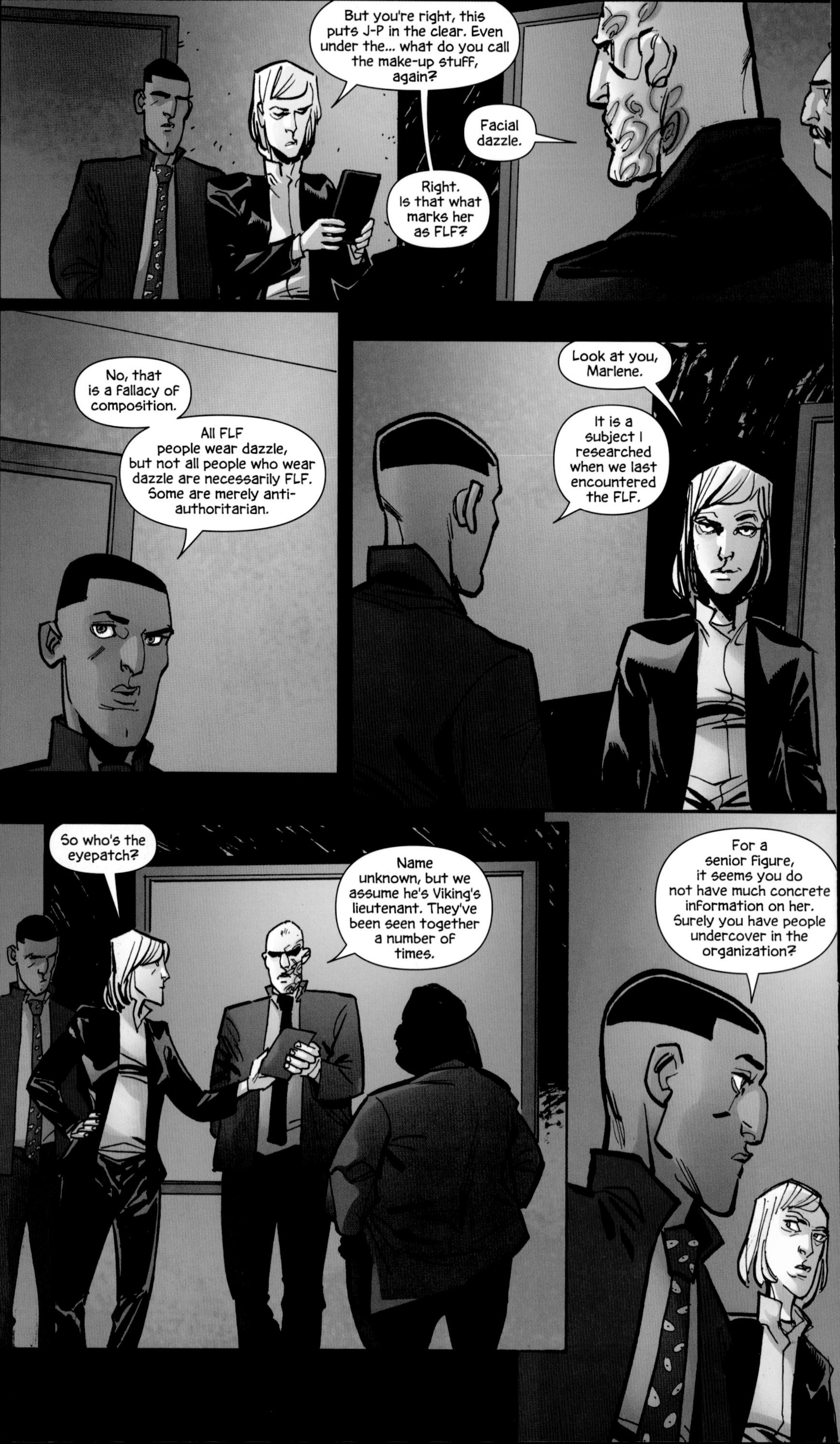
But you're right, this puts J-P in the clear. Even under the... what do you call the make-up stuff, again?
Facial dazzle.
Right. Is that what marks her as FLF?
No, that is a fallacy of composition.
All FLF people wear dazzle, but not all people who wear dazzle are necessarily FLF. Some are merely anti-authoritarian.
Look at you, Marlene.
It is a subject I researched when we last encountered the FLF.
So who's the eyepatch?
Name unknown, but we assume he's Viking's lieutenant. They've been seen together a number of times.
For a senior figure, it seems you do not have much concrete information on her. Surely you have people undercover in the organization?

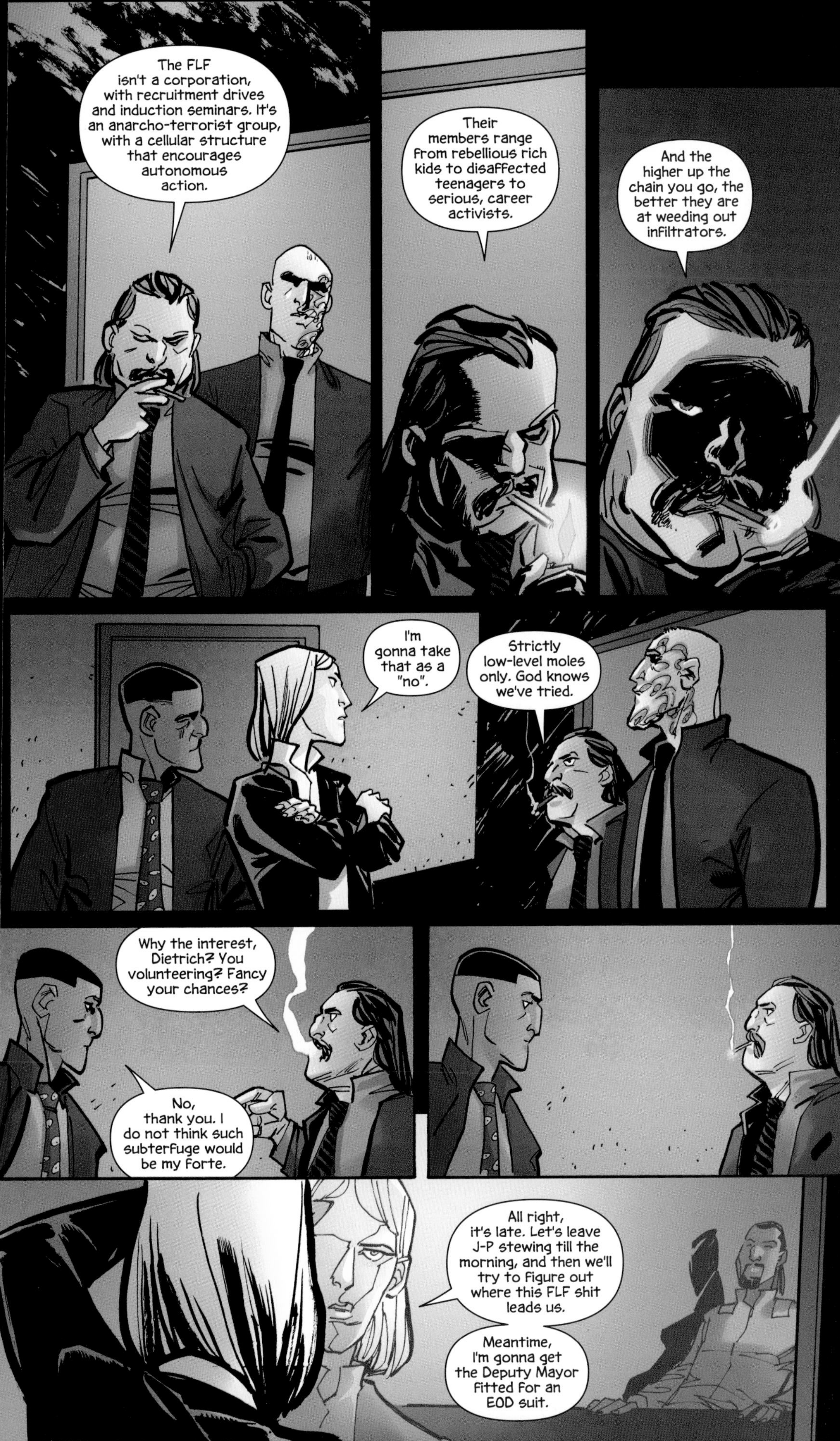
The FLF isn't a corporation, with recruitment drives and induction seminars. It's an anarcho-terrorist group, with a cellular structure that encourages autonomous action.
Their members range from rebellious rich kids to disaffected teenagers to serious, career activists.
And the higher up the chain you go, the better they are at weeding out infiltrators.
I'm gonna take that as a "no".
Strictly low-level moles only. God knows we've tried.
Why the interest, Dietrich? You volunteering? Fancy your chances?
No, thank you. I do not think such subterfuge would be my forte.
All right, it's late. Let's leave J-P stewing till the morning, and then we'll try to figure out where this FLF shit leads us.
Meantime, I'm gonna get the Deputy Mayor fitted for an EOD suit.

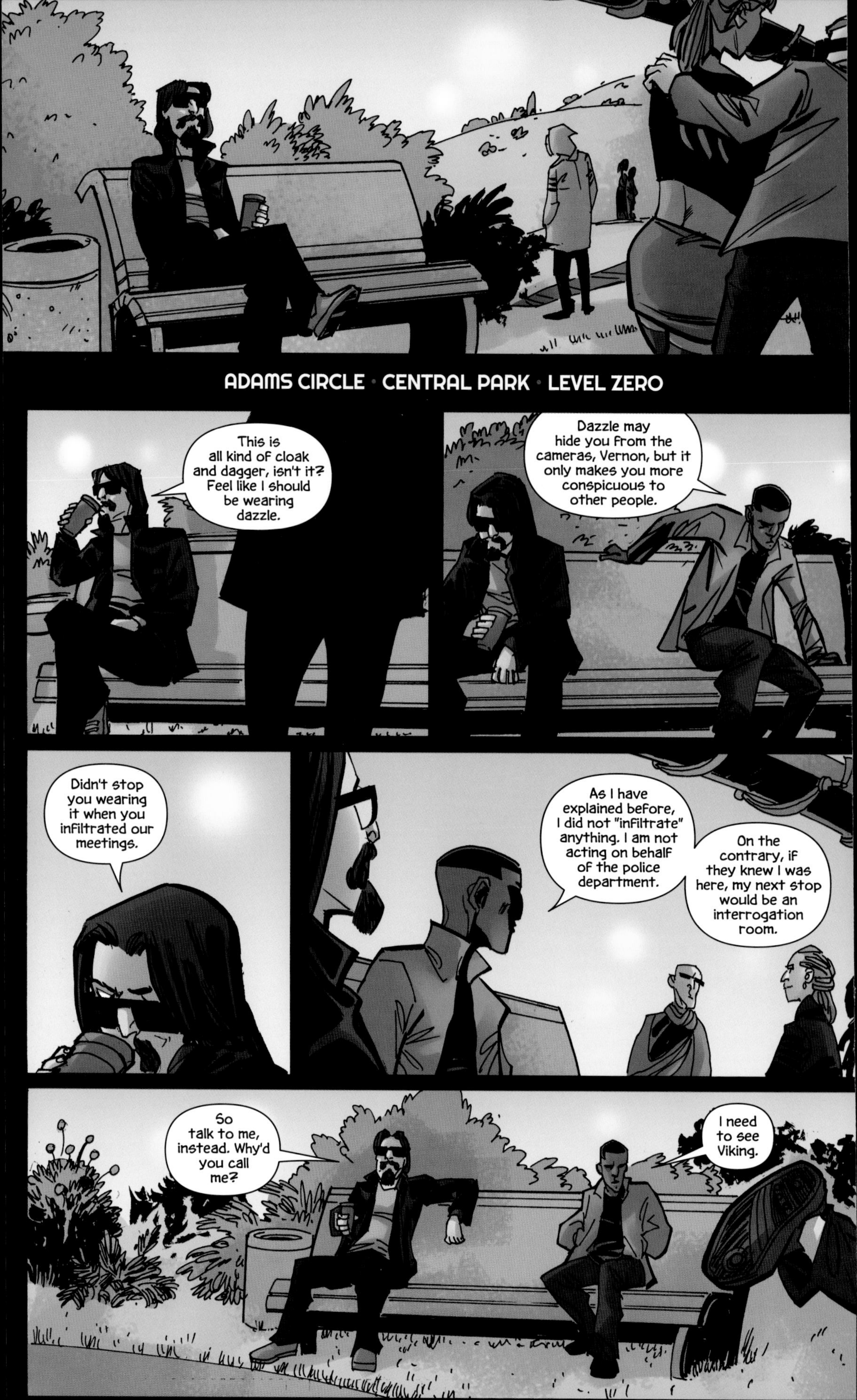
ADAMS CIRCLE · CENTRAL PARK · LEVEL ZERO
This is all kind of cloak and dagger, isn't it? Feel like I should be wearing dazzle.
Dazzle may hide you from the cameras, Vernon, but it only makes you more conspicuous to other people.
Didn't stop you wearing it when you infiltrated our meetings.
As I have explained before, I did not "infiltrate" anything. I am not acting on behalf of the police department.
On the contrary, if they knew I was here, my next stop would be an interrogation room.
So talk to me, instead. Why'd you call me?
I need to see Viking.

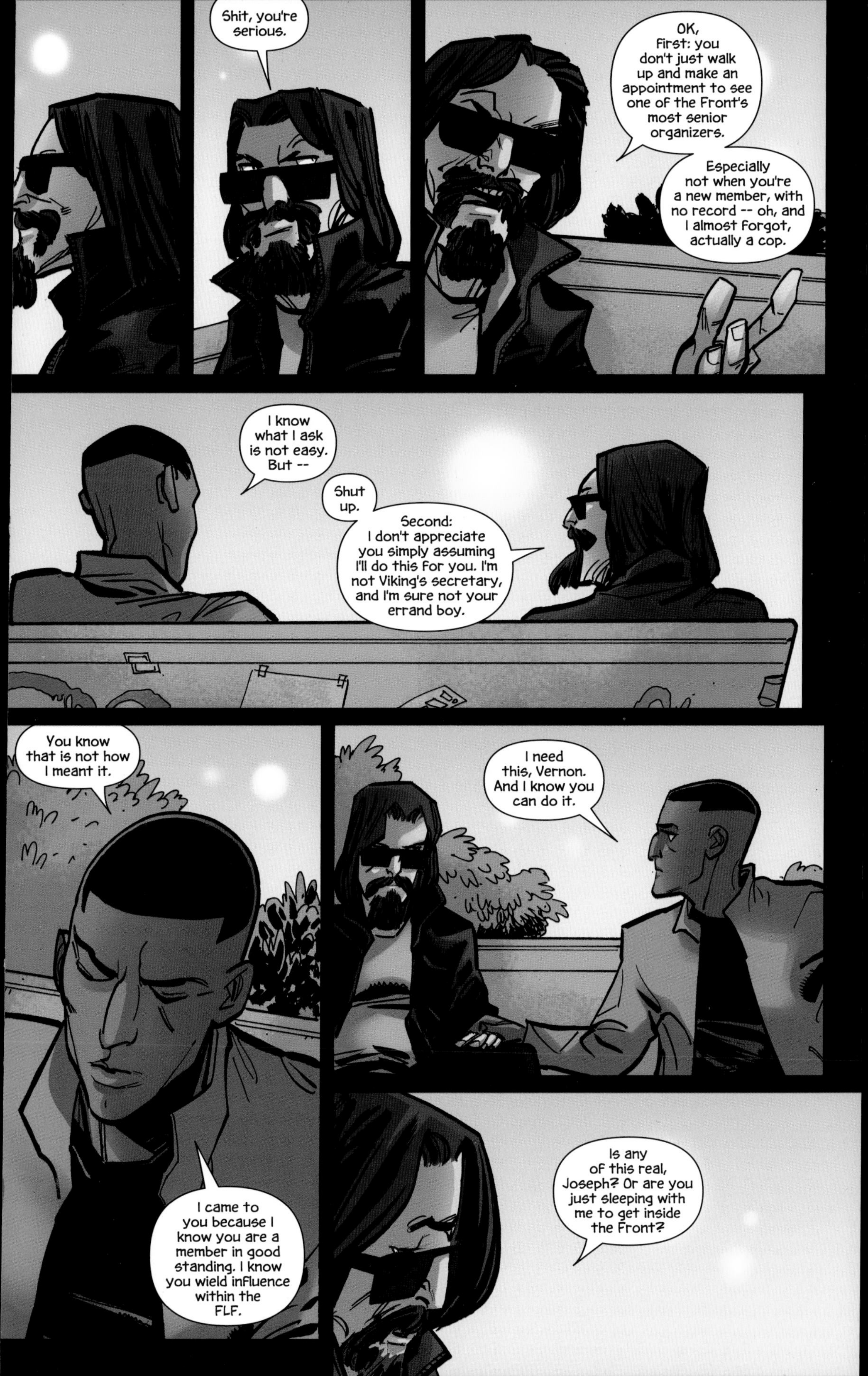
Shit, you're serious.
OK, First: you don't just walk up and make an appointment to see one of the Front's most senior organizers.
Especially not when you're a new member, with no record -- oh, and I almost forgot, actually a cop.
I know what I ask is not easy. But --
Shut up.
Second: I don't appreciate you simply assuming I'll do this for you. I'm not Viking's secretary, and I'm sure not your errand boy.
You know that is not how I meant it.
I came to you because I know you are a member in good standing. I know you wield influence within the FLF.
I need this, Vernon. And I know you can do it.
Is any of this real, Joseph? Or are you just sleeping with me to get inside the Front?

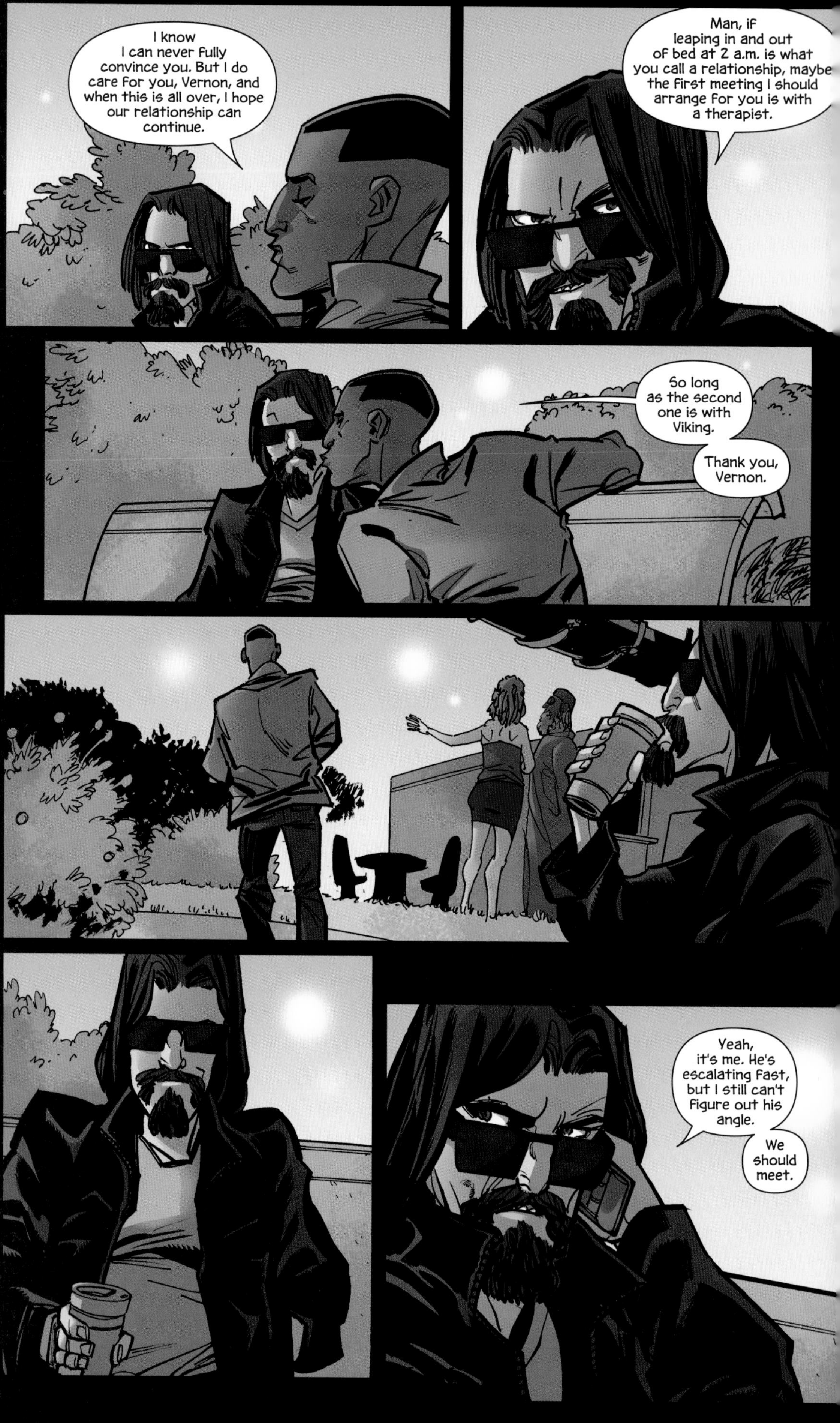
I know I can never fully convince you. But I do care for you, Vernon, and when this is all over, I hope our relationship can continue.
Man, if leaping in and out of bed at 2 a.m. is what you call a relationship, maybe the first meeting I should arrange for you is with a therapist.
So long as the second one is with Viking.
Thank you, Vernon.
Yeah, it's me. He's escalating fast, but I still can't figure out his angle.
We should meet.

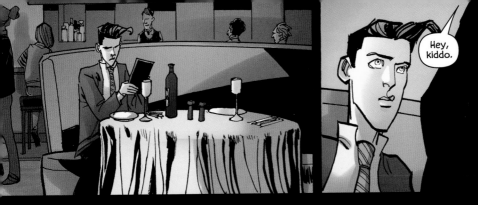

Hey, kiddo.

CHEZ GASPAR · PROTHEROE & 2ND · LEVEL ZERO

Hey, Mom. So good to see you.

Uh... whoa.

When you insisted on picking the place, I half-expected Fusion Burger over on 5th.

Mom, please. Give me some credit.

I know, but you and Nyal loved that place when you were kids.

Uh-oh. I don't see any prices, and that only ever means one thing.

Will you relax? I'm paying. Or rather, my expense account is.

I'll have the swordfish, Maurice. Easy on the salt.

Oui, Monsieur Zhirov. And for Madame?

Ce viande, c'est vraiment la chair d'un animal, oui? Par conséquent, les prix élevés.

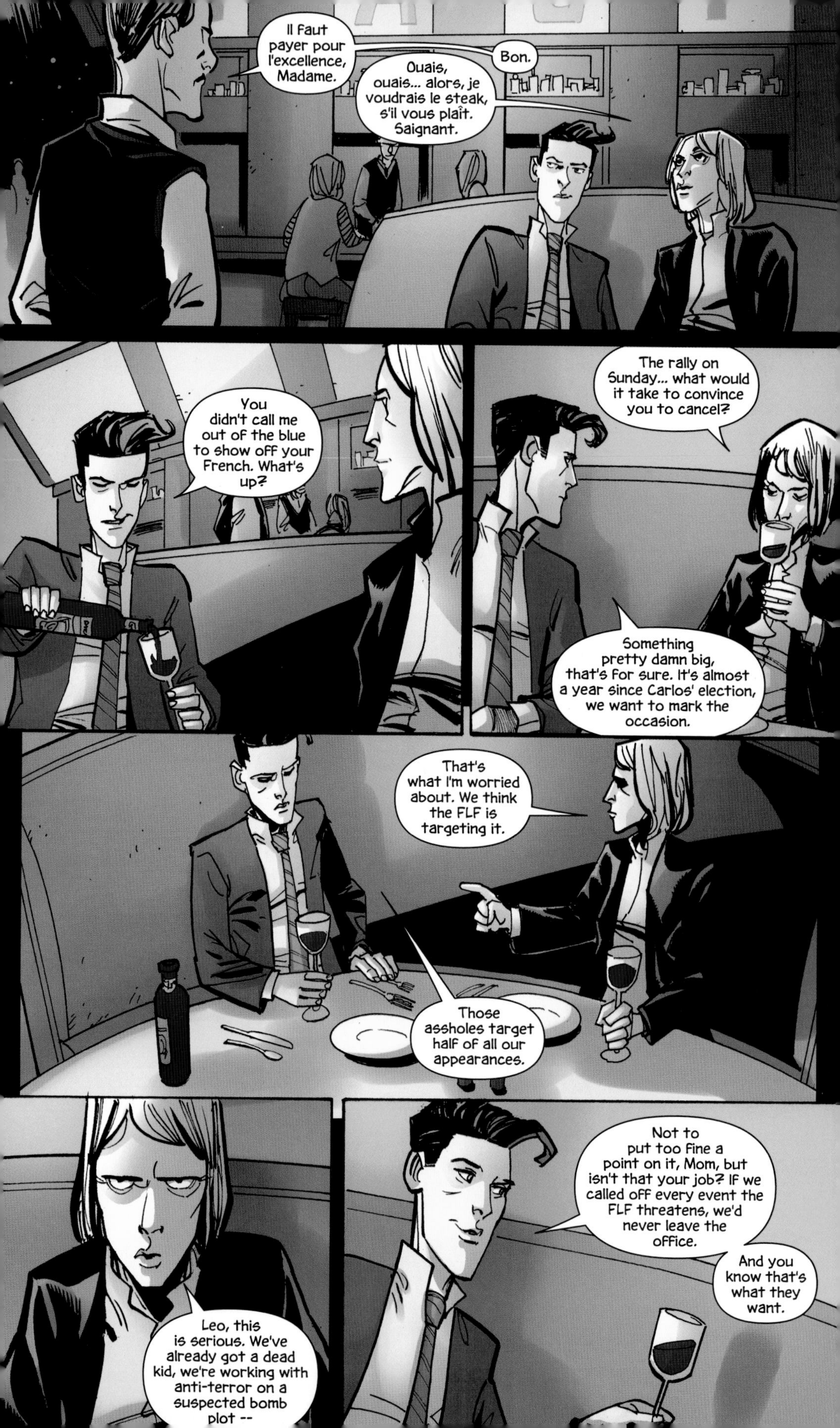
Il faut payer pour l'excellence, Madame.
Bon.
Ouais, ouais... alors, je voudrais le steak, s'il vous plaît. Saignant.
You didn't call me out of the blue to show off your French. What's up?
The rally on Sunday... what would it take to convince you to cancel?
Something pretty damn big, that's for sure. It's almost a year since Carlos' election, we want to mark the occasion.
That's what I'm worried about. We think the FLF is targeting it.
Those assholes target half of all our appearances.
Leo, this is serious. We've already got a dead kid, we're working with anti-terror on a suspected bomb plot --
Not to put too fine a point on it, Mom, but isn't that your job? If we called off every event the FLF threatens, we'd never leave the office.
And you know that's what they want.

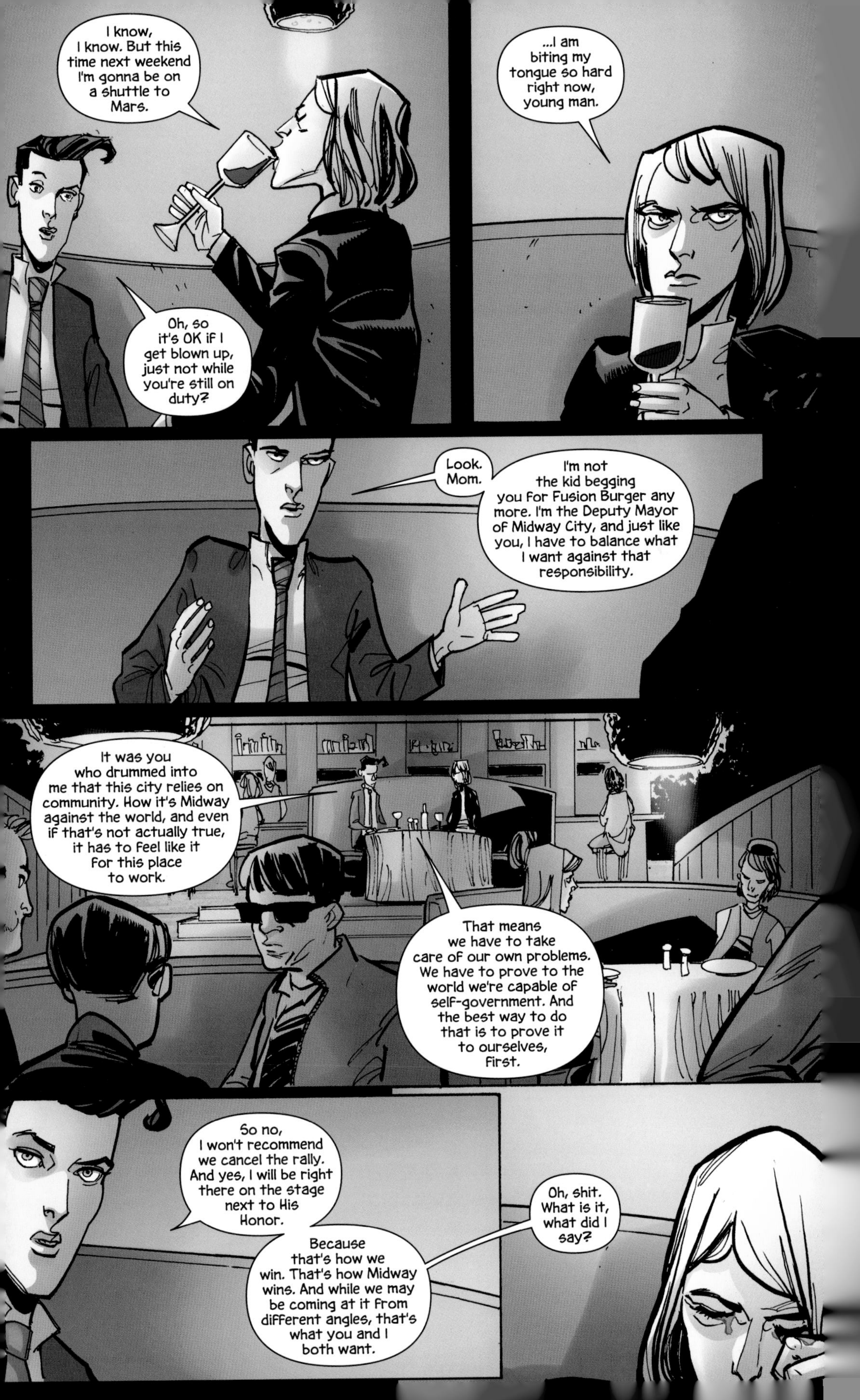
I know, I know. But this time next weekend I'm gonna be on a shuttle to Mars.
Oh, so it's OK if I get blown up, just not while you're still on duty?
...I am biting my tongue so hard right now, young man.
Look. Mom.
I'm not the kid begging you for Fusion Burger any more. I'm the Deputy Mayor of Midway City, and just like you, I have to balance what I want against that responsibility.
It was you who drummed into me that this city relies on community. How it's Midway against the world, and even if that's not actually true, it has to feel like it for this place to work.
That means we have to take care of our own problems. We have to prove to the world we're capable of self-government. And the best way to do that is to prove it to ourselves, first.
So no, I won't recommend we cancel the rally. And yes, I will be right there on the stage next to His Honor.
Because that's how we win. That's how Midway wins. And while we may be coming at it from different angles, that's what you and I both want.
Oh, shit. What is it, what did I say?

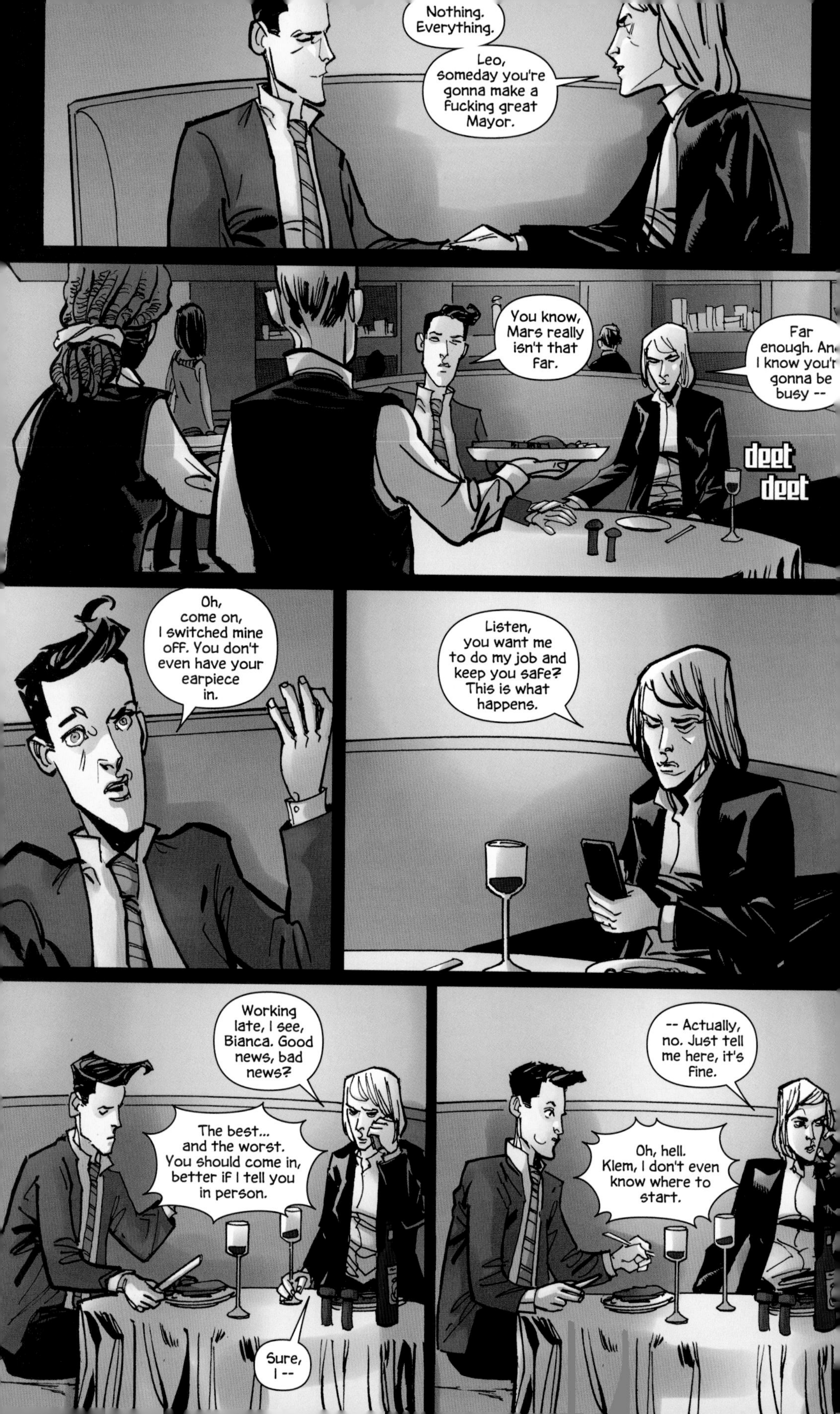
Nothing. Everything.
Leo, someday you're gonna make a fucking great Mayor.
You know, Mars really isn't that far.
Far enough. An
I know you'r
gonna be busy --
deet deet
Oh, come on, I switched mine off. You don't even have your earpiece in.
Listen, you want me to do my job and keep you safe? This is what happens.
Working late, I see, Bianca. Good news, bad news?
The best... and the worst. You should come in, better if I tell you in person.
Sure, I --
-- Actually, no. Just tell me here, it's fine.
Oh, hell. Klem, I don't even know where to start.

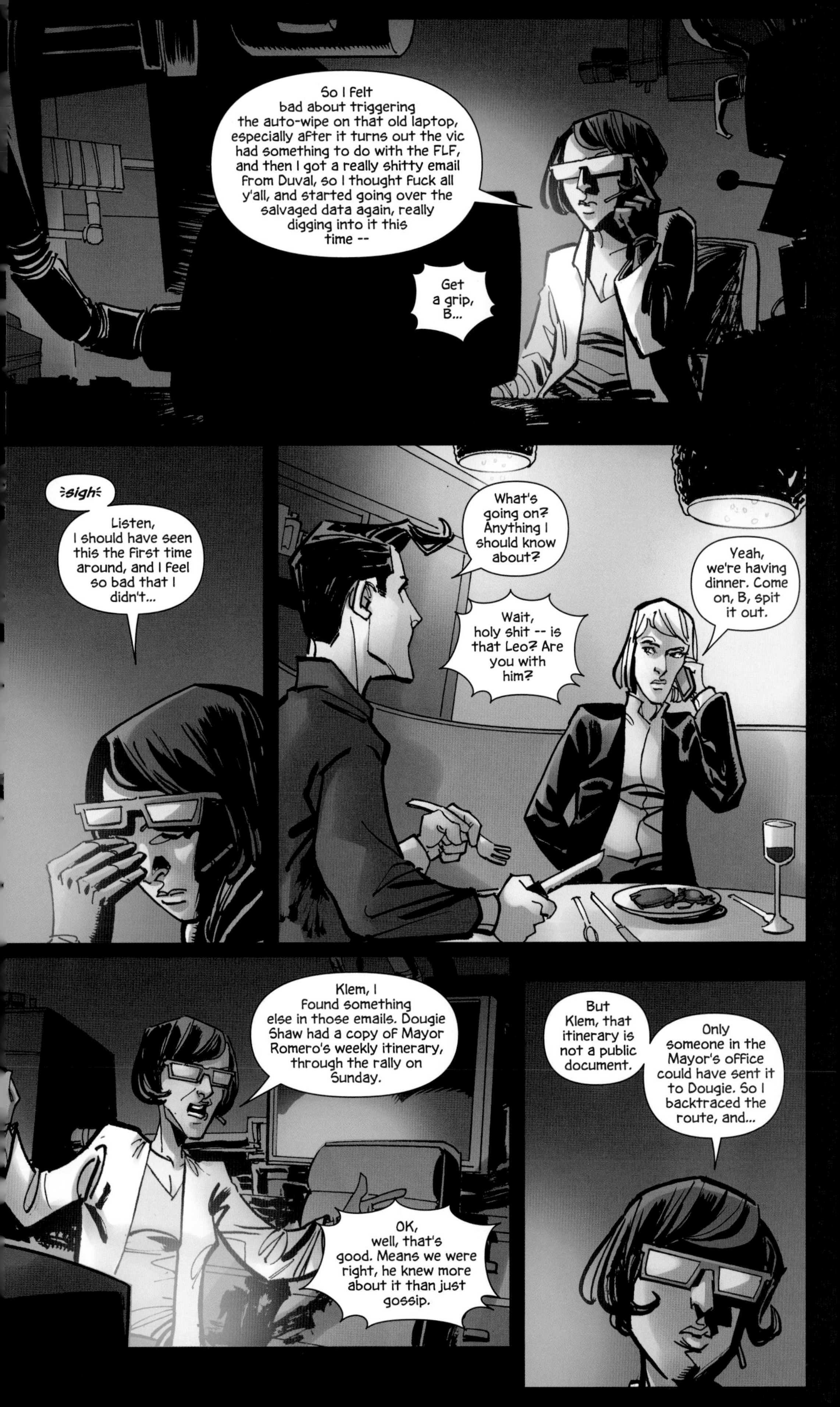
So I felt bad about triggering the auto-wipe on that old laptop, especially after it turns out the vic had something to do with the FLF, and then I got a really shitty email from Duval, so I thought fuck all y'all, and started going over the salvaged data again, really digging into it this time --
Get a grip, B...
sigh
Listen, I should have seen this the first time around, and I feel so bad that I didn't...
What's going on? Anything I should know about?
Yeah, we're having dinner. Come on, B, spit it out.
Wait, holy shit -- is that Leo? Are you with him?
Klem, I found something else in those emails. Dougie Shaw had a copy of Mayor Romero's weekly itinerary, through the rally on Sunday.
OK, well, that's good. Means we were right, he knew more about it than just gossip.
But Klem, that itinerary is not a public document.
Only someone in the Mayor's office could have sent it to Dougie. So I backtraced the route, and...

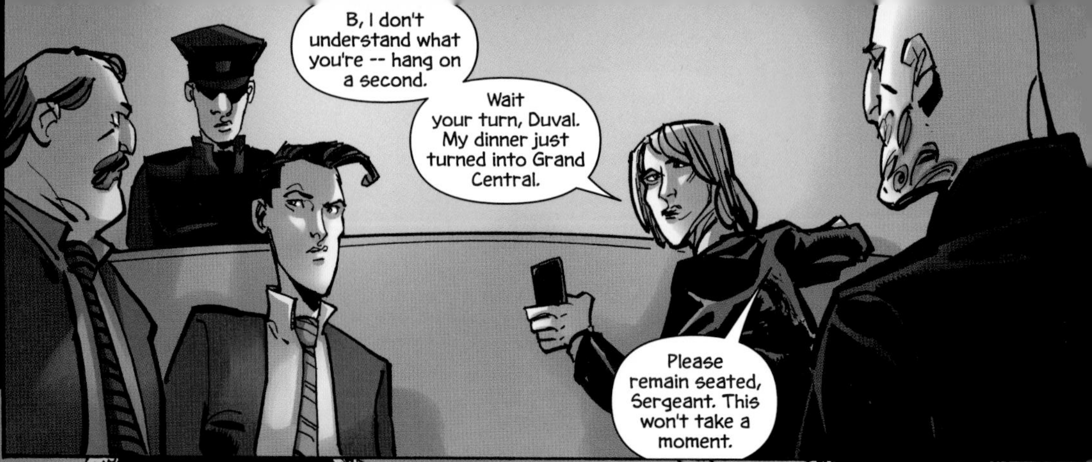
B, I don't understand what you're -- hang on a second.
Wait your turn, Duval. My dinner just turned into Grand Central.
Please remain seated, Sergeant. This won't take a moment.
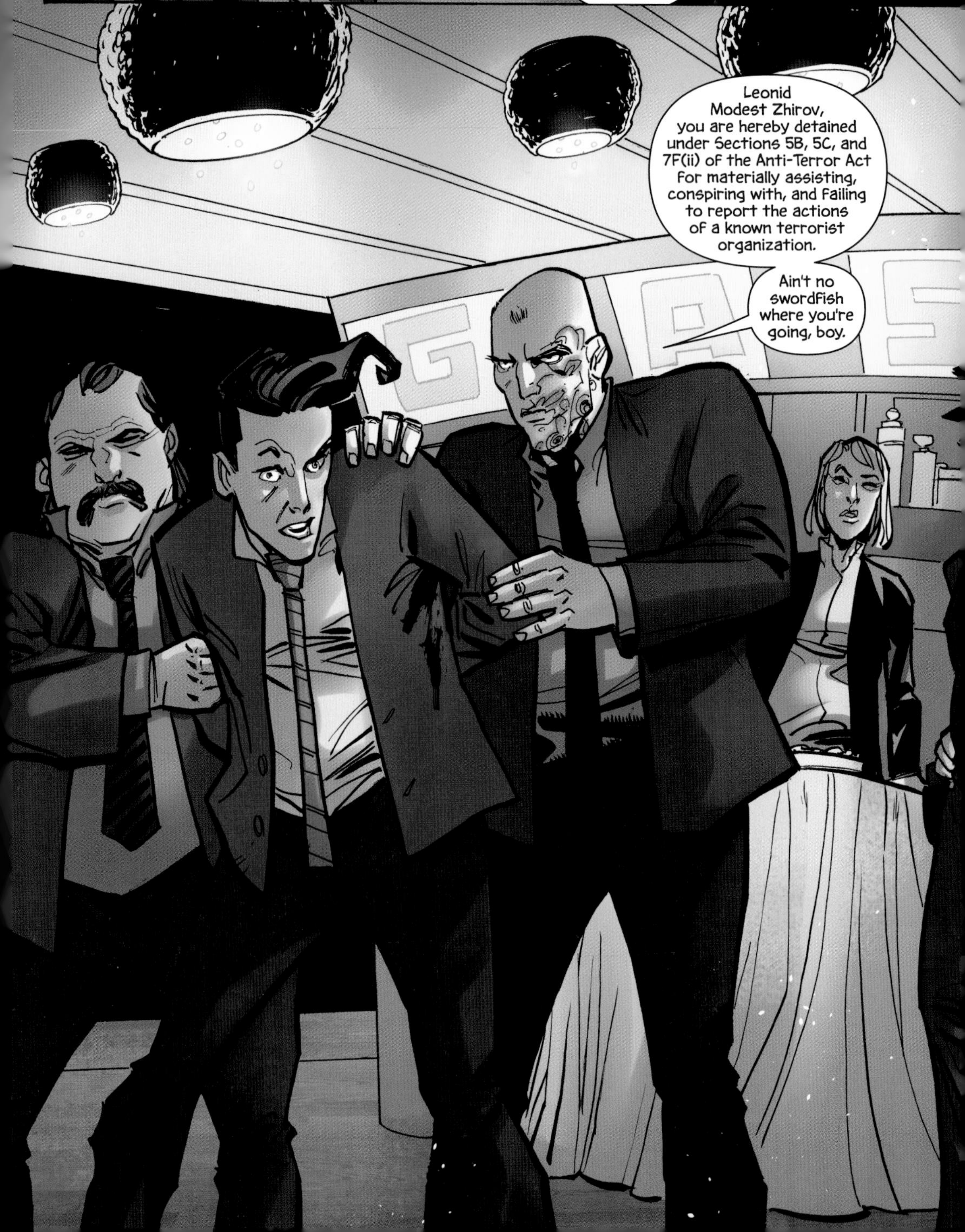
Leonid Modest Zhirov, you are hereby detained under Sections 5B, 5C, and 7F(ii) of the Anti-Terror Act for materially assisting, conspiring with, and failing to report the actions of a known terrorist organization.
Ain't no swordfish where you're going, boy.

PART 3

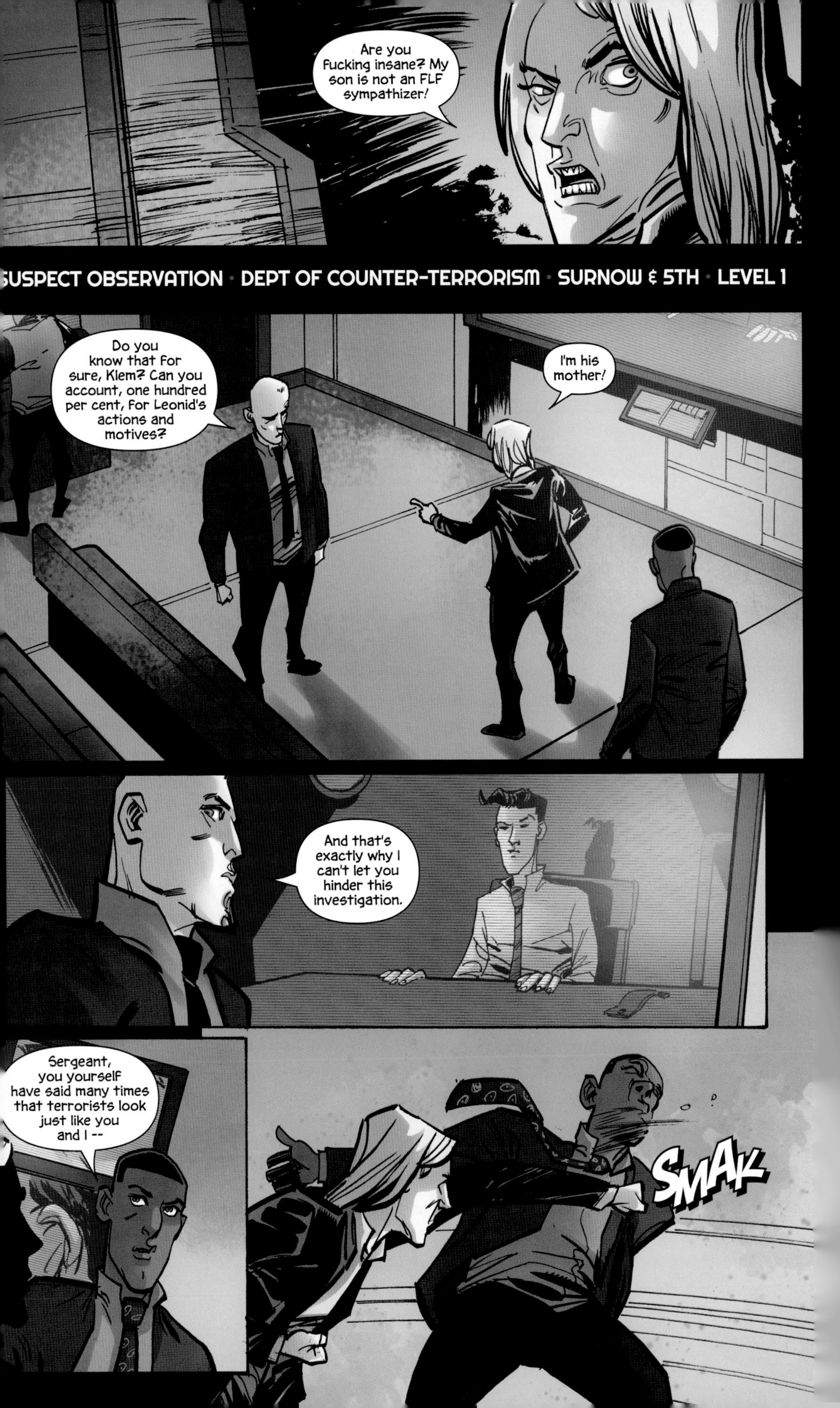
Are you fucking insane? My son is not an FLF sympathizer!
SUSPECT OBSERVATION · DEPT OF COUNTER-TERRORISM · SURNOW & 5TH · LEVEL 1
Do you know that for sure, Klem? Can you account, one hundred per cent, for Leonid's actions and motives?
I'm his mother!
And that's exactly why I can't let you hinder this investigation.
Sergeant, you yourself have said many times that terrorists look just like you and I --
SMAK

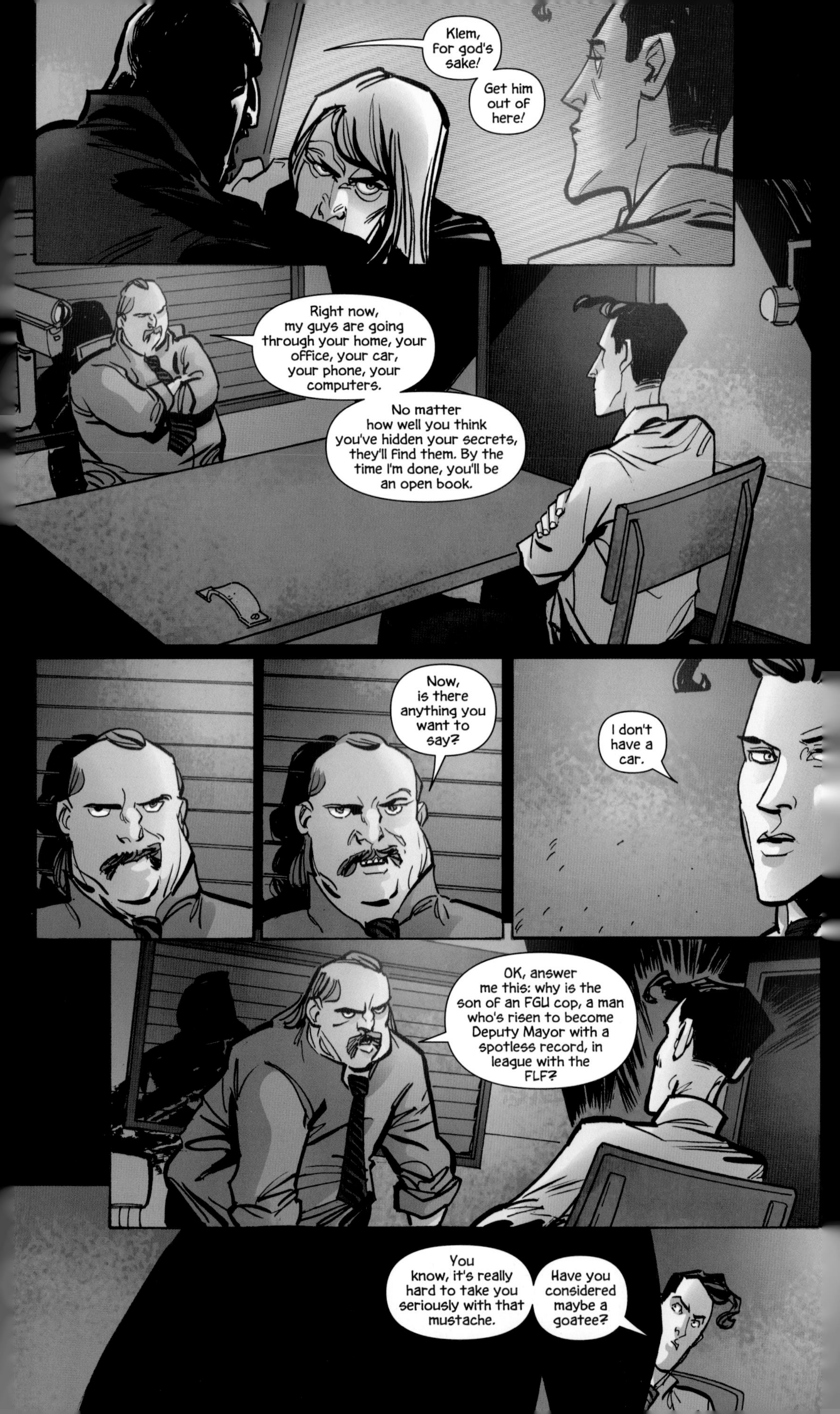

Klem, for god's sake!
Get him out of here!
Right now, my guys are going through your home, your office, your car, your phone, your computers.
No matter how well you think you've hidden your secrets, they'll find them. By the time I'm done, you'll be an open book.
Now, is there anything you want to say?
I don't have a car.
OK, answer me this: why is the son of an FGU cop, a man who's risen to become Deputy Mayor with a spotless record, in league with the FLF?
You know, it's really hard to take you seriously with that mustache.
Have you considered maybe a goatee?

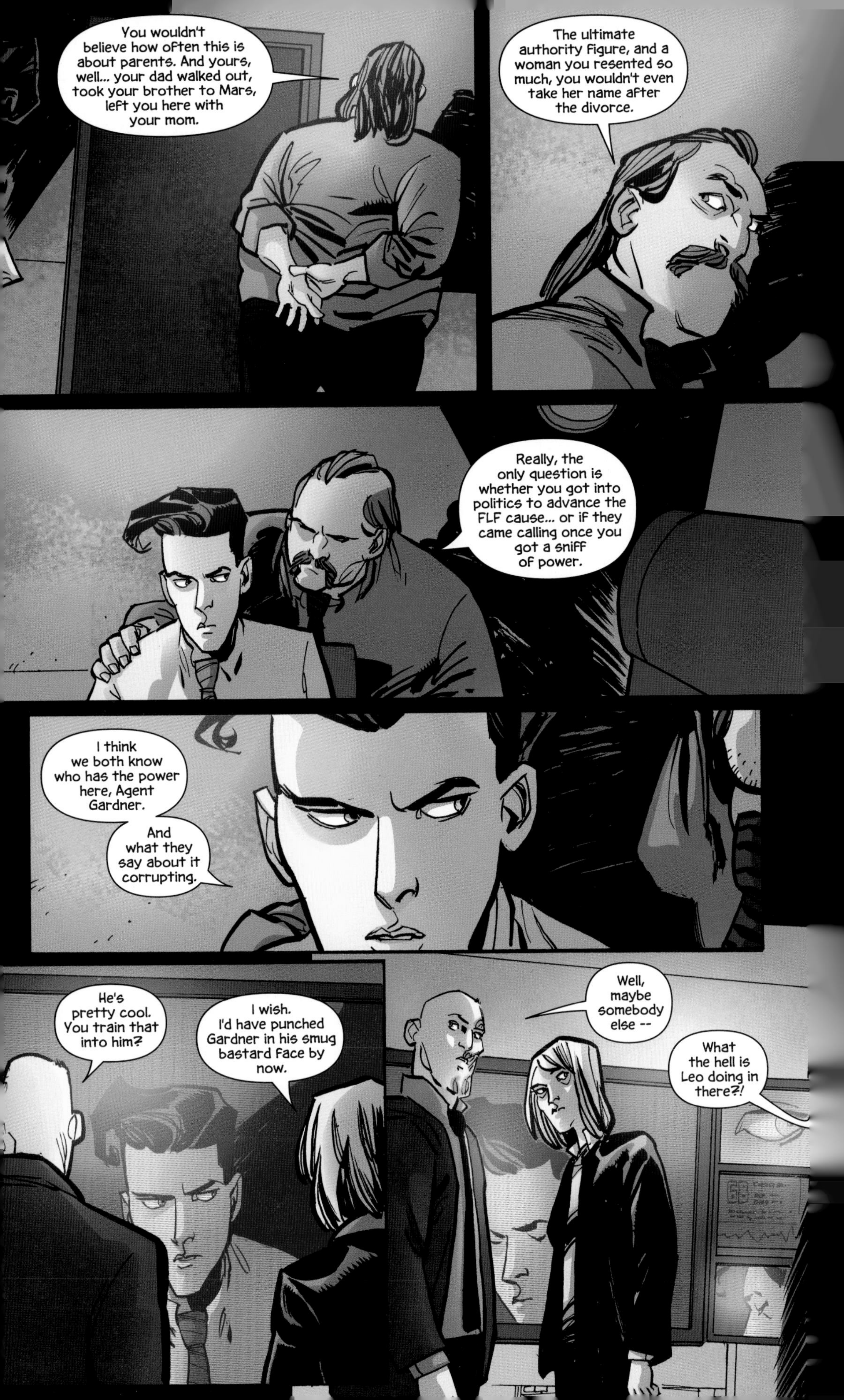
You wouldn't believe how often this is about parents. And yours, well... your dad walked out, took your brother to Mars, left you here with your mom.
The ultimate authority figure, and a woman you resented so much, you wouldn't even take her name after the divorce.
Really, the only question is whether you got into politics to advance the FLF cause... or if they came calling once you got a sniff of power.
I think we both know who has the power here, Agent Gardner.
And what they say about it corrupting.
He's pretty cool. You train that into him?
I wish. I'd have punched Gardner in his smug bastard face by now.
Well, maybe somebody else --
What the hell is Leo doing in there?!

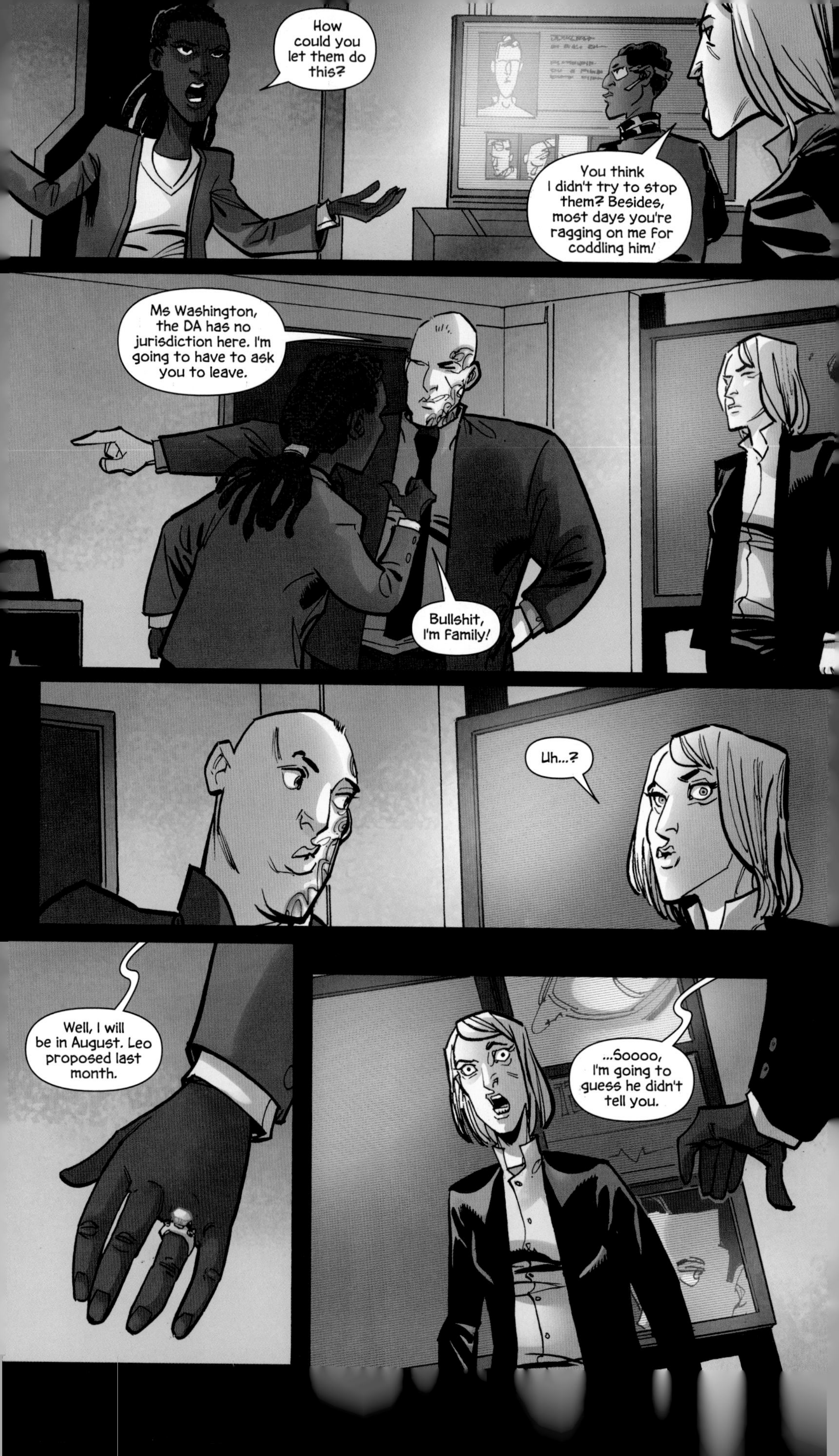
How could you let them do this?
You think I didn't try to stop them? Besides, most days you're ragging on me for coddling him!
Ms Washington, the DA has no jurisdiction here. I'm going to have to ask you to leave.
Bullshit, I'm Family!
Uh...?
Well, I will be in August. Leo proposed last month.
...Soooo, I'm going to guess he didn't tell you.

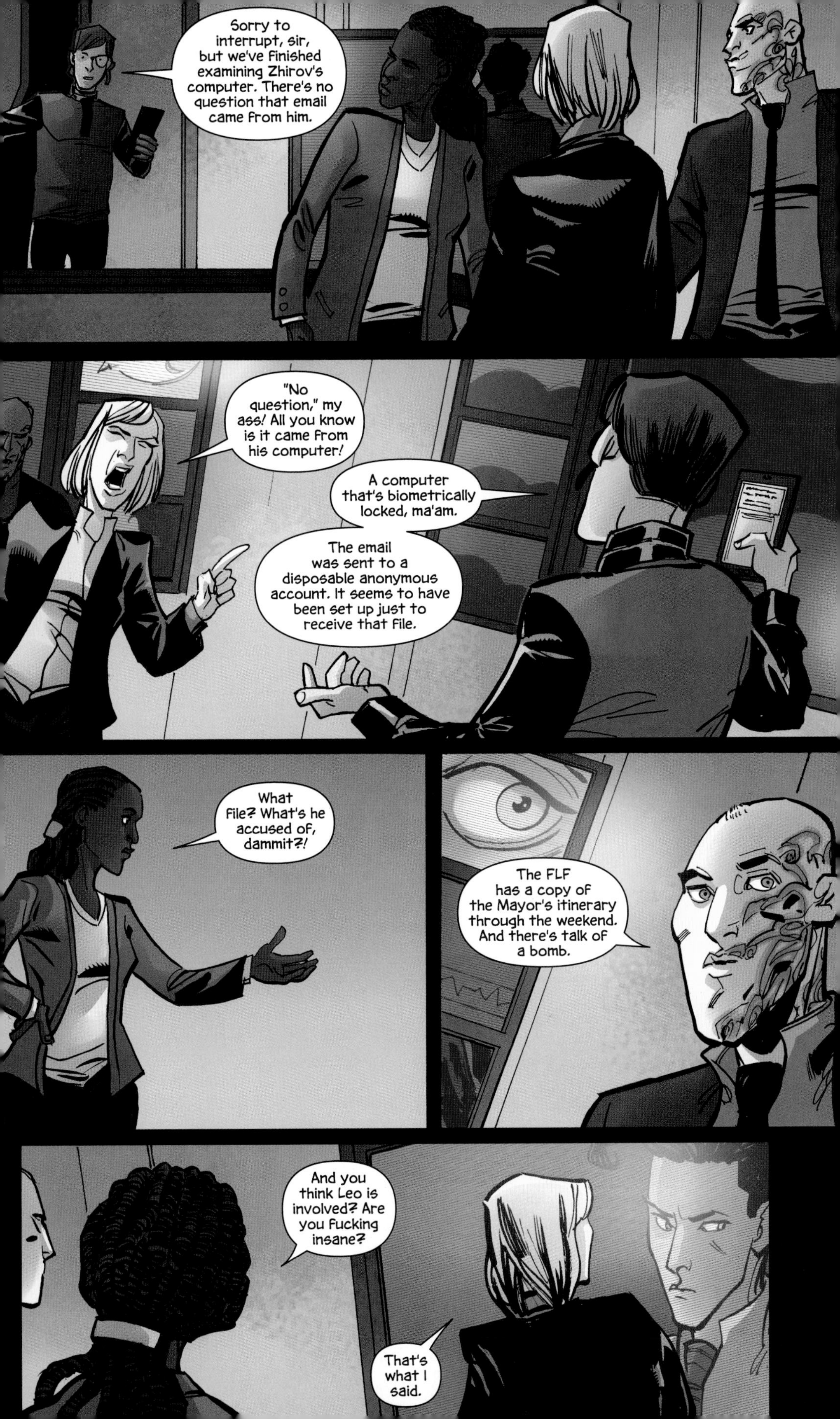
Sorry to interrupt, sir, but we've finished examining Zhirov's computer. There's no question that email came from him.
"No question," my ass! All you know is it came from his computer!
A computer that's biometrically locked, ma'am.
The email was sent to a disposable anonymous account. It seems to have been set up just to receive that file.
What file? What's he accused of, dammit?!
The FLF has a copy of the Mayor's itinerary through the weekend. And there's talk of a bomb.
And you think Leo is involved? Are you fucking insane?
That's what I said.

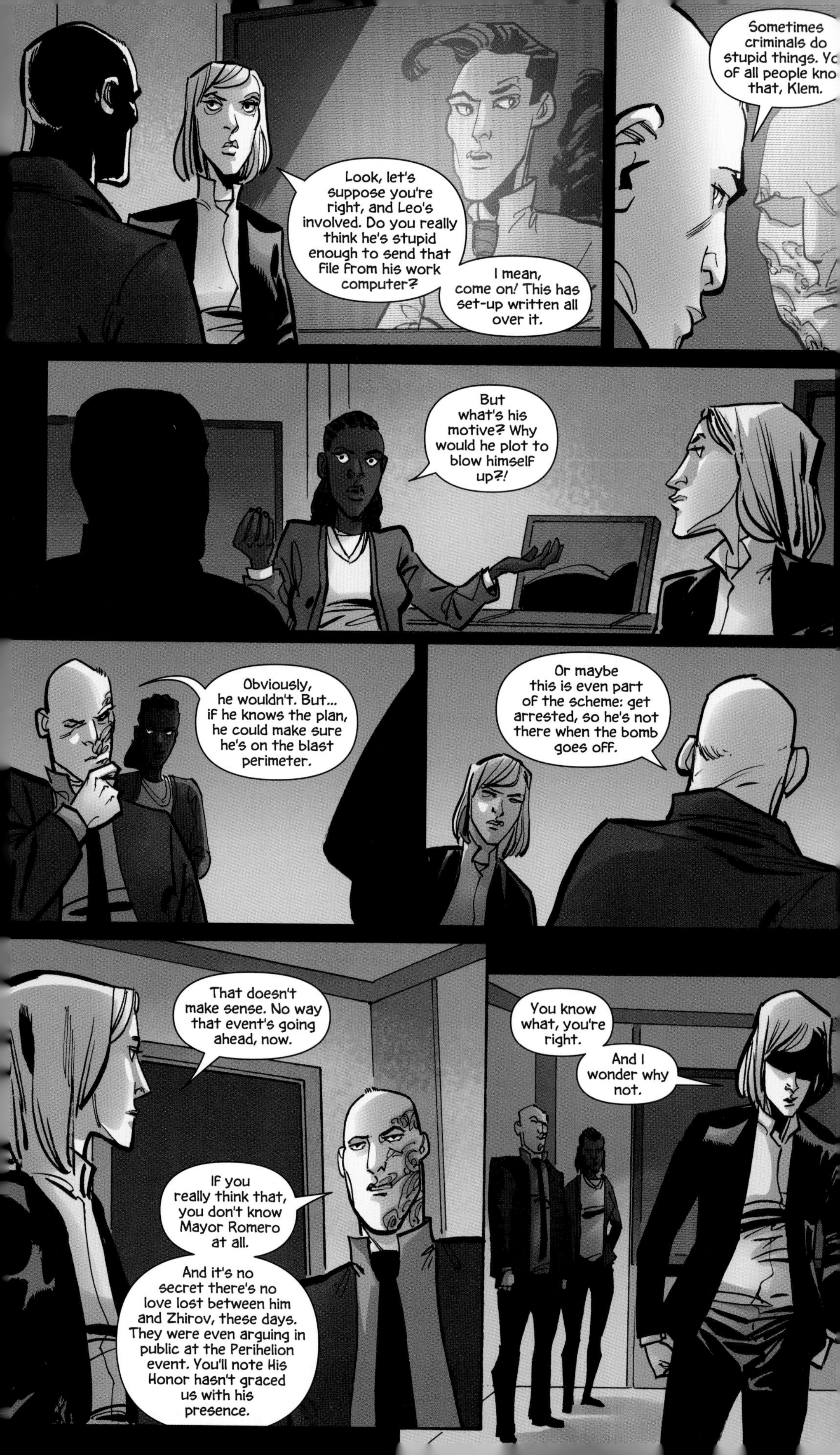

Look, let's suppose you're right, and Leo's involved. Do you really think he's stupid enough to send that file from his work computer?
I mean, come on! This has set-up written all over it.
Sometimes criminals do stupid things. Yo of all people kno that, Klem.
But what's his motive? Why would he plot to blow himself up?!
Obviously, he wouldn't. But... if he knows the plan, he could make sure he's on the blast perimeter.
Or maybe this is even part of the scheme: get arrested, so he's not there when the bomb goes off.
That doesn't make sense. No way that event's going ahead, now.
If you really think that, you don't know Mayor Romero at all.
And it's no secret there's no love lost between him and Zhirov, these days. They were even arguing in public at the Perihelion event. You'll note His Honor hasn't graced us with his presence.
You know what, you're right.
And I wonder why not.

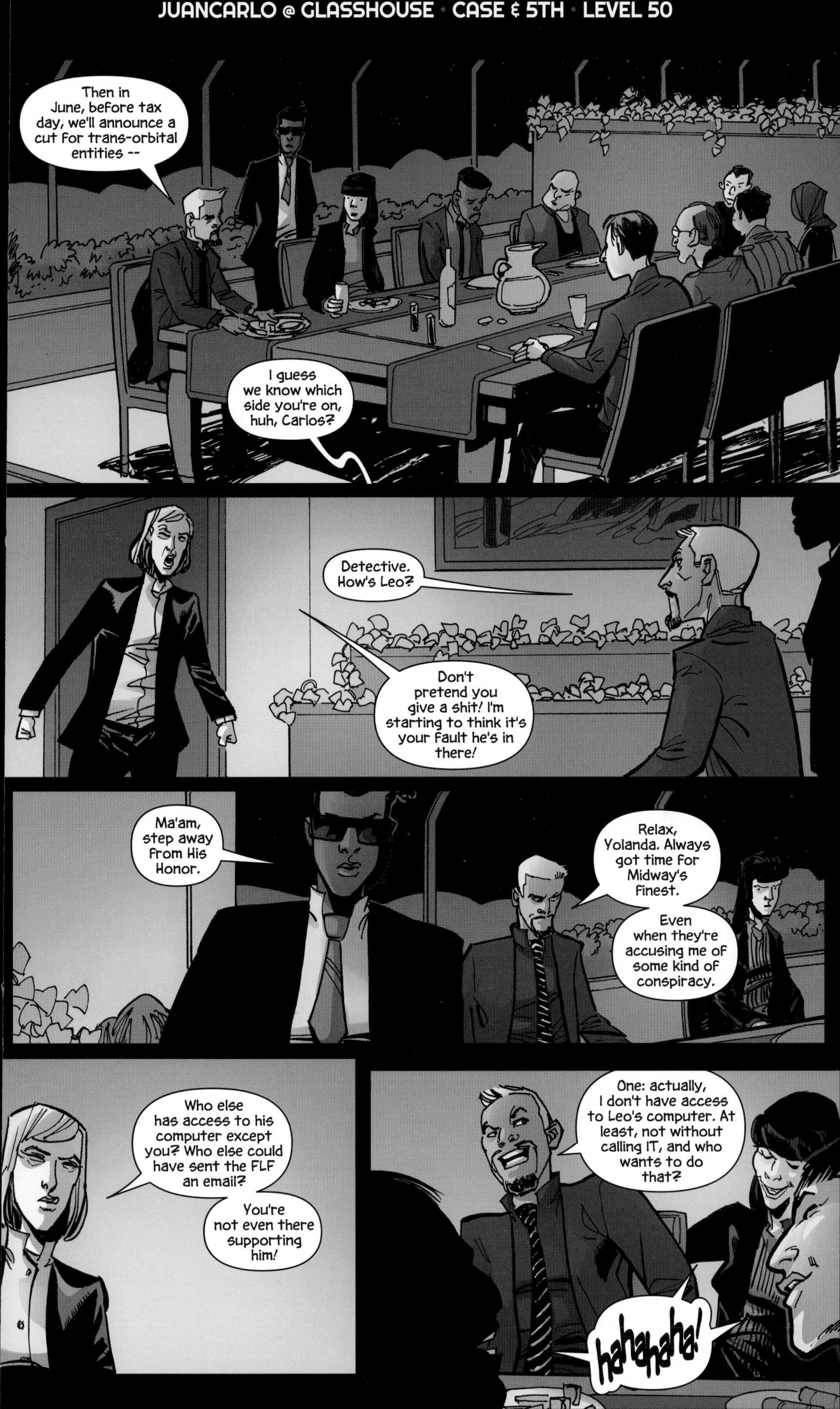

JUANCARLO @ GLASSHOUSE • CASE & 5TH • LEVEL 50
Then in June, before tax day, we'll announce a cut for trans-orbital entities --
I guess we know which side you're on, huh, Carlos?
Detective. How's Leo?
Don't pretend you give a shit! I'm starting to think it's your fault he's in there!
Ma'am, step away from His Honor.
Relax, Yolanda. Always got time for Midway's Finest.
Even when they're accusing me of some kind of conspiracy.
Who else has access to his computer except you? Who else could have sent the FLF an email?
You're not even there supporting him!
One: actually, I don't have access to Leo's computer. At least, not without calling IT, and who wants to do that?
hahahaha!

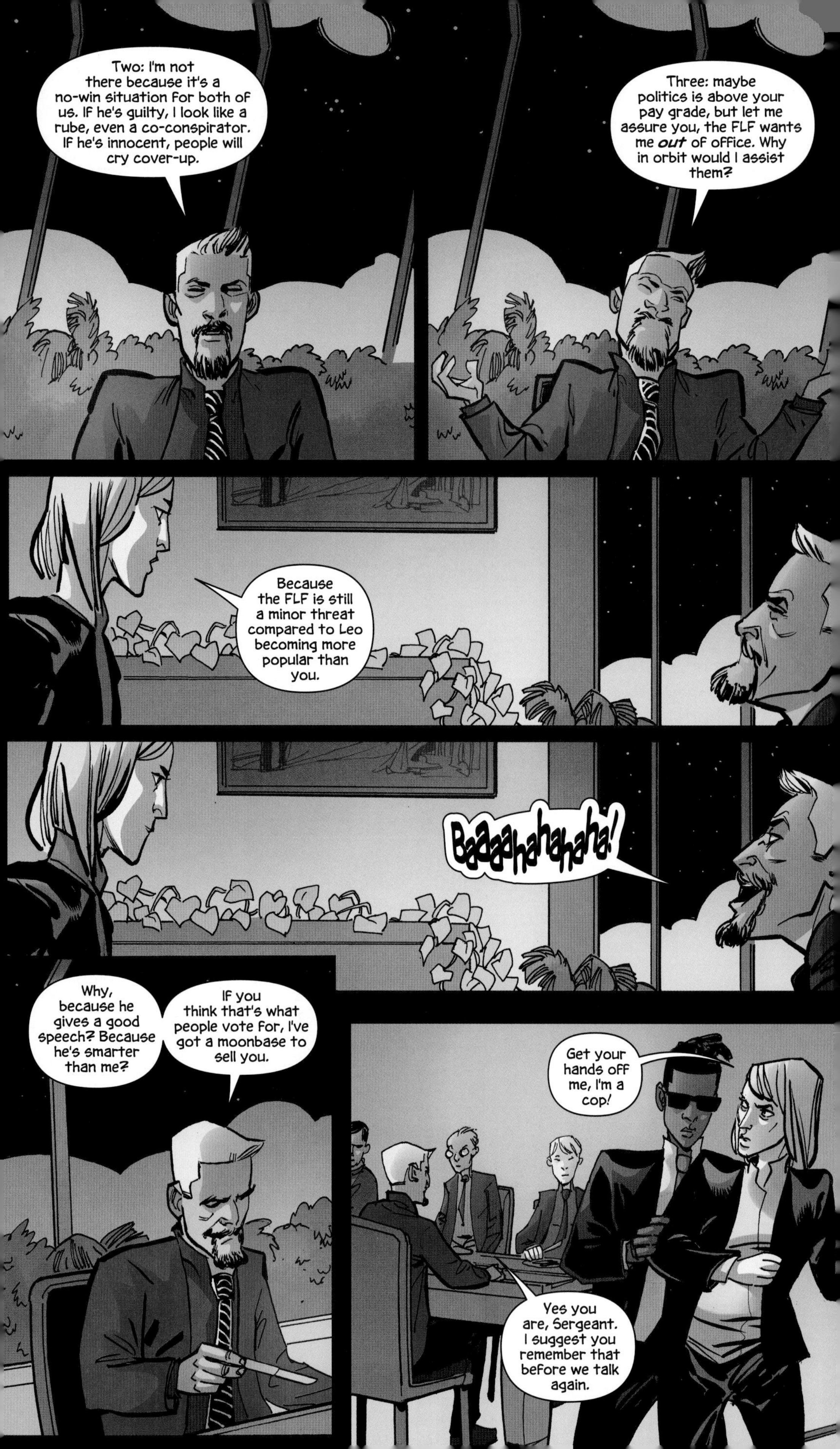
Two: I'm not there because it's a no-win situation for both of us. If he's guilty, I look like a rube, even a co-conspirator. If he's innocent, people will cry cover-up.
Three: maybe politics is above your pay grade, but let me assure you, the FLF wants me *out* of office. Why in orbit would I assist them?
Because the FLF is still a minor threat compared to Leo becoming more popular than you.
Baaaahahahaha!
Why, because he gives a good speech? Because he's smarter than me?
If you think that's what people vote for, I've got a moonbase to sell you.
Get your hands off me, I'm a cop!
Yes you are, Sergeant. I suggest you remember that before we talk again.

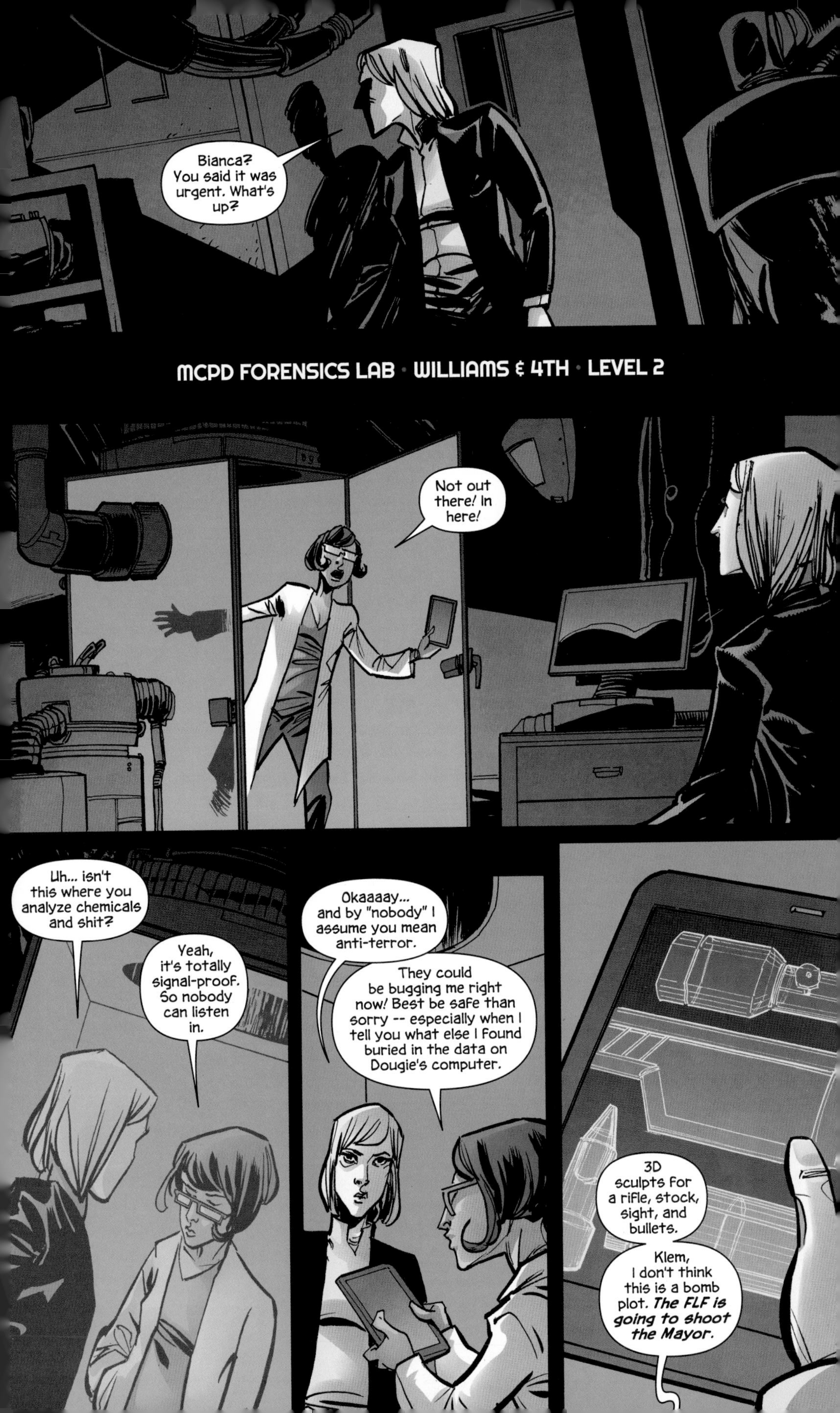

Bianca? You said it was urgent. What's up?
MCPD FORENSICS LAB • WILLIAMS & 4TH • LEVEL 2
Not out there! In here!
Uh... isn't this where you analyze chemicals and shit?
Yeah, it's totally signal-proof. So nobody can listen in.
Okaaaay... and by "nobody" I assume you mean anti-terror.
They could be bugging me right now! Best be safe than sorry -- especially when I tell you what else I found buried in the data on Dougie's computer.
3D sculpts for a rifle, stock, sight, and bullets.
Klem, I don't think this is a bomb plot. *The FLF is going to shoot the Mayor*.

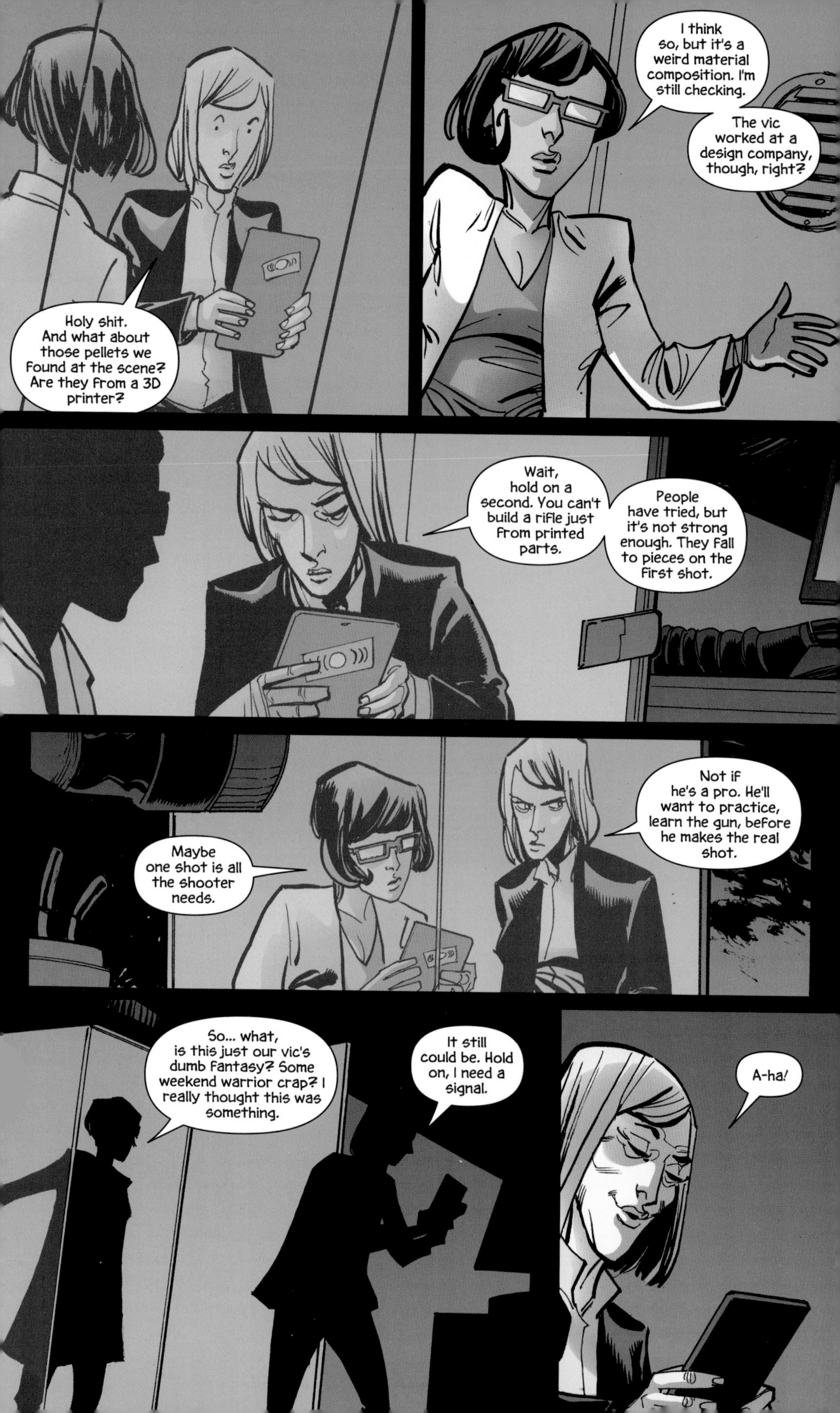
Holy shit. And what about those pellets we found at the scene? Are they from a 3D printer?
I think so, but it's a weird material composition. I'm still checking.
The vic worked at a design company, though, right?
Wait, hold on a second. You can't build a rifle just from printed parts.
People have tried, but it's not strong enough. They fall to pieces on the first shot.
Maybe one shot is all the shooter needs.
Not if he's a pro. He'll want to practice, learn the gun, before he makes the real shot.
So... what, is this just our vic's dumb fantasy? Some weekend warrior crap? I really thought this was something.
It still could be. Hold on, I need a signal.
A-ha!

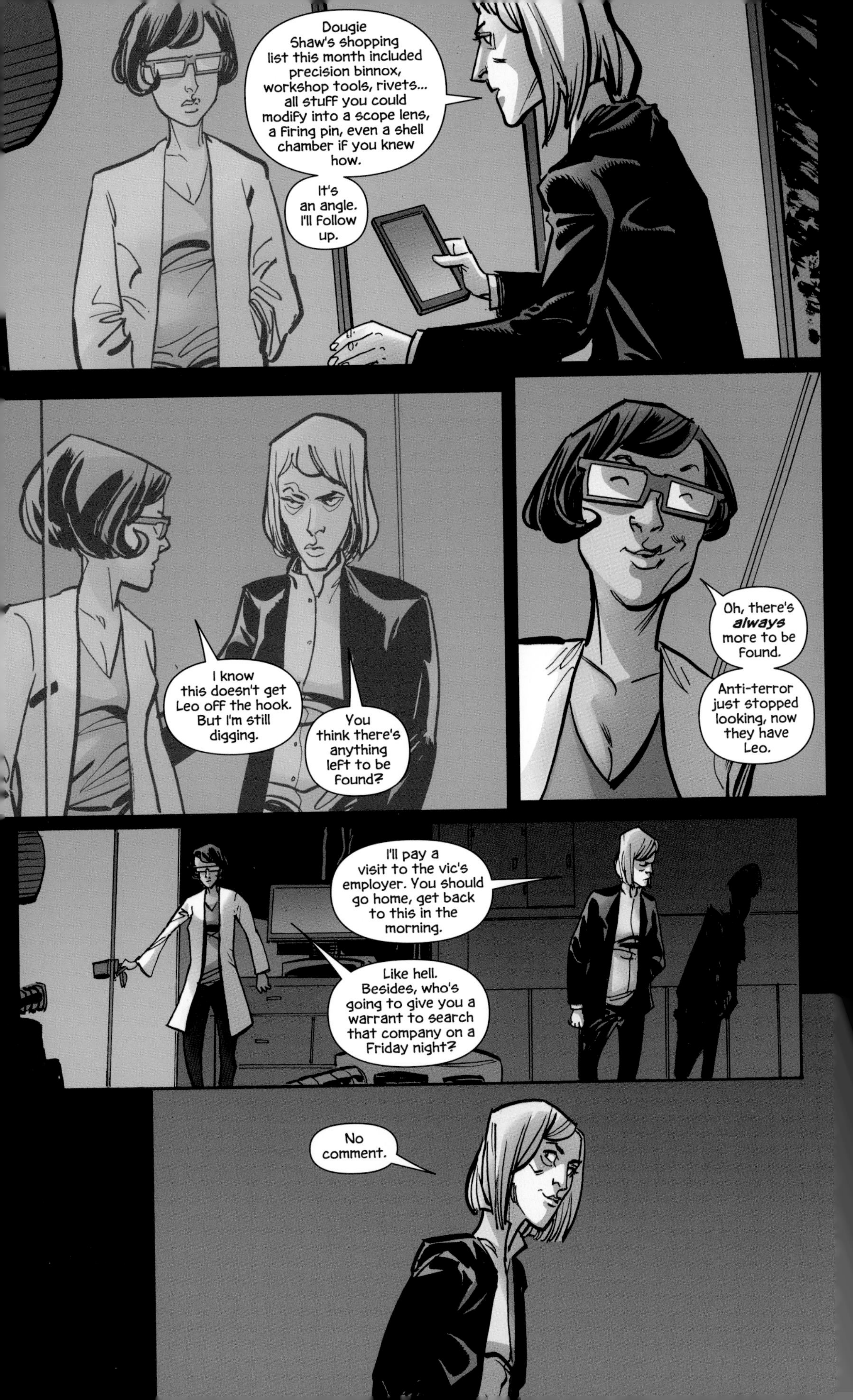
Dougie Shaw's shopping list this month included precision binnox, workshop tools, rivets... all stuff you could modify into a scope lens, a firing pin, even a shell chamber if you knew how.
It's an angle. I'll follow up.
I know this doesn't get Leo off the hook. But I'm still digging.
You think there's anything left to be found?
Oh, there's *always* more to be found.
Anti-terror just stopped looking, now they have Leo.
I'll pay a visit to the vic's employer. You should go home, get back to this in the morning.
Like hell. Besides, who's going to give you a warrant to search that company on a Friday night?
No comment.

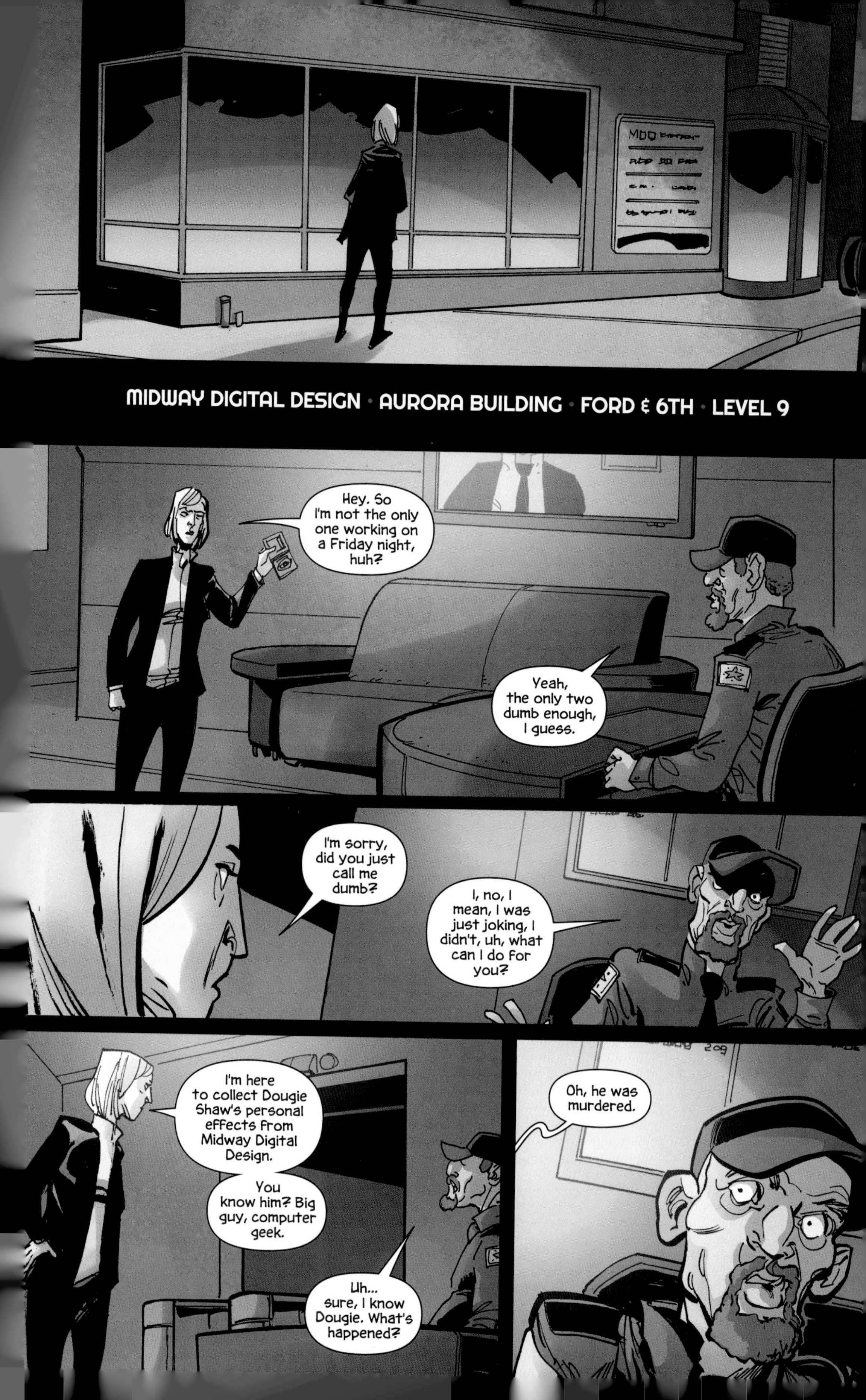
MIDWAY DIGITAL DESIGN • AURORA BUILDING • FORD & 6TH • LEVEL 9
Hey. So I'm not the only one working on a Friday night, huh?
Yeah, the only two dumb enough, I guess.
I'm sorry, did you just call me dumb?
I, no, I mean, I was just joking, I didn't, uh, what can I do for you?
I'm here to collect Dougie Shaw's personal effects from Midway Digital Design.
You know him? Big guy, computer geek.
Uh... sure, I know Dougie. What's happened?
Oh, he was murdered.

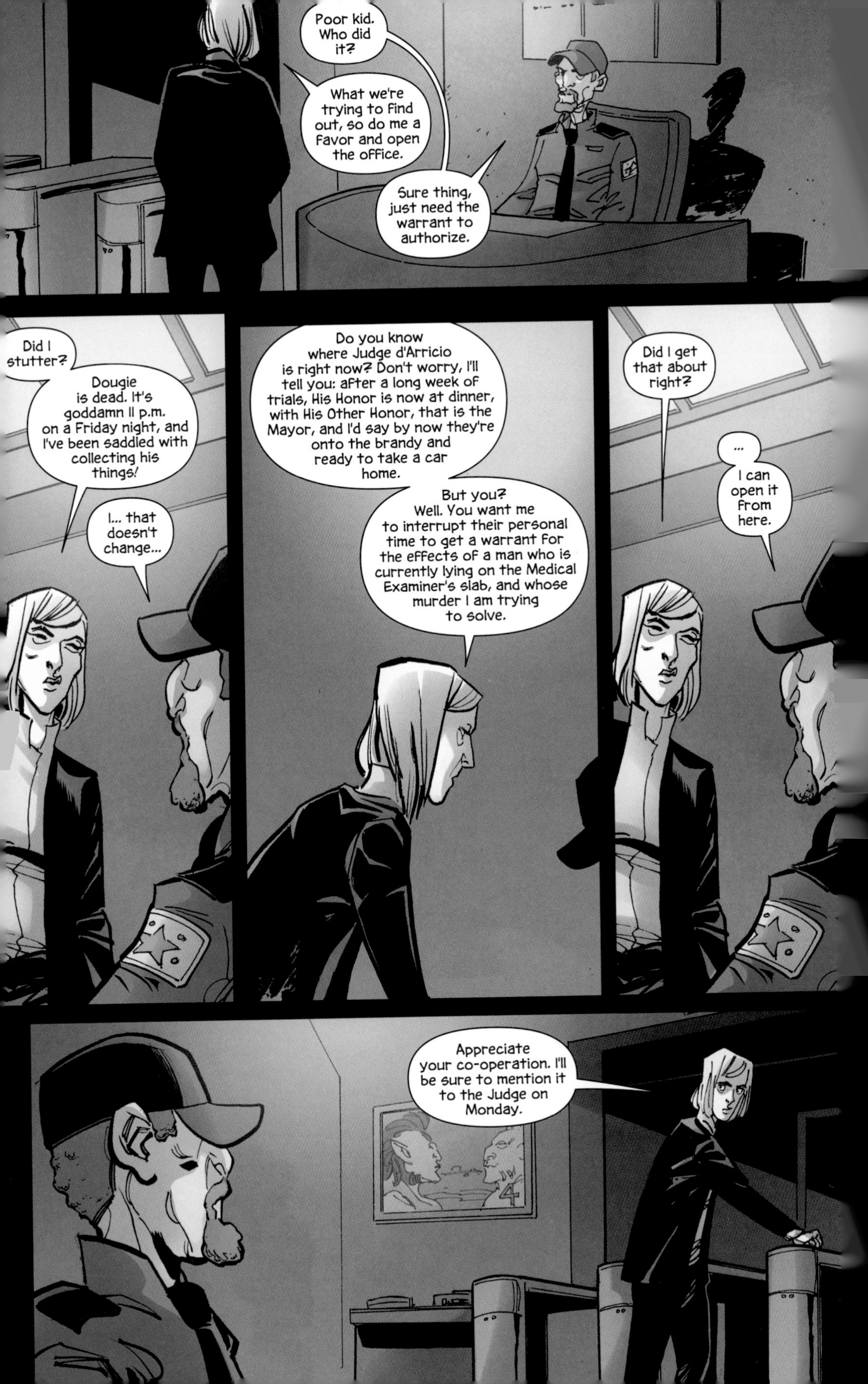
Poor kid. Who did it?
What we're trying to find out, so do me a favor and open the office.
Sure thing, just need the warrant to authorize.
Did I stutter?
Dougie is dead. It's goddamn 11 p.m. on a Friday night, and I've been saddled with collecting his things!
I... that doesn't change...
Do you know where Judge d'Arricio is right now? Don't worry, I'll tell you: after a long week of trials, His Honor is now at dinner, with His Other Honor, that is the Mayor, and I'd say by now they're onto the brandy and ready to take a car home.
But you? Well. You want me to interrupt their personal time to get a warrant for the effects of a man who is currently lying on the Medical Examiner's slab, and whose murder I am trying to solve.
Did I get that about right?
...
I can open it from here.
Appreciate your co-operation. I'll be sure to mention it to the Judge on Monday.

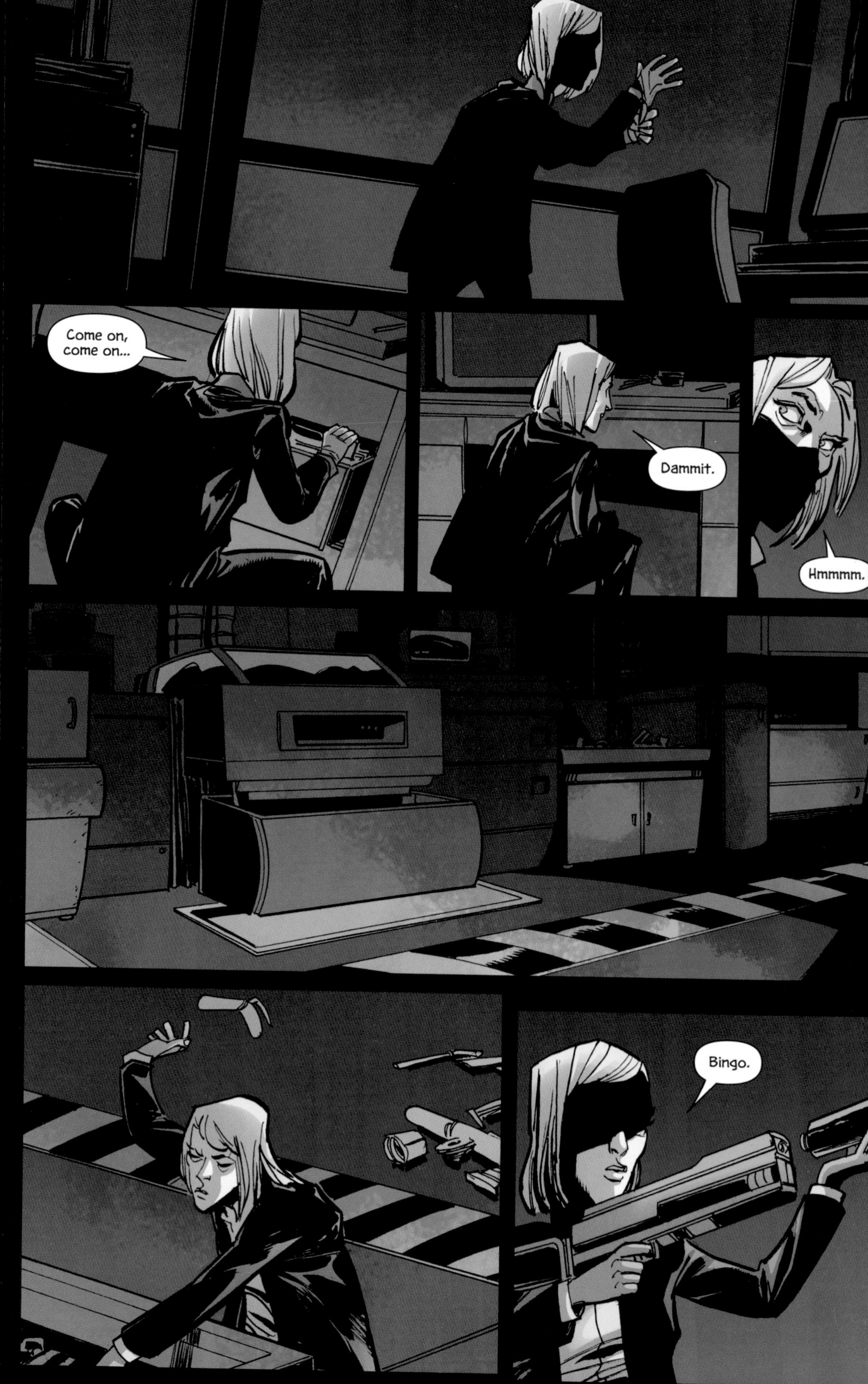
Come on,
come on...
Dammit.
Hmmmm.
Bingo.

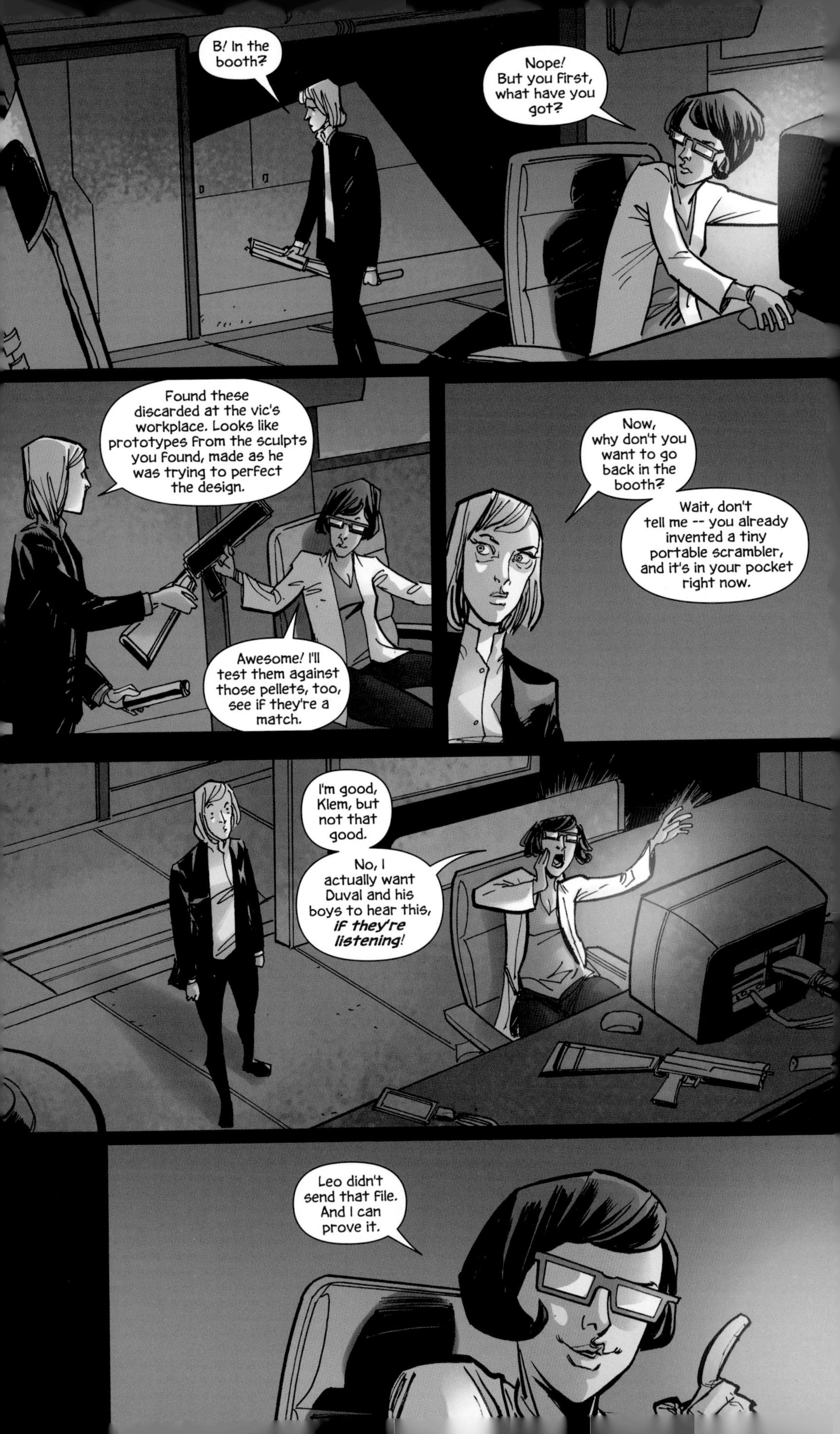
B! In the booth?
Nope! But you first, what have you got?
Found these discarded at the vic's workplace. Looks like prototypes from the sculpts you found, made as he was trying to perfect the design.
Awesome! I'll test them against those pellets, too, see if they're a match.
Now, why don't you want to go back in the booth?
Wait, don't tell me -- you already invented a tiny portable scrambler, and it's in your pocket right now.
I'm good, Klem, but not that good.
No, I actually want Duval and his boys to hear this, *if they're listening*!
Leo didn't send that file. And I can prove it.

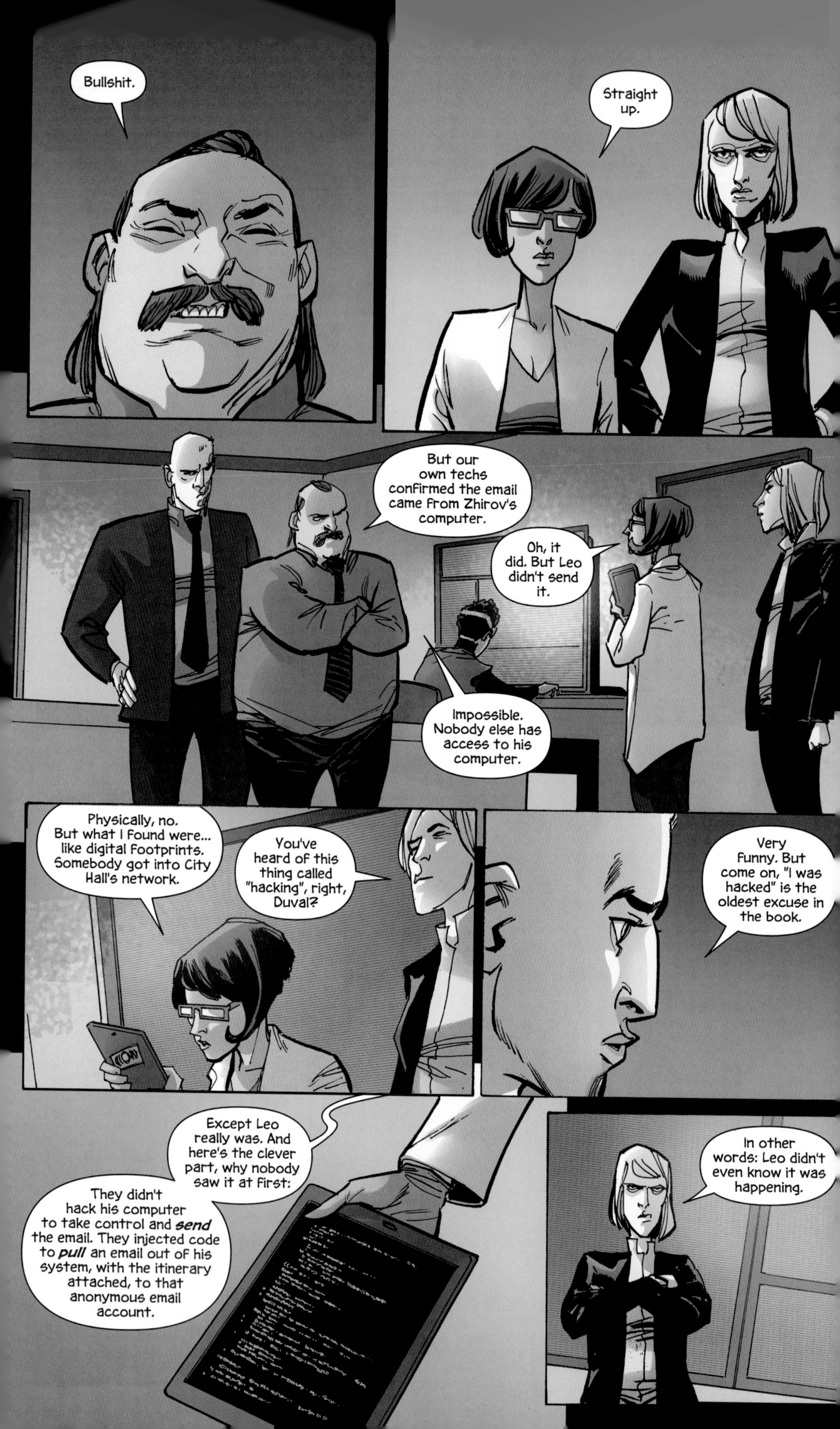
Bullshit.
Straight up.
But our own techs confirmed the email came from Zhirov's computer.
Oh, it did. But Leo didn't send it.
Impossible. Nobody else has access to his computer.
Physically, no. But what I found were... like digital footprints. Somebody got into City Hall's network.
You've heard of this thing called "hacking", right, Duval?
Very funny. But come on, "I was hacked" is the oldest excuse in the book.
Except Leo really was. And here's the clever part, why nobody saw it at first:
They didn't hack his computer to take control and *send* the email. They injected code to ***pull*** an email out of his system, with the itinerary attached, to that anonymous email account.
In other words: Leo didn't even know it was happening.

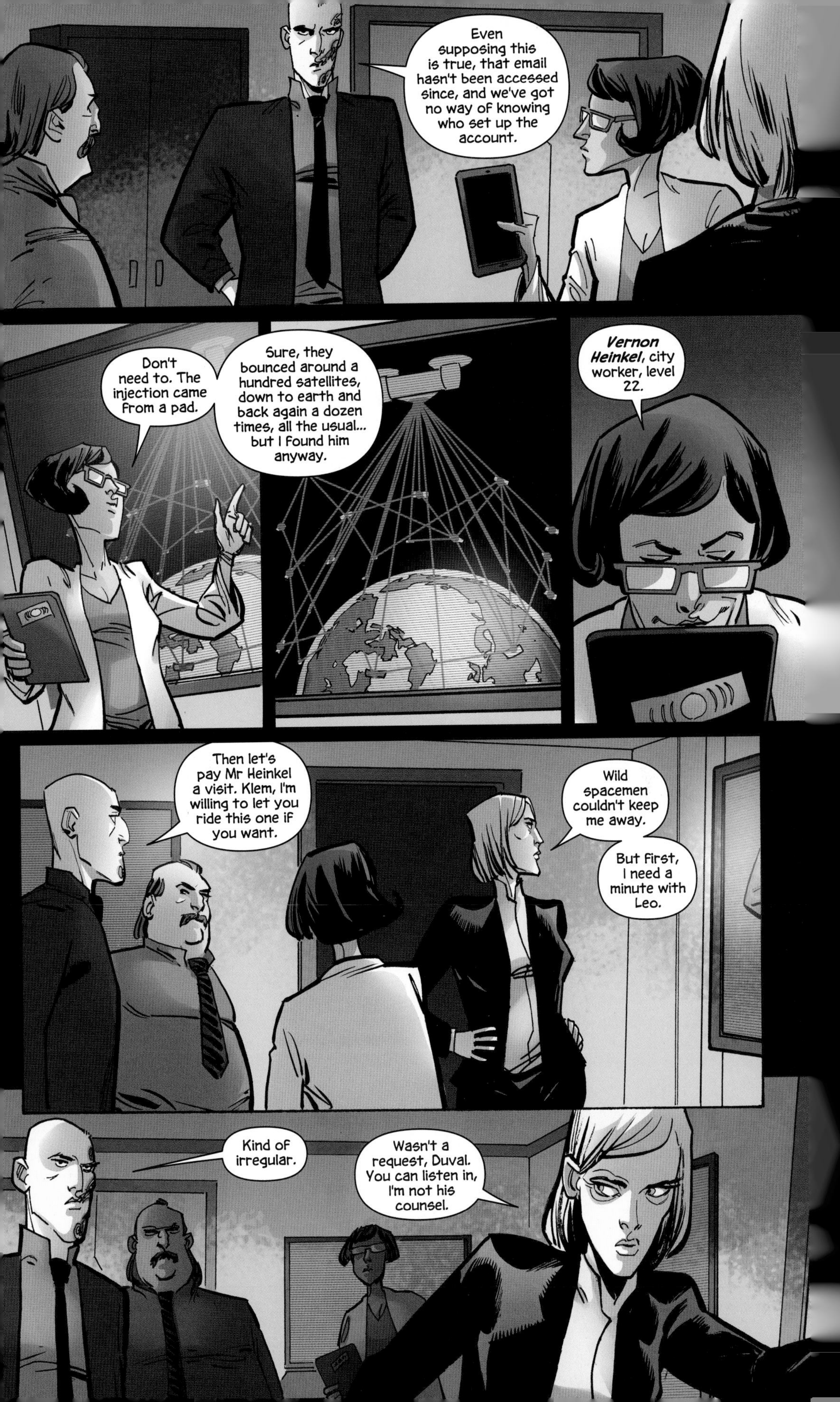
Even supposing this is true, that email hasn't been accessed since, and we've got no way of knowing who set up the account.
Don't need to. The injection came from a pad.
Sure, they bounced around a hundred satellites, down to earth and back again a dozen times, all the usual... but I found him anyway.
Vernon Heinkel, city worker, level 22.
Then let's pay Mr Heinkel a visit. Klem, I'm willing to let you ride this one if you want.
Wild spacemen couldn't keep me away.
But first, I need a minute with Leo.
Kind of irregular.
Wasn't a request, Duval. You can listen in, I'm not his counsel.

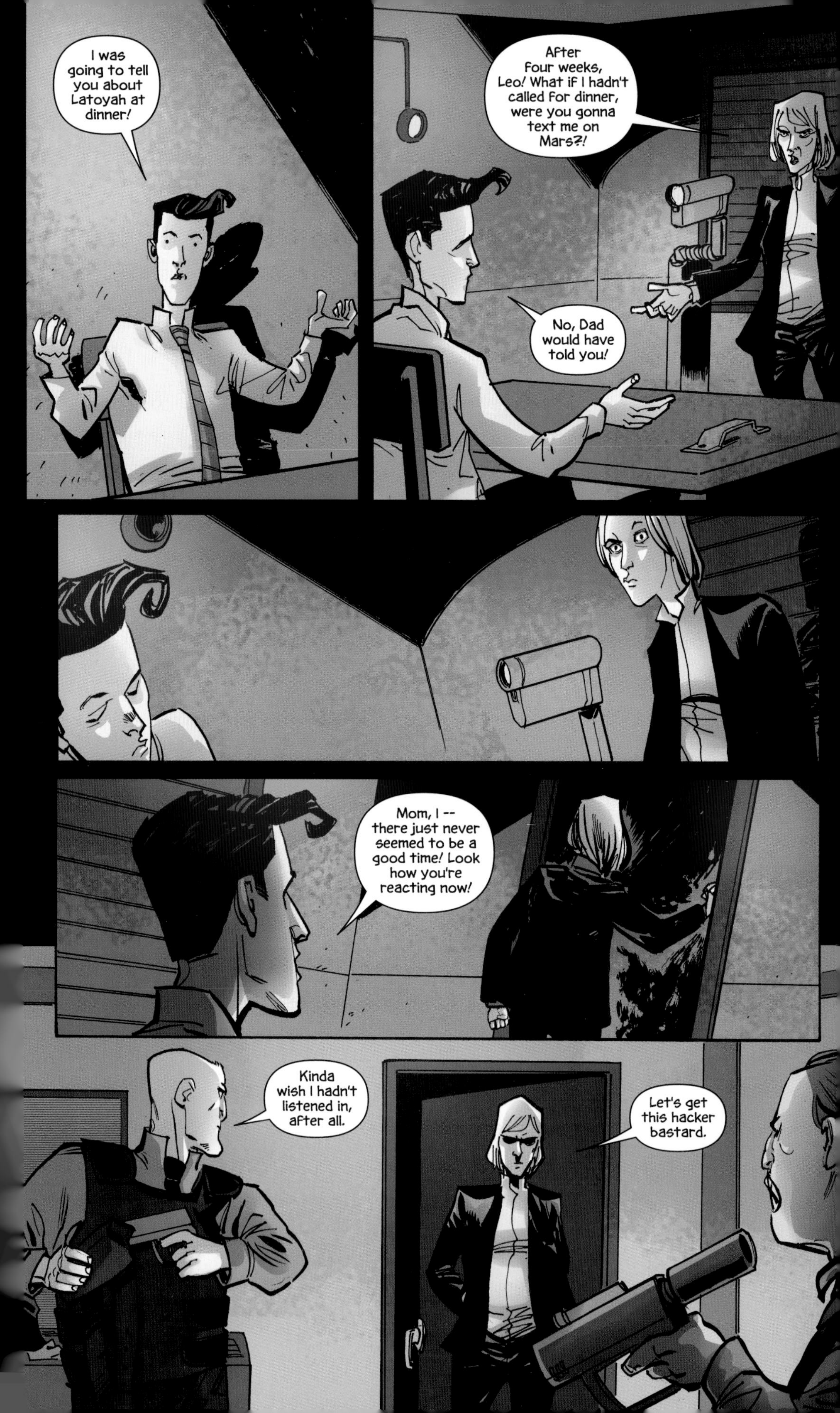
I was going to tell you about Latoyah at dinner!
After four weeks, Leo! What if I hadn't called for dinner, were you gonna text me on Mars?!
No, Dad would have told you!
Mom, I -- there just never seemed to be a good time! Look how you're reacting now!
Kinda wish I hadn't listened in, after all.
Let's get this hacker bastard.

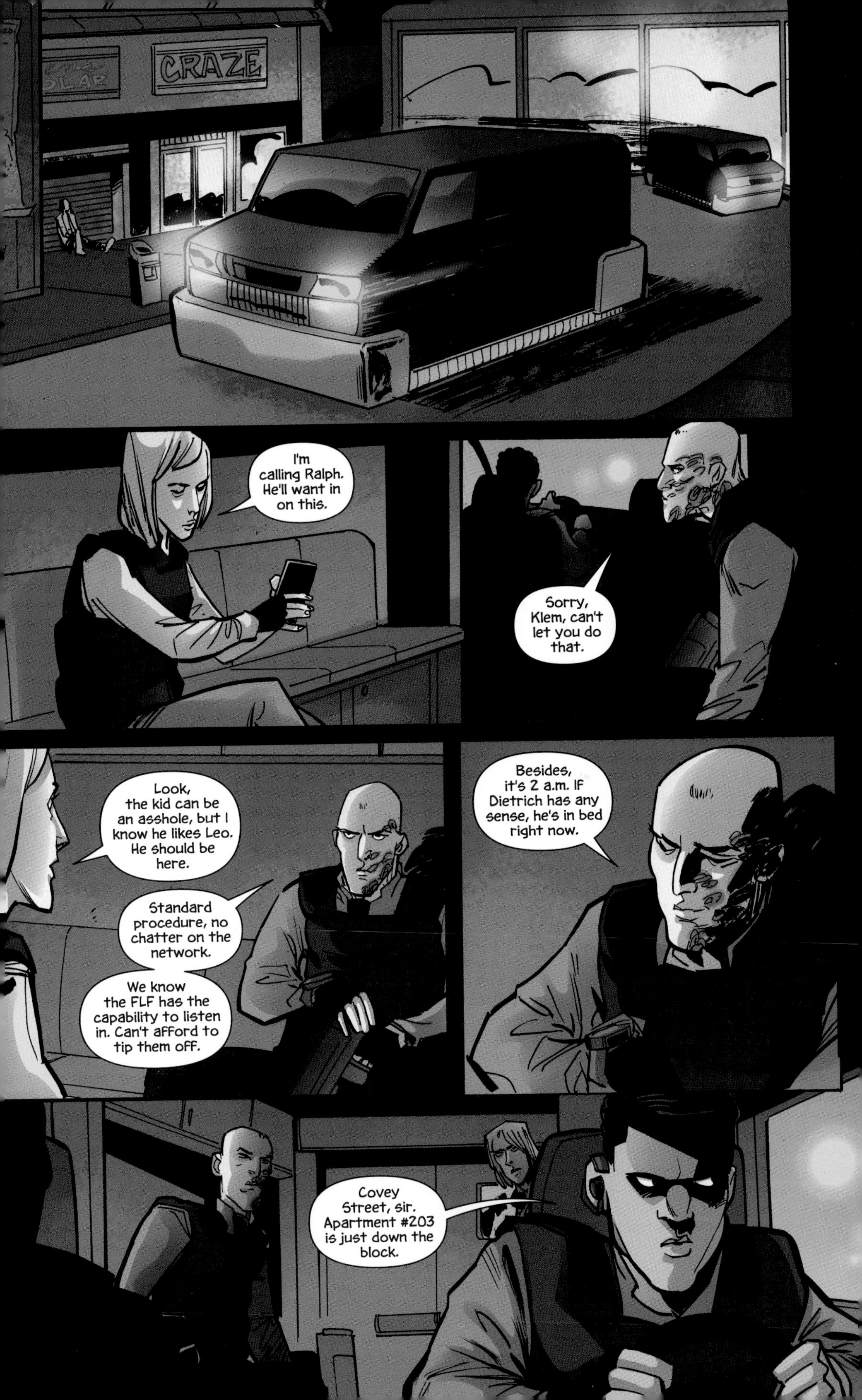
CRAZE
I'm calling Ralph. He'll want in on this.
Sorry, Klem, can't let you do that.
Look, the kid can be an asshole, but I know he likes Leo. He should be here.
Standard procedure, no chatter on the network.
We know the FLF has the capability to listen in. Can't afford to tip them off.
Besides, it's 2 a.m. If Dietrich has any sense, he's in bed right now.
Covey Street, sir. Apartment #203 is just down the block.

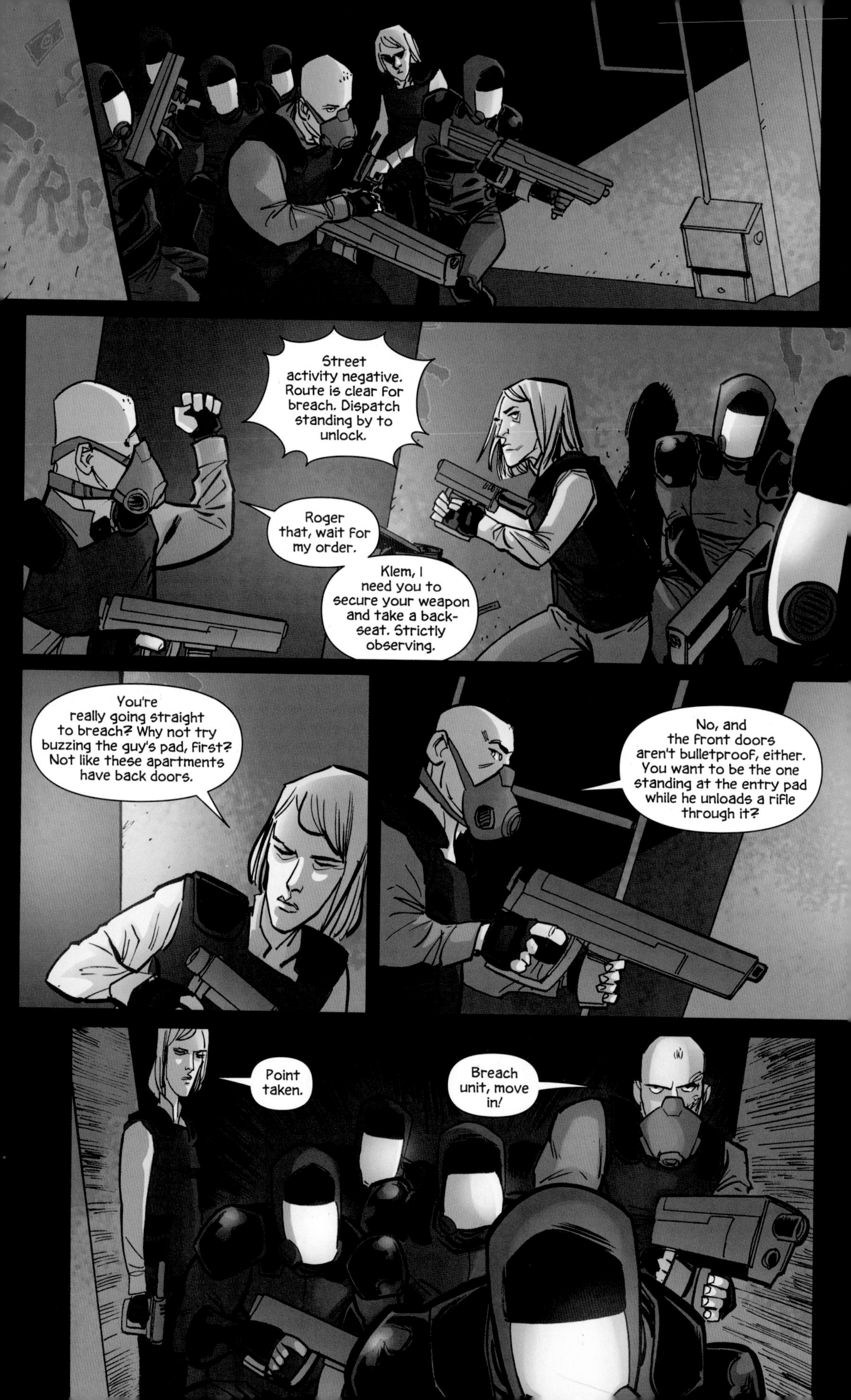

Street activity negative. Route is clear for breach. Dispatch standing by to unlock.
Roger that, wait for my order.
Klem, I need you to secure your weapon and take a back-seat. Strictly observing.
You're really going straight to breach? Why not try buzzing the guy's pad, first? Not like these apartments have back doors.
No, and the front doors aren't bulletproof, either. You want to be the one standing at the entry pad while he unloads a rifle through it?
Point taken.
Breach unit, move in!

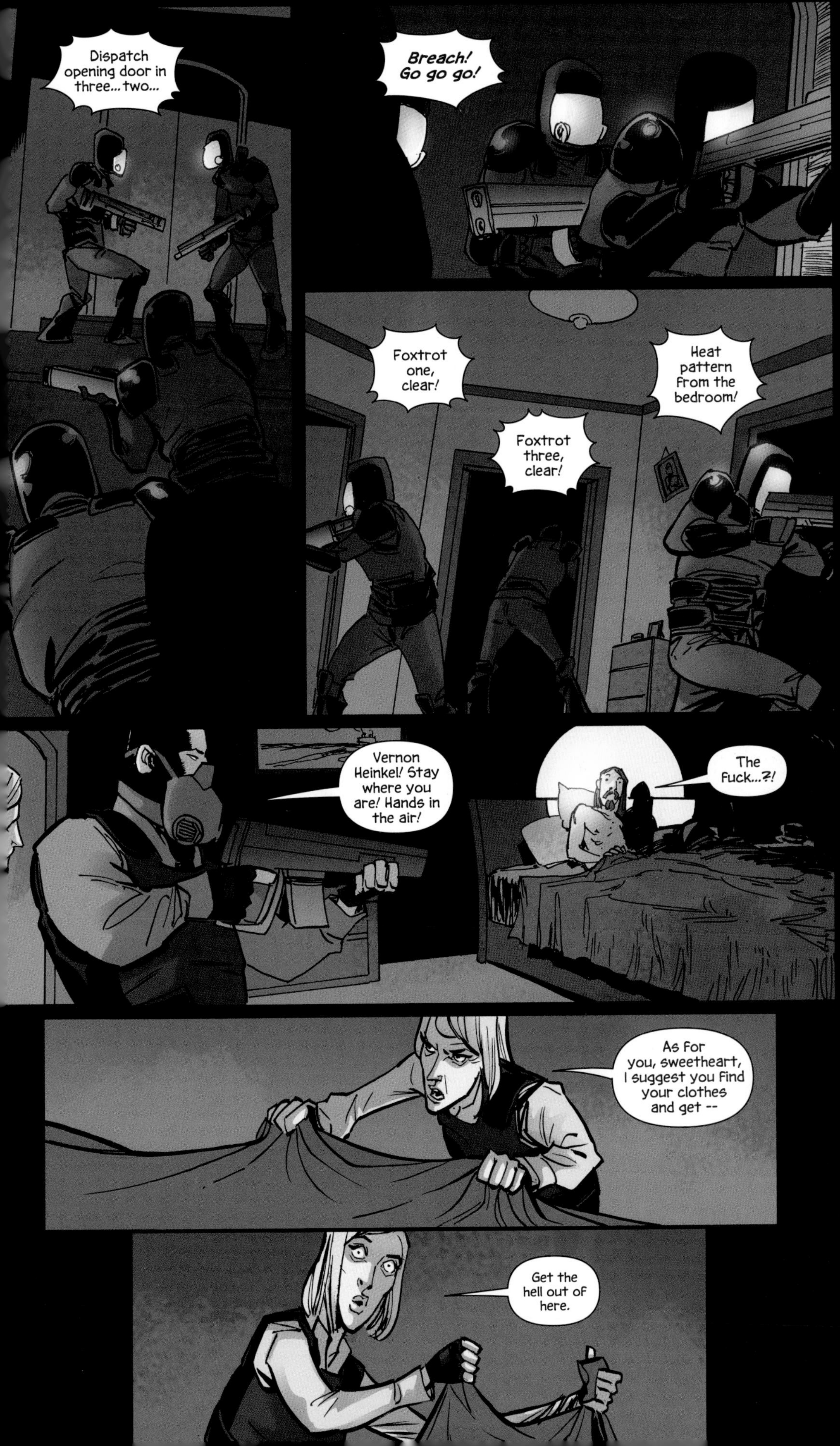
Dispatch opening door in three... two...
Breach! Go go go!
Foxtrot one, clear!
Heat pattern from the bedroom!
Foxtrot three, clear!
Vernon Heinkel! Stay where you are! Hands in the air!
The Fuck...?!
As for you, sweetheart, I suggest you find your clothes and get --
Get the hell out of here.

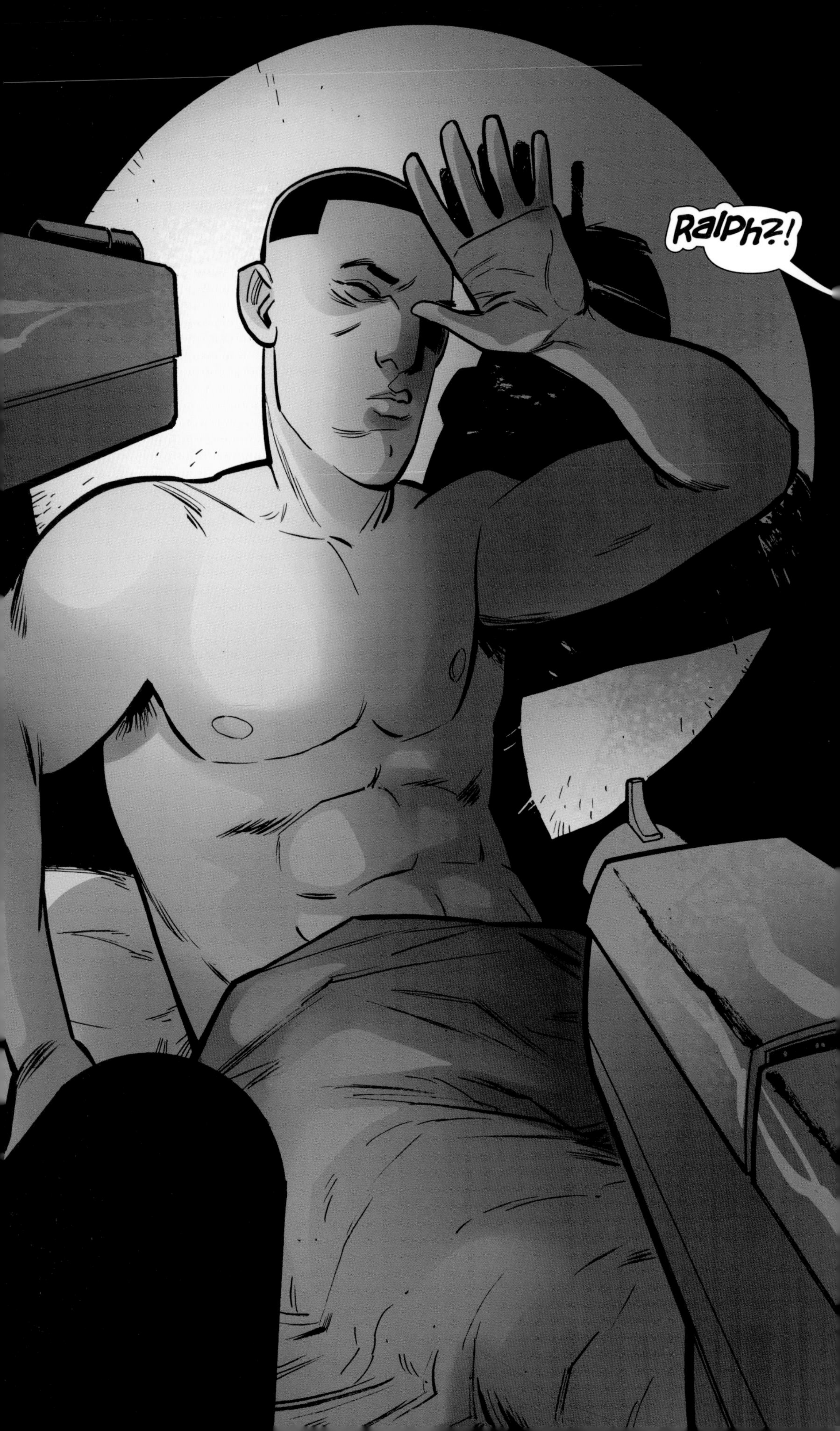
Ralph?!

PART 4

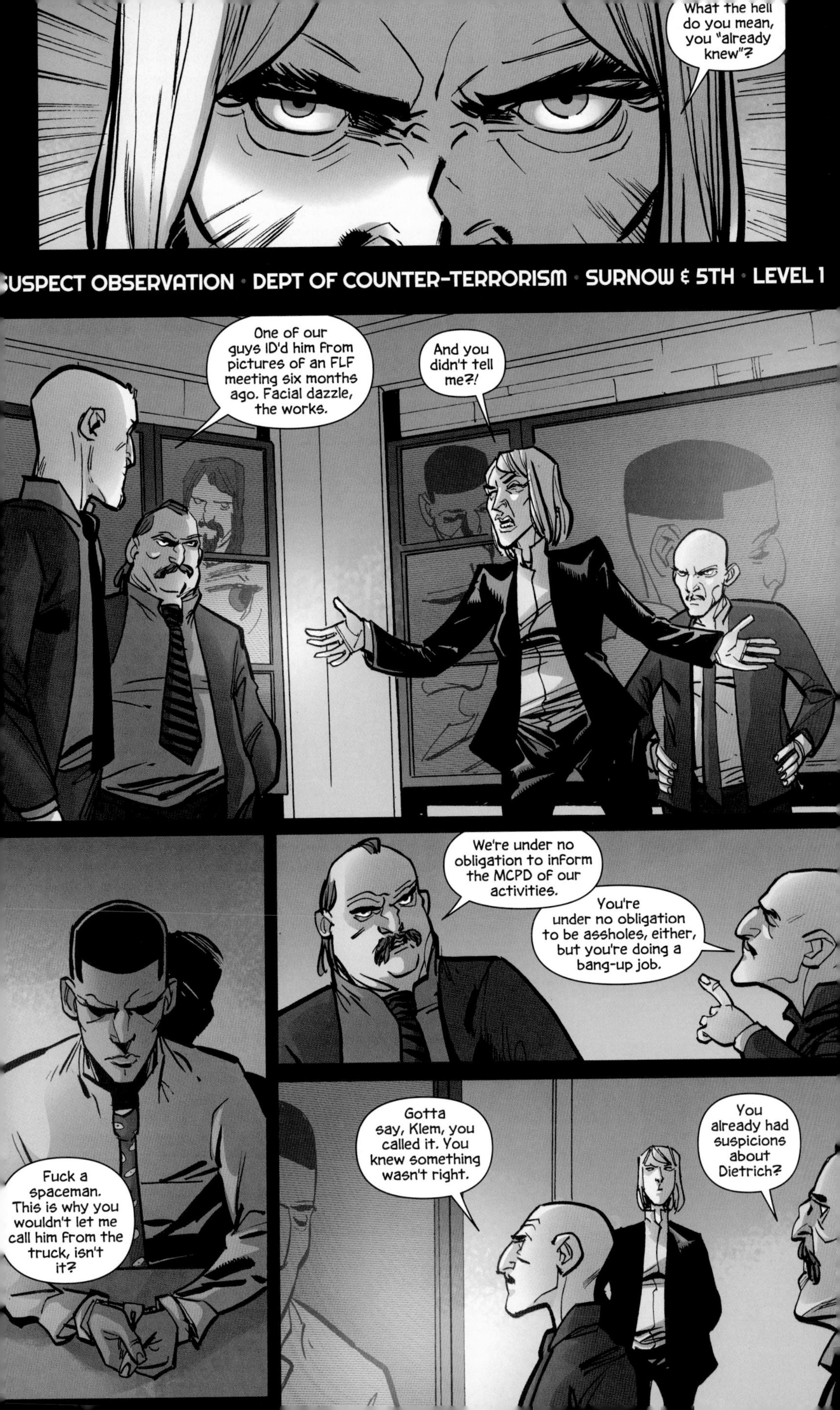
What the hell do you mean, you "already knew"?
SUSPECT OBSERVATION · DEPT OF COUNTER-TERRORISM · SURNOW & 5TH · LEVEL 1
One of our guys ID'd him from pictures of an FLF meeting six months ago. Facial dazzle, the works.
And you didn't tell me?!
We're under no obligation to inform the MCPD of our activities.
You're under no obligation to be assholes, either, but you're doing a bang-up job.
Fuck a spaceman. This is why you wouldn't let me call him from the truck, isn't it?
Gotta say, Klem, you called it. You knew something wasn't right.
You already had suspicions about Dietrich?

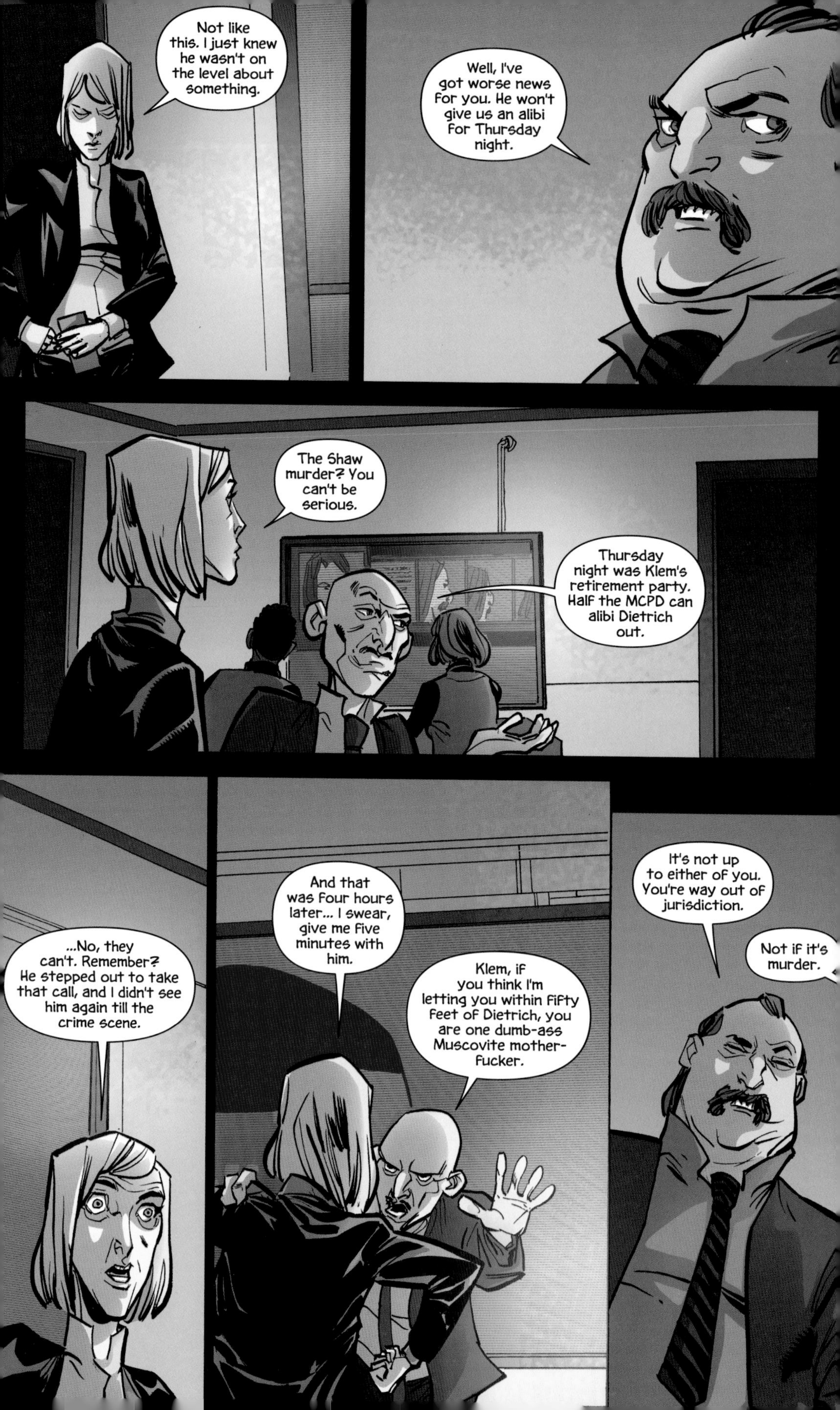

Not like this. I just knew he wasn't on the level about something.
Well, I've got worse news for you. He won't give us an alibi for Thursday night.
The Shaw murder? You can't be serious.
Thursday night was Klem's retirement party. Half the MCPD can alibi Dietrich out.
...No, they can't. Remember? He stepped out to take that call, and I didn't see him again till the crime scene.
And that was four hours later... I swear, give me five minutes with him.
Klem, if you think I'm letting you within fifty feet of Dietrich, you are one dumb-ass Muscovite mother-fucker.
It's not up to either of you. You're way out of jurisdiction.
Not if it's murder.

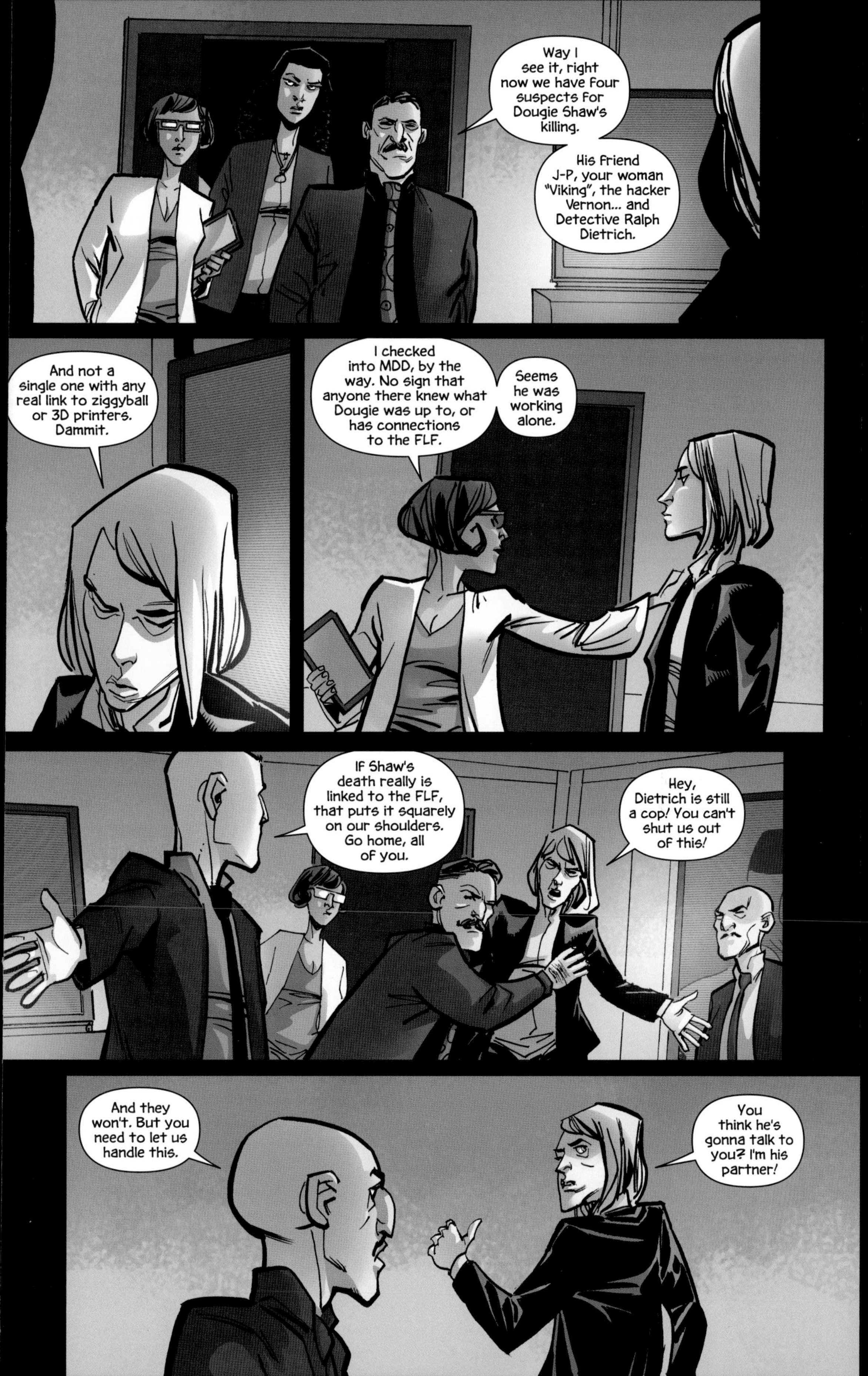
Way I see it, right now we have four suspects for Dougie Shaw's killing.
His friend J-P, your woman "Viking", the hacker Vernon... and Detective Ralph Dietrich.
And not a single one with any real link to ziggyball or 3D printers. Dammit.
I checked into MDD, by the way. No sign that anyone there knew what Dougie was up to, or has connections to the FLF.
Seems he was working alone.
If Shaw's death really is linked to the FLF, that puts it squarely on our shoulders. Go home, all of you.
Hey, Dietrich is still a cop! You can't shut us out of this!
And they won't. But you need to let us handle this.
You think he's gonna talk to you? I'm his partner!

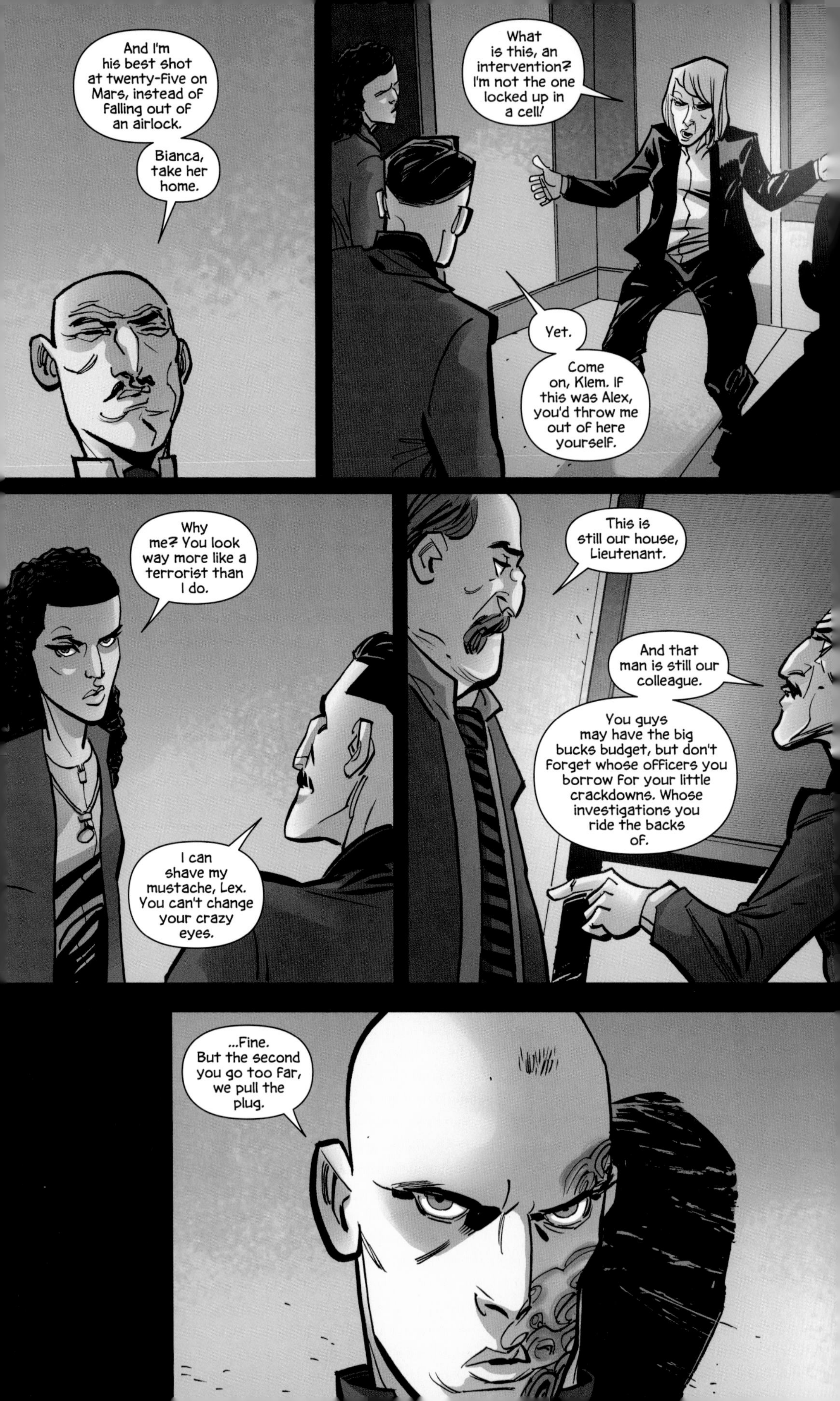

And I'm his best shot at twenty-five on Mars, instead of falling out of an airlock.
Bianca, take her home.
What is this, an intervention? I'm not the one locked up in a cell!
Yet.
Come on, Klem. If this was Alex, you'd throw me out of here yourself.
Why me? You look way more like a terrorist than I do.
I can shave my mustache, Lex. You can't change your crazy eyes.
This is still our house, Lieutenant.
And that man is still our colleague.
You guys may have the big bucks budget, but don't forget whose officers you borrow for your little crackdowns. Whose investigations you ride the backs of.
...Fine. But the second you go too far, we pull the plug.

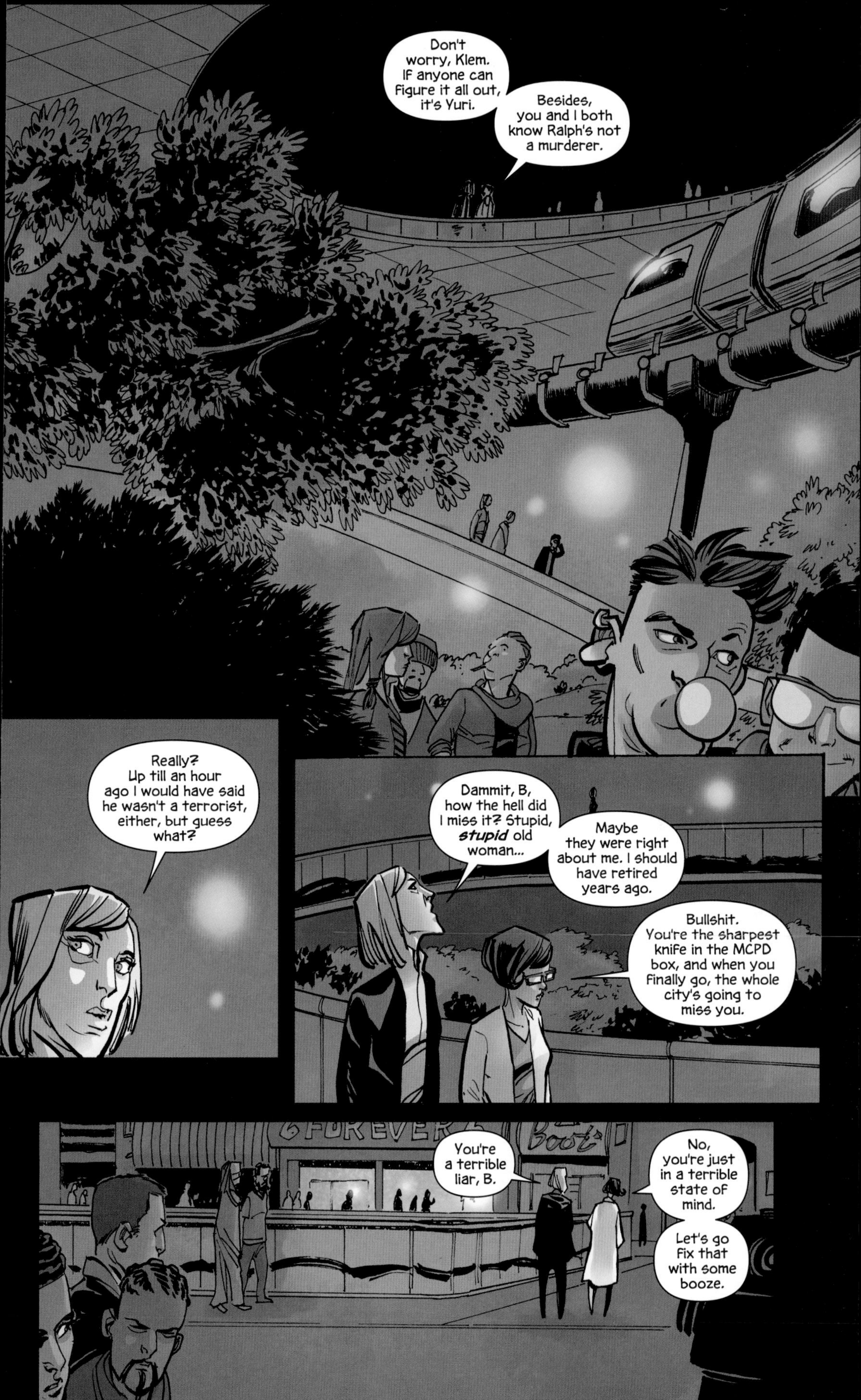
Don't worry, Klem. If anyone can figure it all out, it's Yuri.
Besides, you and I both know Ralph's not a murderer.
Really? Up till an hour ago I would have said he wasn't a terrorist, either, but guess what?
Dammit, B, how the hell did I miss it? Stupid, *stupid* old woman...
Maybe they were right about me. I should have retired years ago.
Bullshit. You're the sharpest knife in the MCPD box, and when you finally go, the whole city's going to miss you.
FOREVER
Boot
You're a terrible liar, B.
No, you're just in a terrible state of mind.
Let's go fix that with some booze.

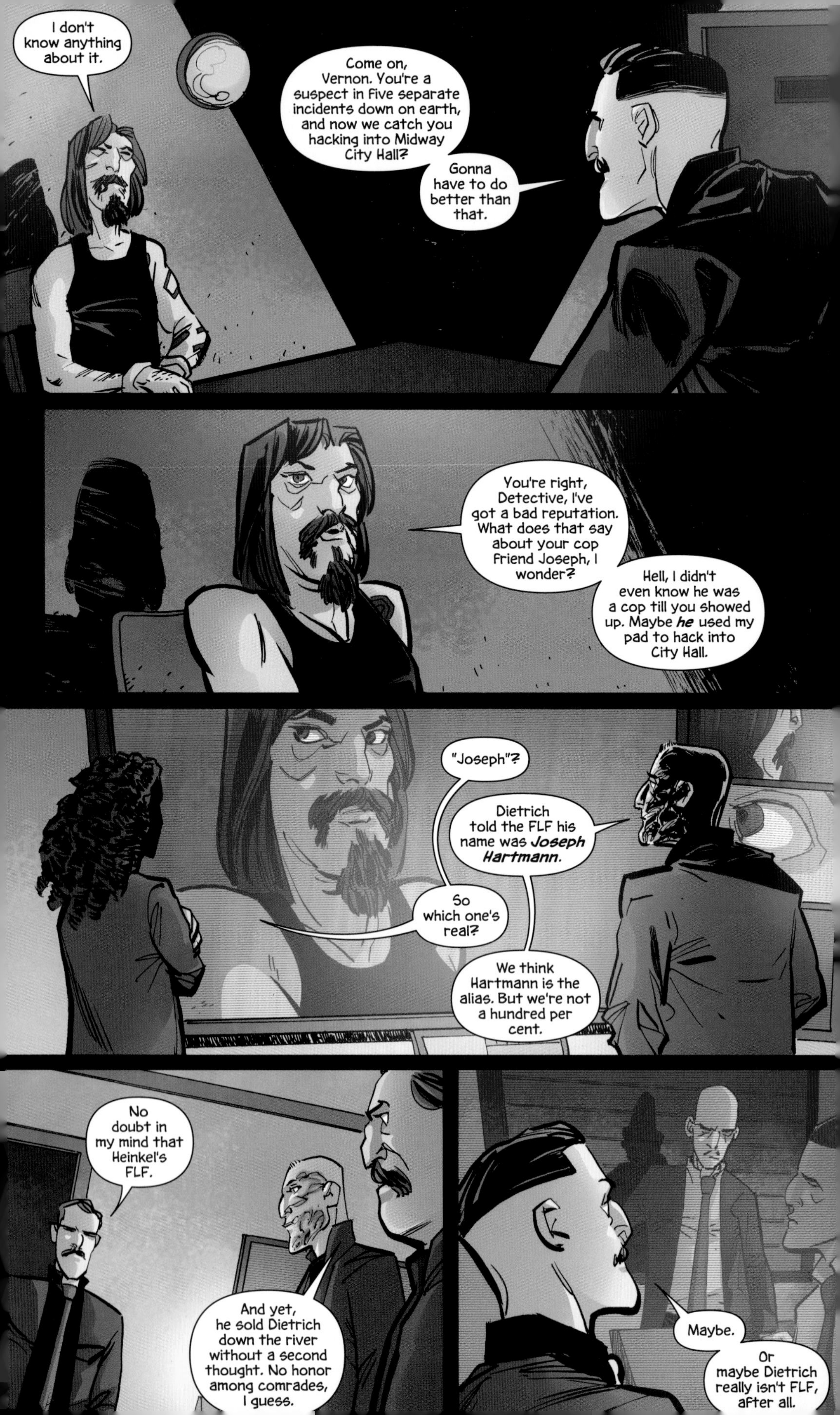
I don't know anything about it.
Come on, Vernon. You're a suspect in five separate incidents down on earth, and now we catch you hacking into Midway City Hall?
Gonna have to do better than that.
You're right, Detective, I've got a bad reputation. What does that say about your cop friend Joseph, I wonder?
Hell, I didn't even know he was a cop till you showed up. Maybe *he* used my pad to hack into City Hall.
"Joseph"?
Dietrich told the FLF his name was ***Joseph Hartmann***.
So which one's real?
We think Hartmann is the alias. But we're not a hundred per cent.
No doubt in my mind that Heinkel's FLF.
And yet, he sold Dietrich down the river without a second thought. No honor among comrades, I guess.
Maybe.
Or maybe Dietrich really isn't FLF, after all.

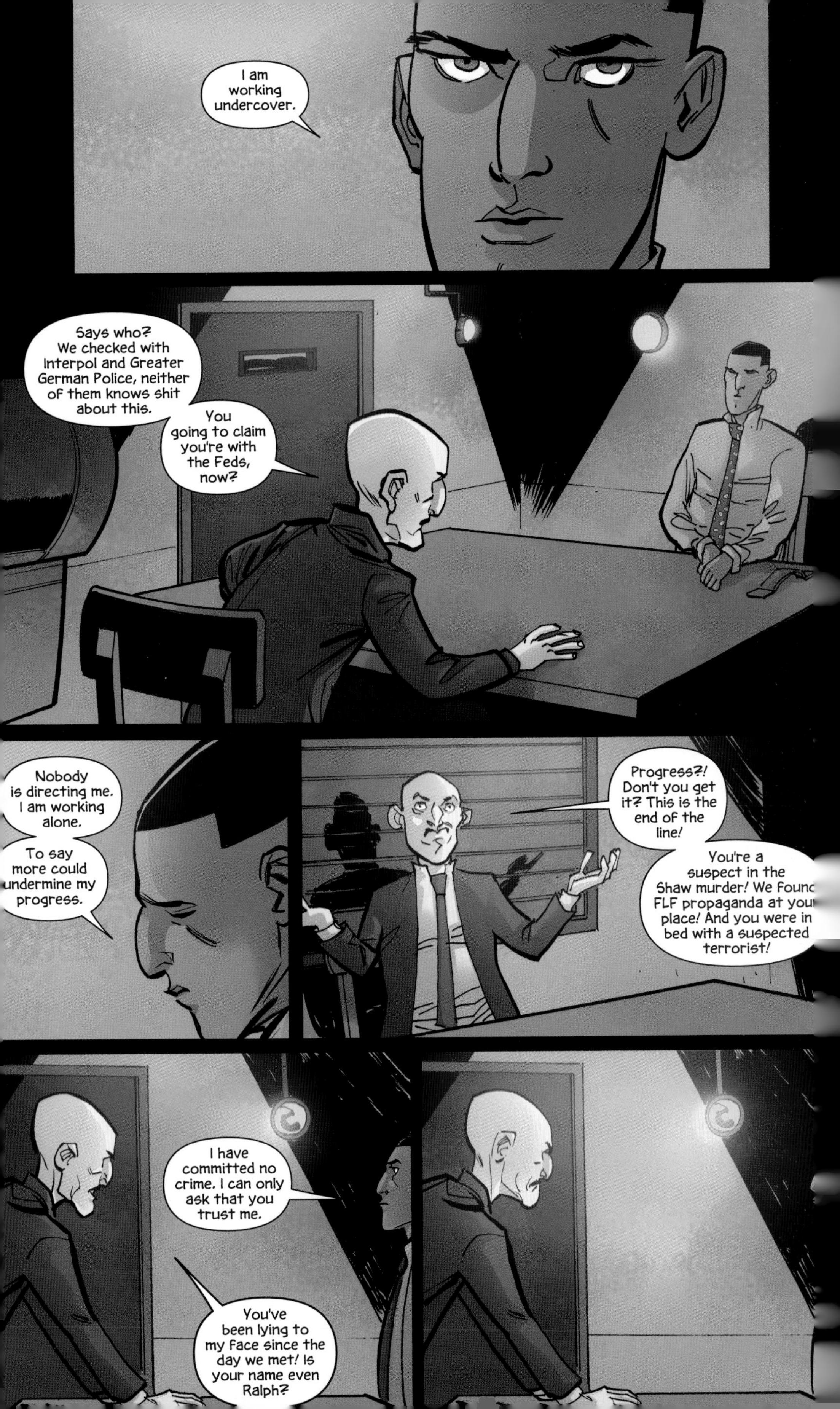
I am working undercover.
Says who? We checked with Interpol and Greater German Police, neither of them knows shit about this.
You going to claim you're with the Feds, now?
Nobody is directing me. I am working alone.
To say more could undermine my progress.
Progress?! Don't you get it? This is the end of the line!
You're a suspect in the Shaw murder! We found FLF propaganda at your place! And you were in bed with a suspected terrorist!
I have committed no crime. I can only ask that you trust me.
You've been lying to my face since the day we met! Is your name even Ralph?

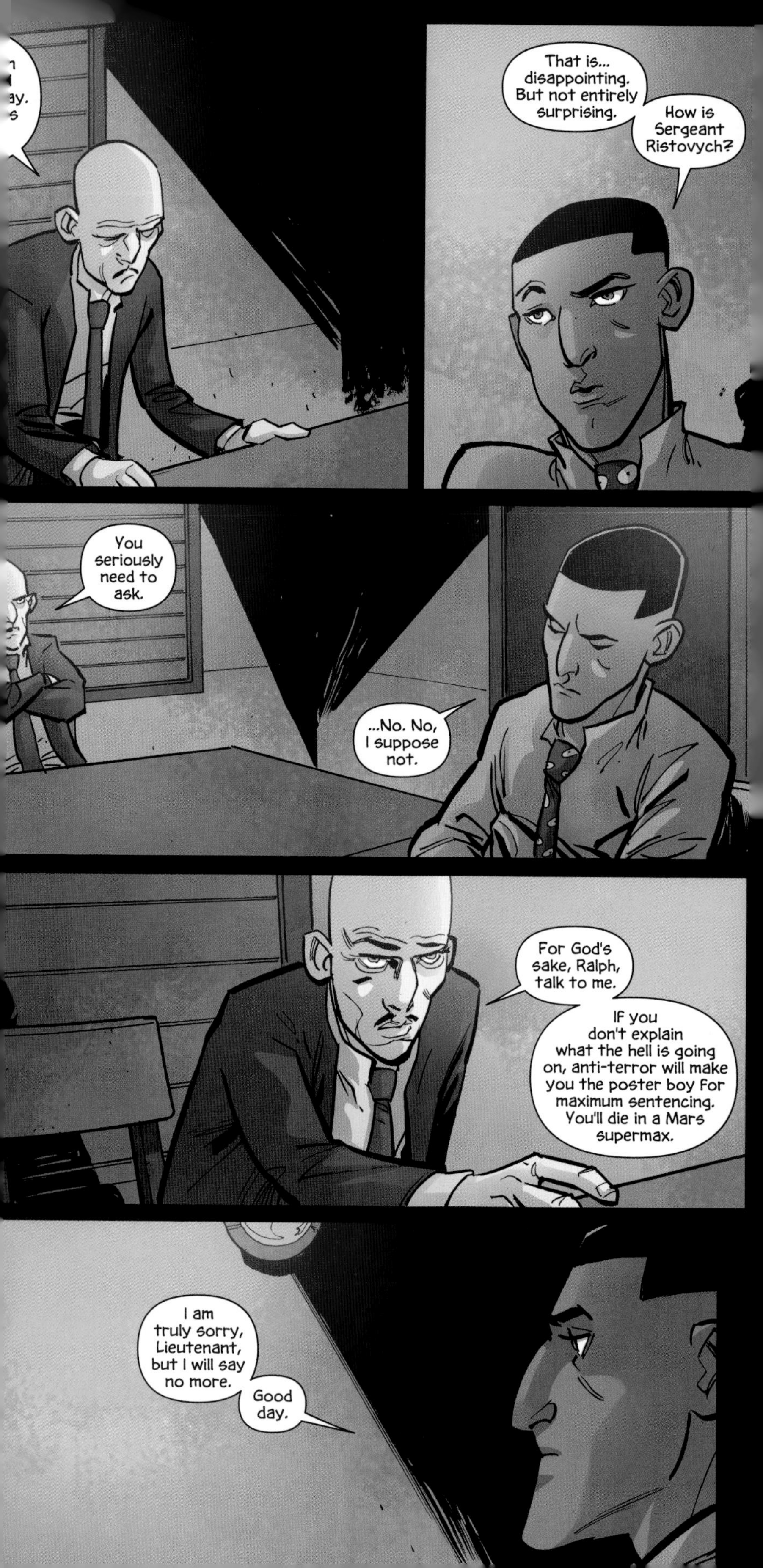
That is... disappointing. But not entirely surprising.
How is Sergeant Ristovych?
You seriously need to ask.
...No. No, I suppose not.
For God's sake, Ralph, talk to me.
If you don't explain what the hell is going on, anti-terror will make you the poster boy for maximum sentencing. You'll die in a Mars supermax.
I am truly sorry, Lieutenant, but I will say no more.
Good day.

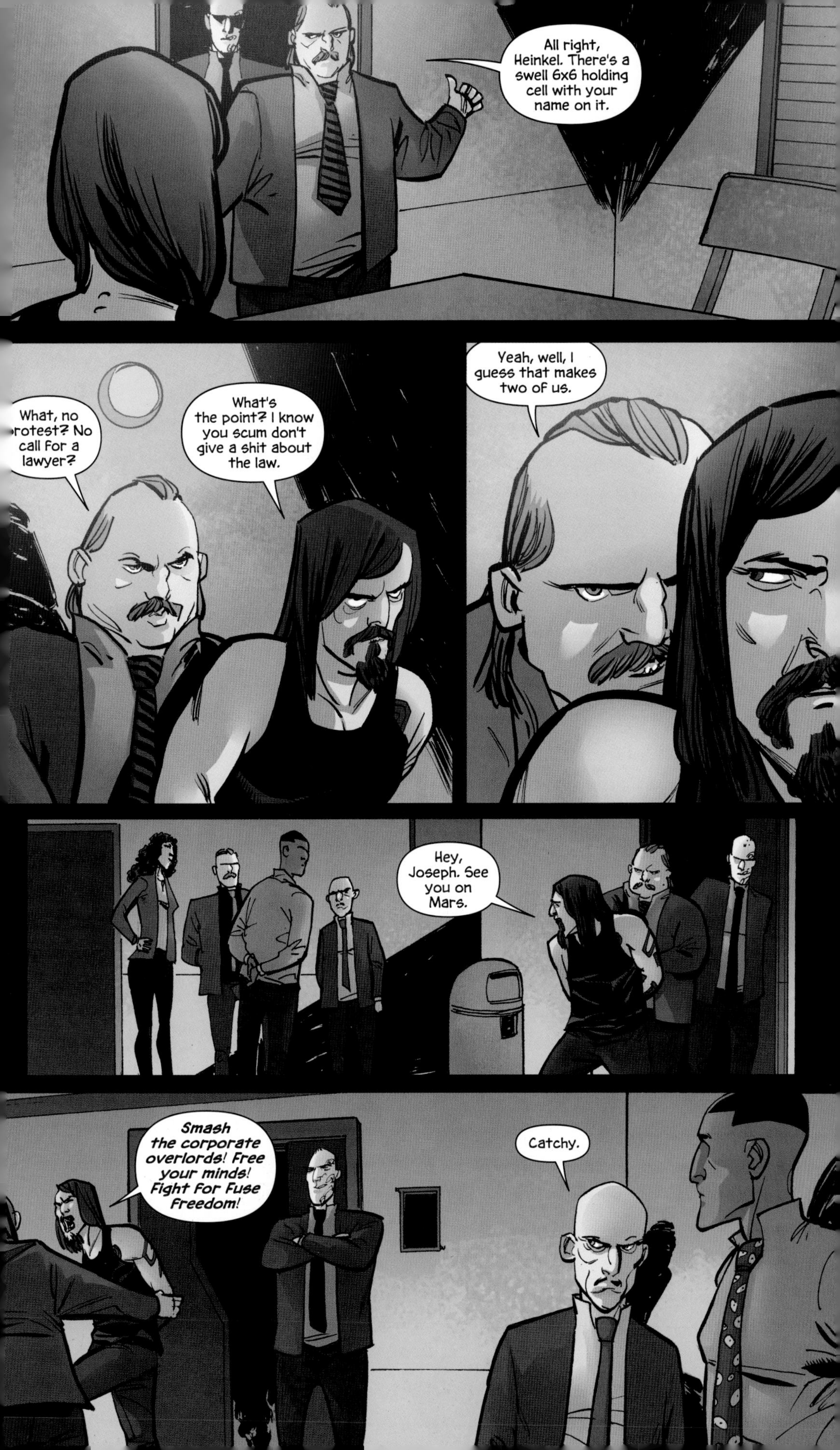
All right, Heinkel. There's a swell 6x6 holding cell with your name on it.
What, no protest? No call for a lawyer?
What's the point? I know you scum don't give a shit about the law.
Yeah, well, I guess that makes two of us.
Hey, Joseph. See you on Mars.
Smash the corporate overlords! Free your minds! Fight for Fuse Freedom!
Catchy.

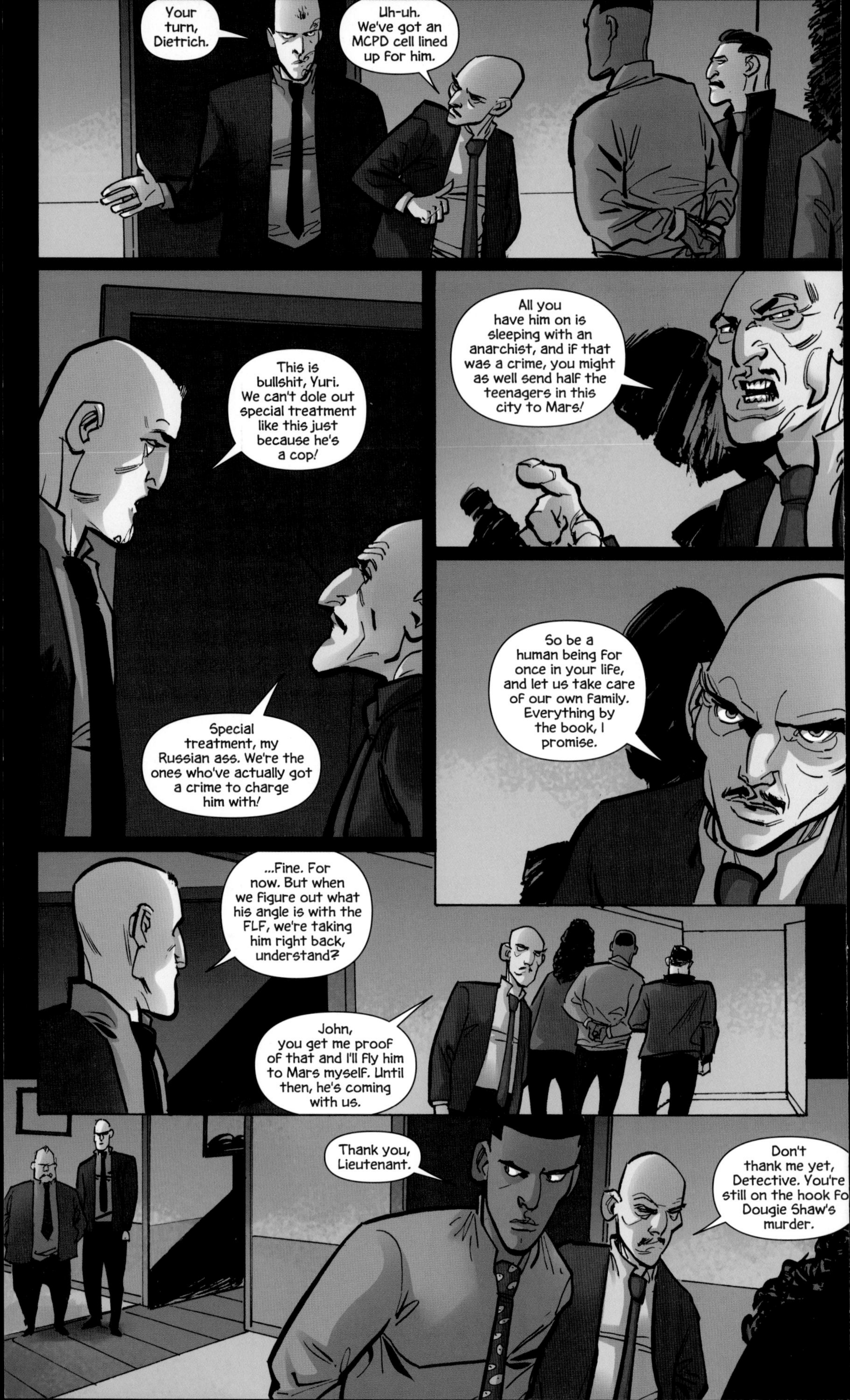
Your turn, Dietrich.
Uh-uh. We've got an MCPD cell lined up for him.
This is bullshit, Yuri. We can't dole out special treatment like this just because he's a cop!
Special treatment, my Russian ass. We're the ones who've actually got a crime to charge him with!
All you have him on is sleeping with an anarchist, and if that was a crime, you might as well send half the teenagers in this city to Mars!
So be a human being for once in your life, and let us take care of our own family. Everything by the book, I promise.
...Fine. For now. But when we figure out what his angle is with the FLF, we're taking him right back, understand?
John, you get me proof of that and I'll fly him to Mars myself. Until then, he's coming with us.
Thank you, Lieutenant.
Don't thank me yet, Detective. You're still on the hook fo Dougie Shaw's murder.

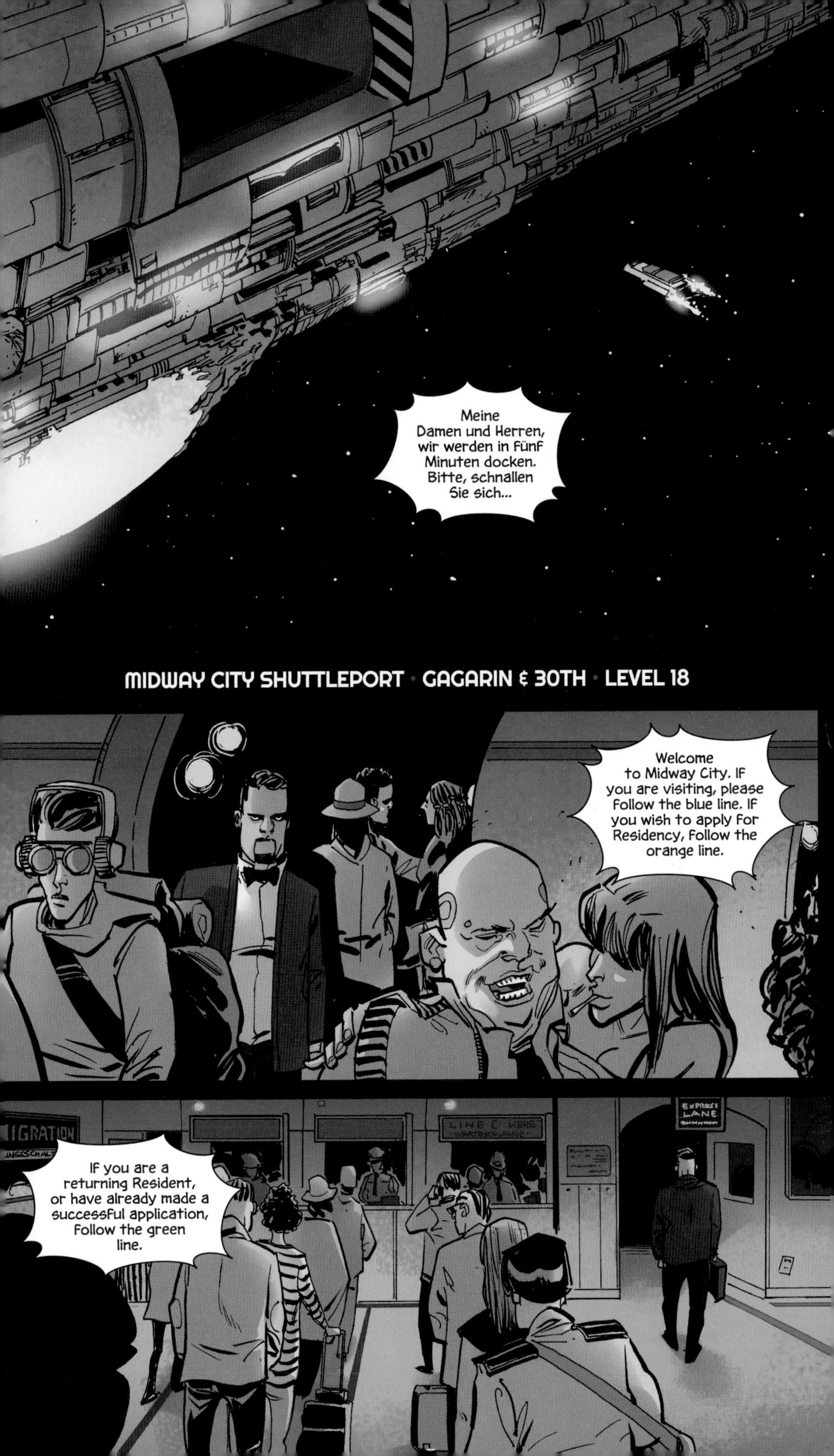
Meine Damen und Herren, wir werden in fünf Minuten docken. Bitte, schnallen Sie sich...
MIDWAY CITY SHUTTLEPORT · GAGARIN & 30TH · LEVEL 18
Welcome to Midway City. If you are visiting, please follow the blue line. If you wish to apply for Residency, follow the orange line.
EXPRESS LANE
If you are a returning Resident, or have already made a successful application, follow the green line.

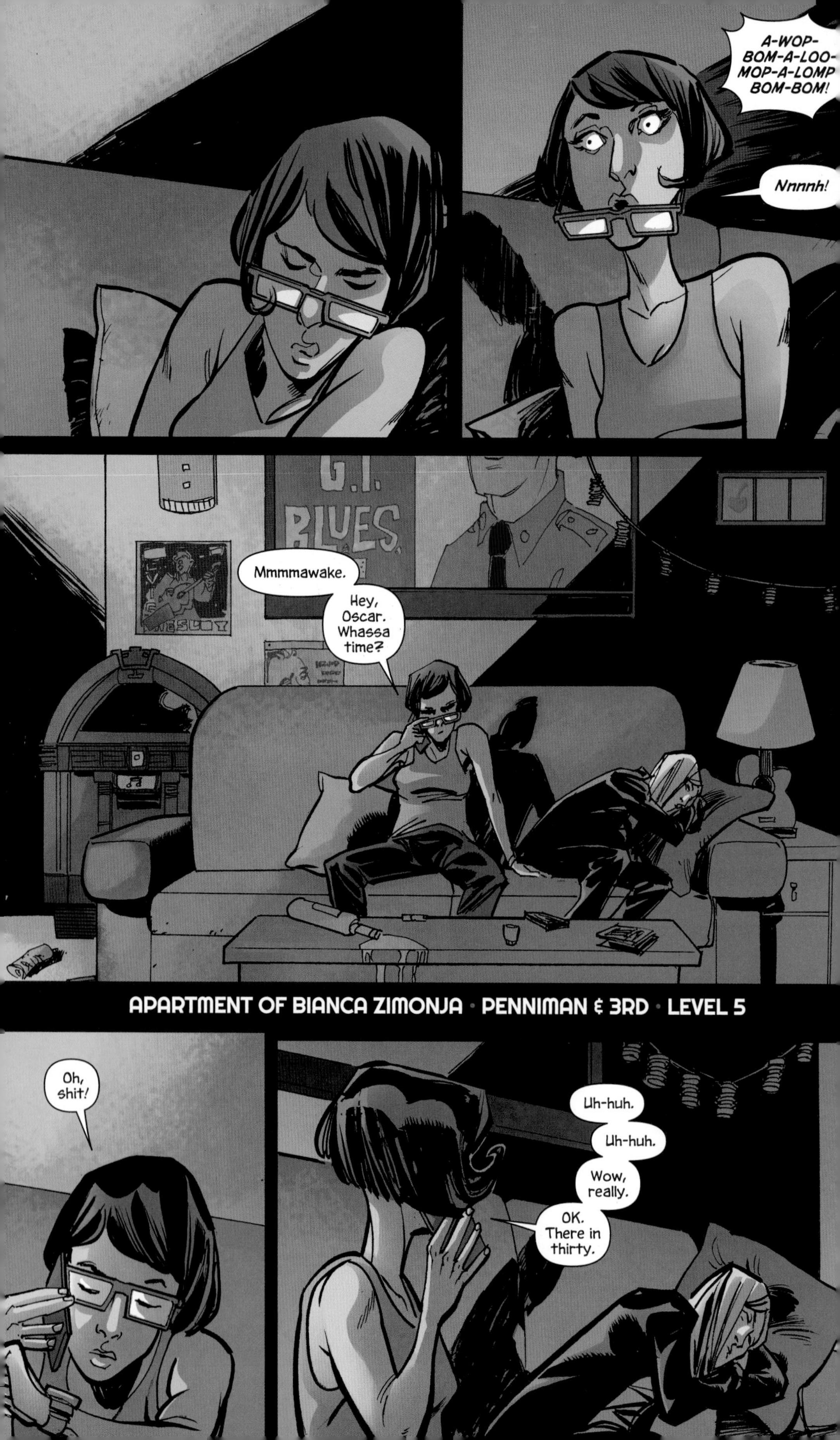
A-WOP-BOM-A-LOO-MOP-A-LOMP BOM-BOM!
Nnnnh!
Mmmmawake.
Hey, Oscar. Whassa time?
APARTMENT OF BIANCA ZIMONJA · PENNIMAN & 3RD · LEVEL 5
Oh, shit!
Uh-huh.
Uh-huh.
Wow, really.
OK. There in thirty.

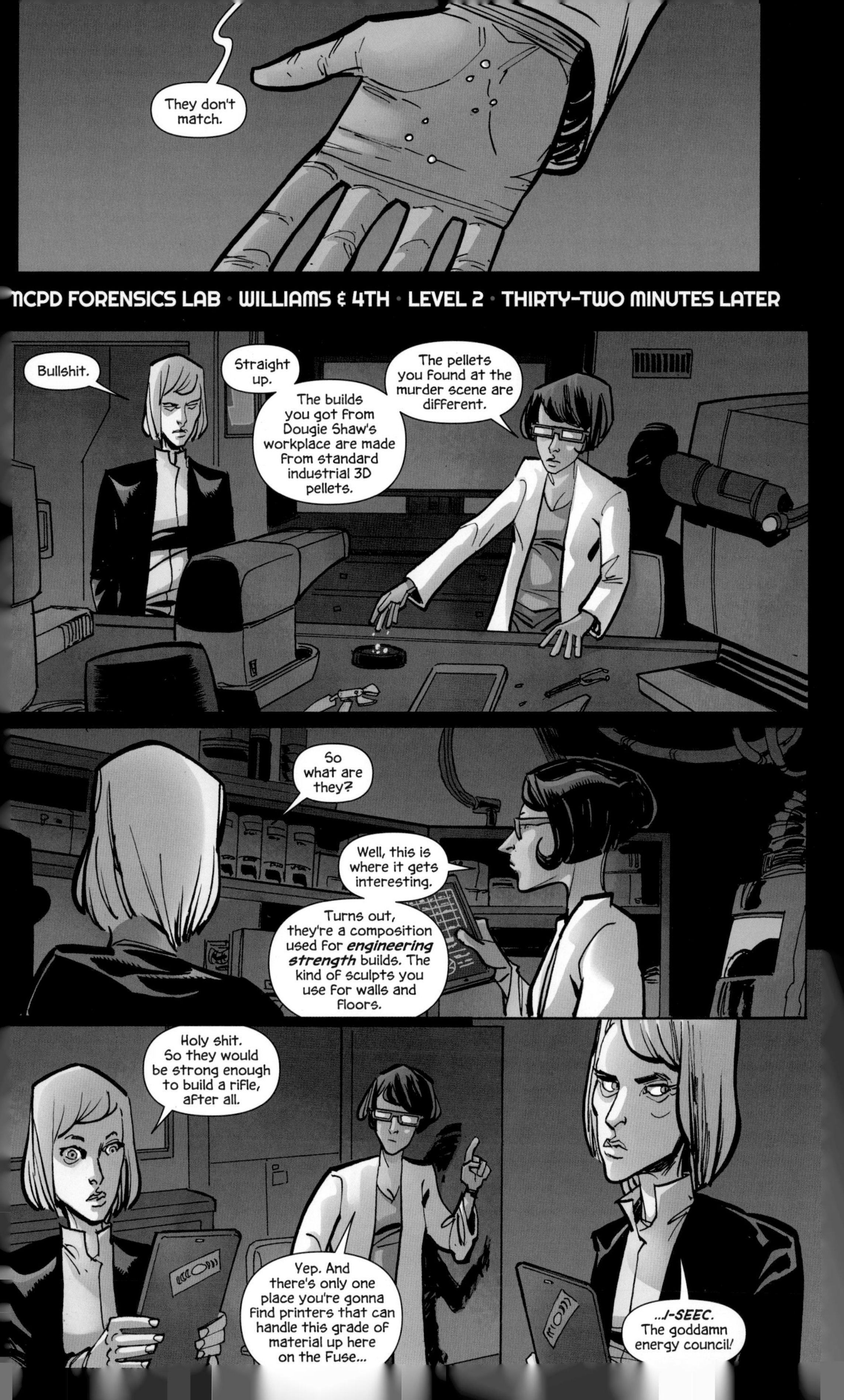
They don't match.
MCPD FORENSICS LAB · WILLIAMS & 4TH · LEVEL 2 · THIRTY-TWO MINUTES LATER
Bullshit.
Straight up.
The pellets you found at the murder scene are different.
The builds you got from Dougie Shaw's workplace are made from standard industrial 3D pellets.
So what are they?
Well, this is where it gets interesting.
Turns out, they're a composition used for *engineering strength* builds. The kind of sculpts you use for walls and floors.
Holy shit. So they would be strong enough to build a rifle, after all.
Yep. And there's only one place you're gonna find printers that can handle this grade of material up here on the Fuse...
...I-SEEC. The goddamn energy council!

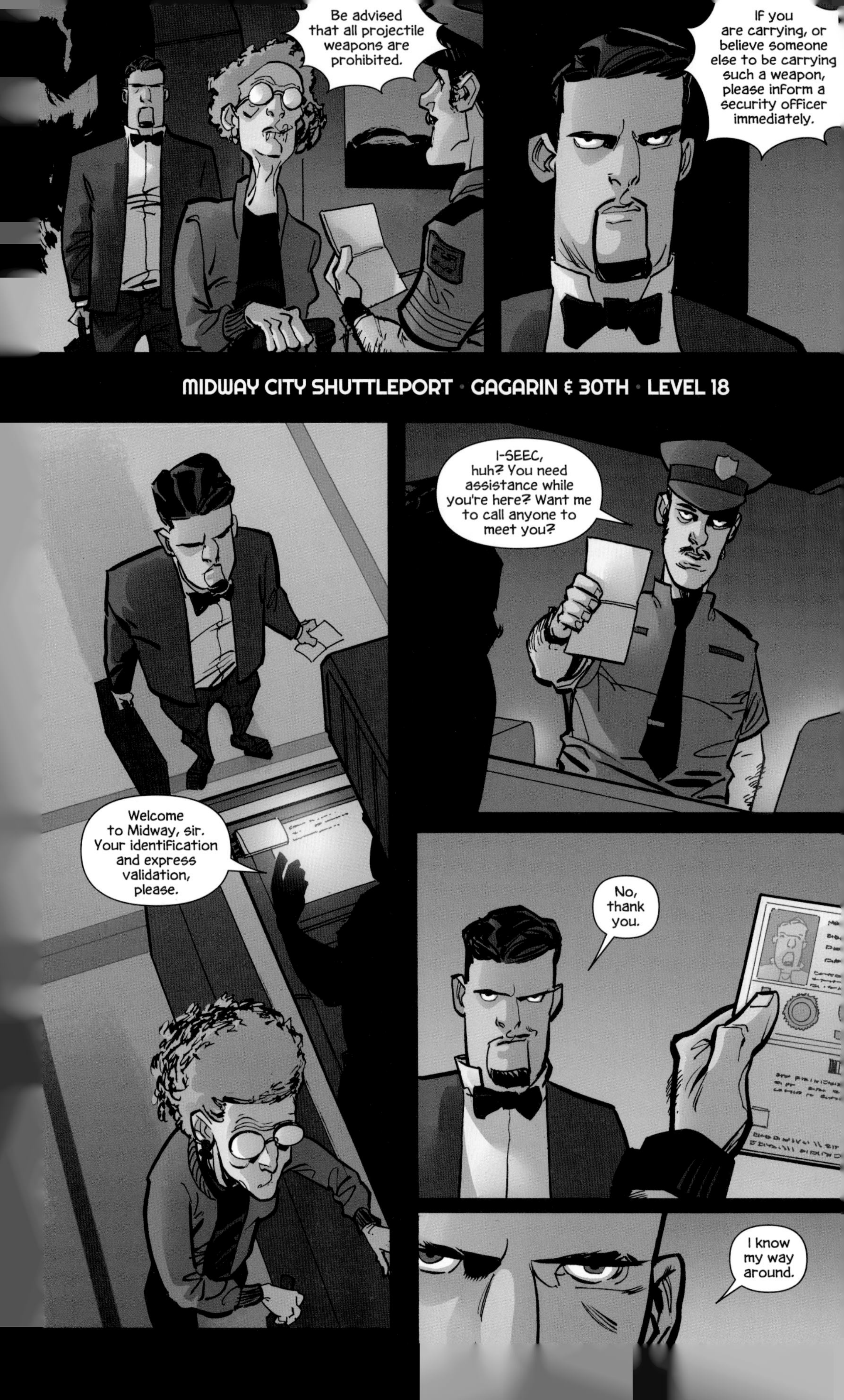
Be advised that all projectile weapons are prohibited.
If you are carrying, or believe someone else to be carrying such a weapon, please inform a security officer immediately.
MIDWAY CITY SHUTTLEPORT · GAGARIN & 30TH · LEVEL 18
Welcome to Midway, sir. Your identification and express validation, please.
I-SEEC, huh? You need assistance while you're here? Want me to call anyone to meet you?
No, thank you.
I know my way around.

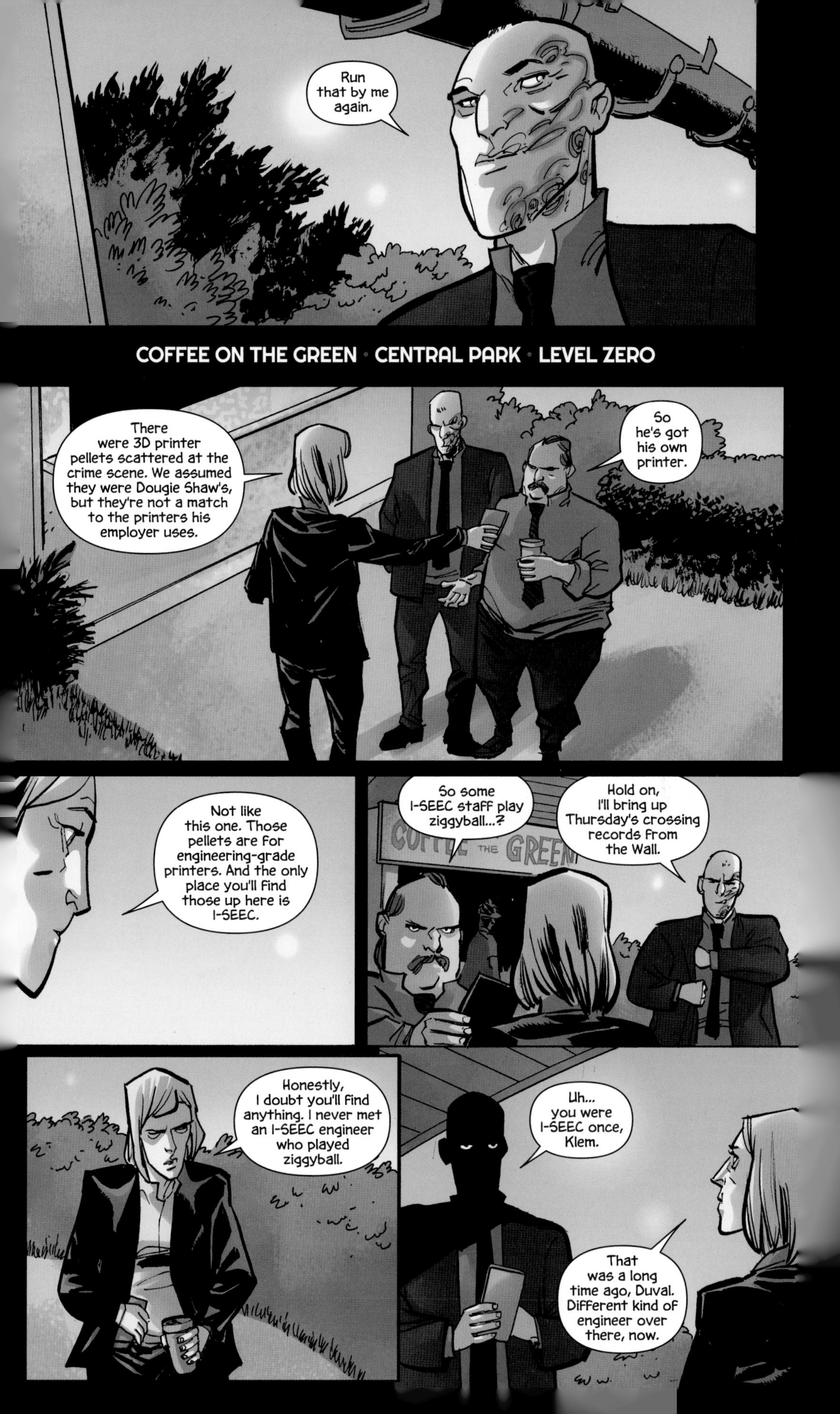
Run that by me again.
COFFEE ON THE GREEN • CENTRAL PARK • LEVEL ZERO
There were 3D printer pellets scattered at the crime scene. We assumed they were Dougie Shaw's, but they're not a match to the printers his employer uses.
So he's got his own printer.
Not like this one. Those pellets are for engineering-grade printers. And the only place you'll find those up here is I-SEEC.
So some I-SEEC staff play ziggyball...?
Hold on, I'll bring up Thursday's crossing records from the Wall.
COFFEE THE GREEN
Honestly, I doubt you'll find anything. I never met an I-SEEC engineer who played ziggyball.
Uh... you were I-SEEC once, Klem.
That was a long time ago, Duval. Different kind of engineer over there, now.

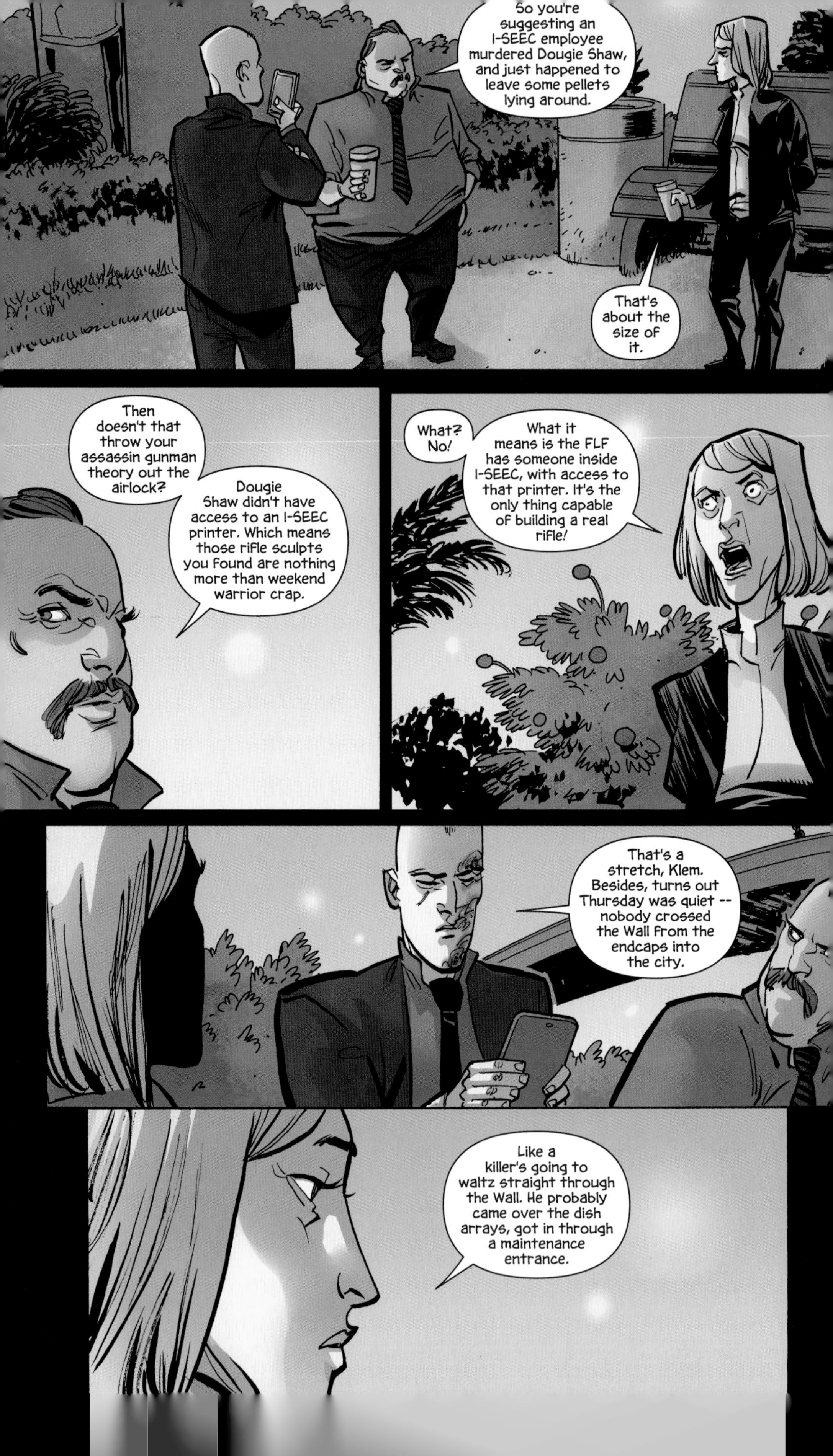
So you're suggesting an I-SEEC employee murdered Dougie Shaw, and just happened to leave some pellets lying around.
That's about the size of it.
Then doesn't that throw your assassin gunman theory out the airlock?
Dougie Shaw didn't have access to an I-SEEC printer. Which means those rifle sculpts you found are nothing more than weekend warrior crap.
What? No!
What it means is the FLF has someone inside I-SEEC, with access to that printer. It's the only thing capable of building a real rifle!
That's a stretch, Klem. Besides, turns out Thursday was quiet -- nobody crossed the Wall from the endcaps into the city.
Like a killer's going to waltz straight through the Wall. He probably came over the dish arrays, got in through a maintenance entrance.

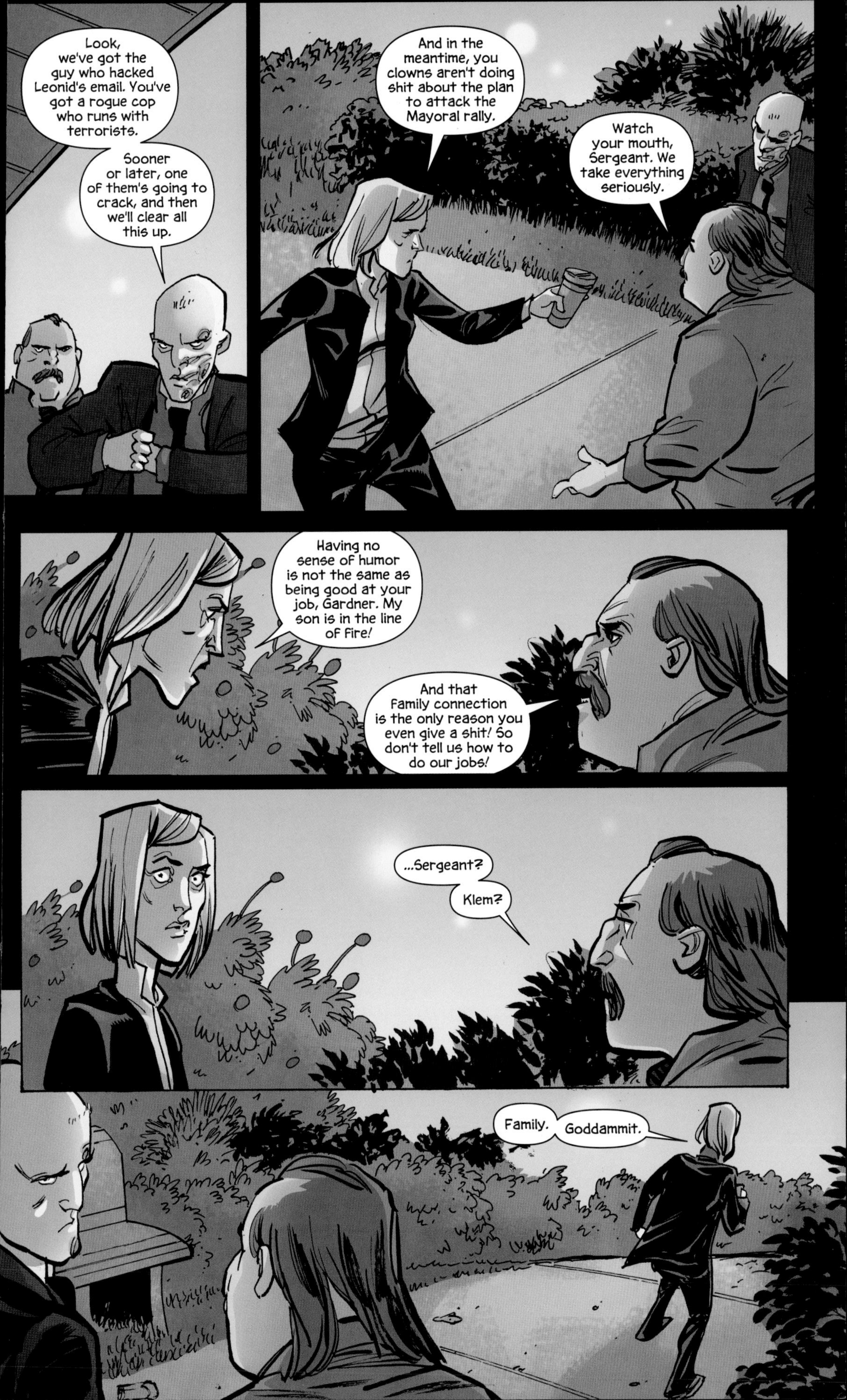
Look, we've got the guy who hacked Leonid's email. You've got a rogue cop who runs with terrorists.
Sooner or later, one of them's going to crack, and then we'll clear all this up.
And in the meantime, you clowns aren't doing shit about the plan to attack the Mayoral rally.
Watch your mouth, Sergeant. We take everything seriously.
Having no sense of humor is not the same as being good at your job, Gardner. My son is in the line of fire!
And that family connection is the only reason you even give a shit! So don't tell us how to do our jobs!
...Sergeant?
Klem?
Family.
Goddammit.

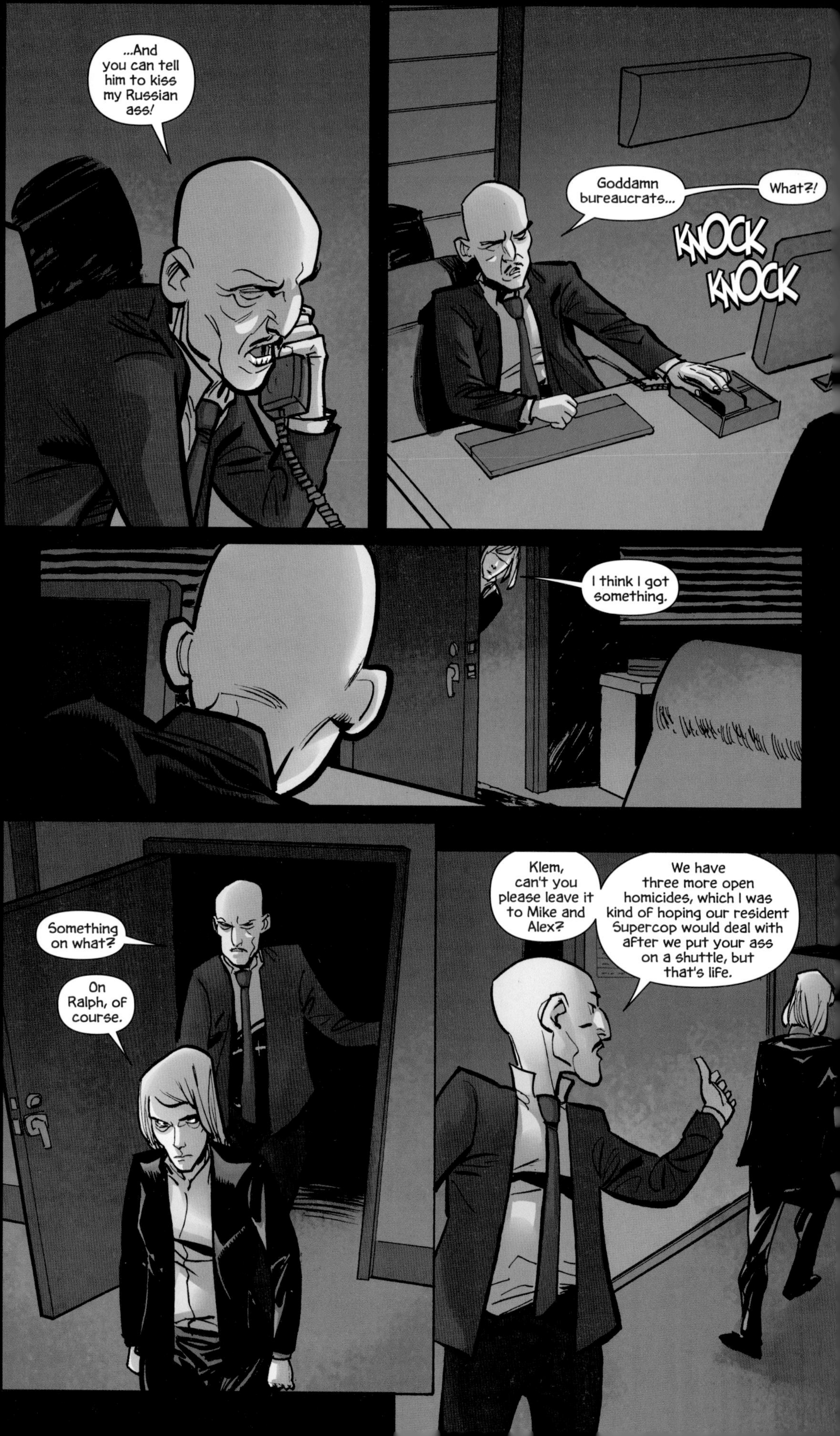
...And you can tell him to kiss my Russian ass!
Goddamn bureaucrats...
What?!
KNOCK KNOCK
I think I got something.
Something on what?
On Ralph, of course.
Klem, can't you please leave it to Mike and Alex?
We have three more open homicides, which I was kind of hoping our resident Supercop would deal with after we put your ass on a shuttle, but that's life.

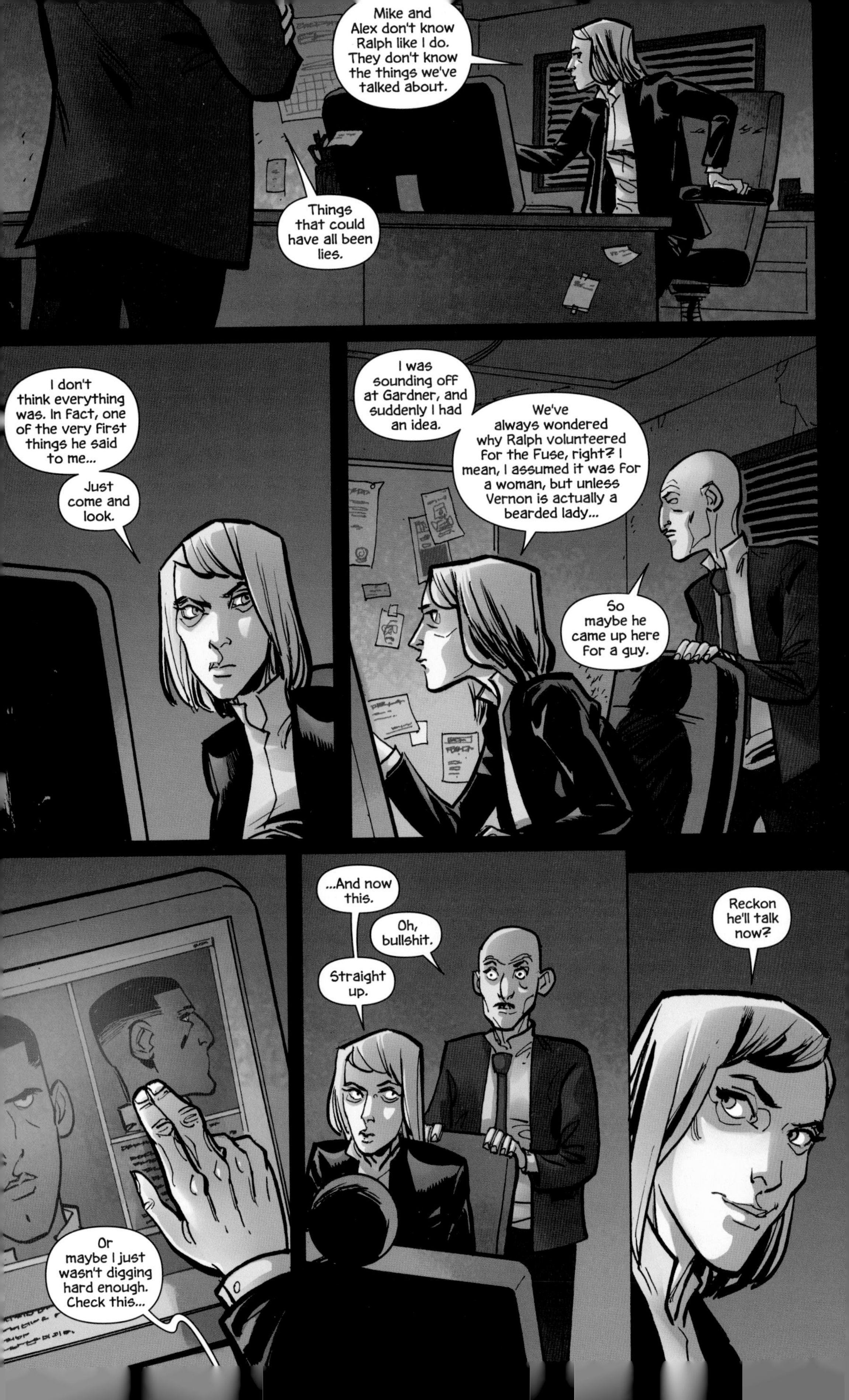
Mike and Alex don't know Ralph like I do. They don't know the things we've talked about.
Things that could have all been lies.
I don't think everything was. In fact, one of the very first things he said to me...
Just come and look.
I was sounding off at Gardner, and suddenly I had an idea.
We've always wondered why Ralph volunteered for the Fuse, right? I mean, I assumed it was for a woman, but unless Vernon is actually a bearded lady...
So maybe he came up here for a guy.
Or maybe I just wasn't digging hard enough. Check this...
...And now this.
Oh, bullshit.
Straight up.
Reckon he'll talk now?

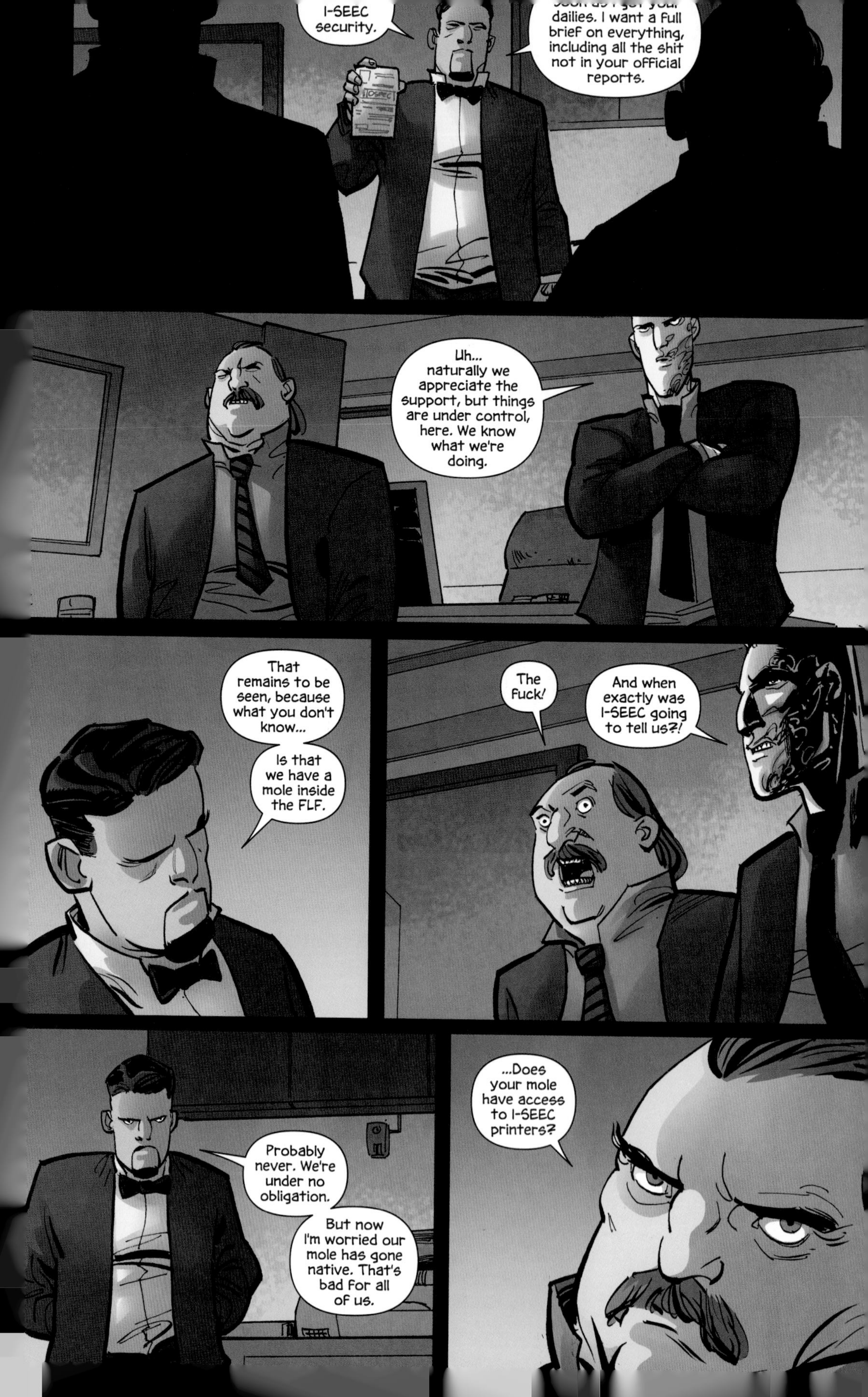
I-SEEC security.
dailies. I want a full brief on everything, including all the shit not in your official reports.
Uh... naturally we appreciate the support, but things are under control, here. We know what we're doing.
That remains to be seen, because what you don't know...
Is that we have a mole inside the FLF.
The Fuck!
And when exactly was I-SEEC going to tell us?!
Probably never. We're under no obligation.
But now I'm worried our mole has gone native. That's bad for all of us.
...Does your mole have access to I-SEEC printers?

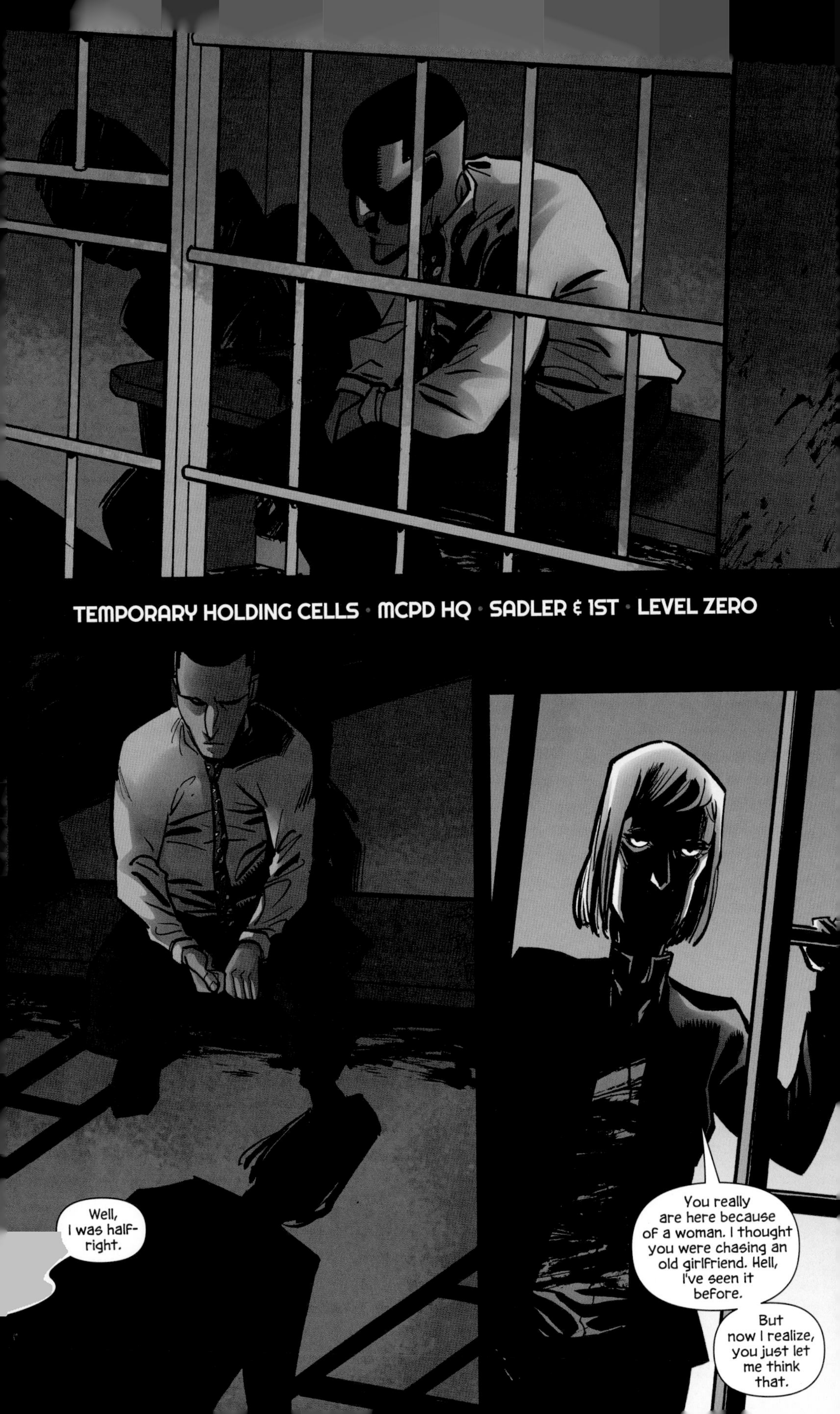
TEMPORARY HOLDING CELLS · MCPD HQ · SADLER & 1ST · LEVEL ZERO
You really are here because of a woman. I thought you were chasing an old girlfriend. Hell, I've seen it before.
But now I realize, you just let me think that.
Well, I was half-right.

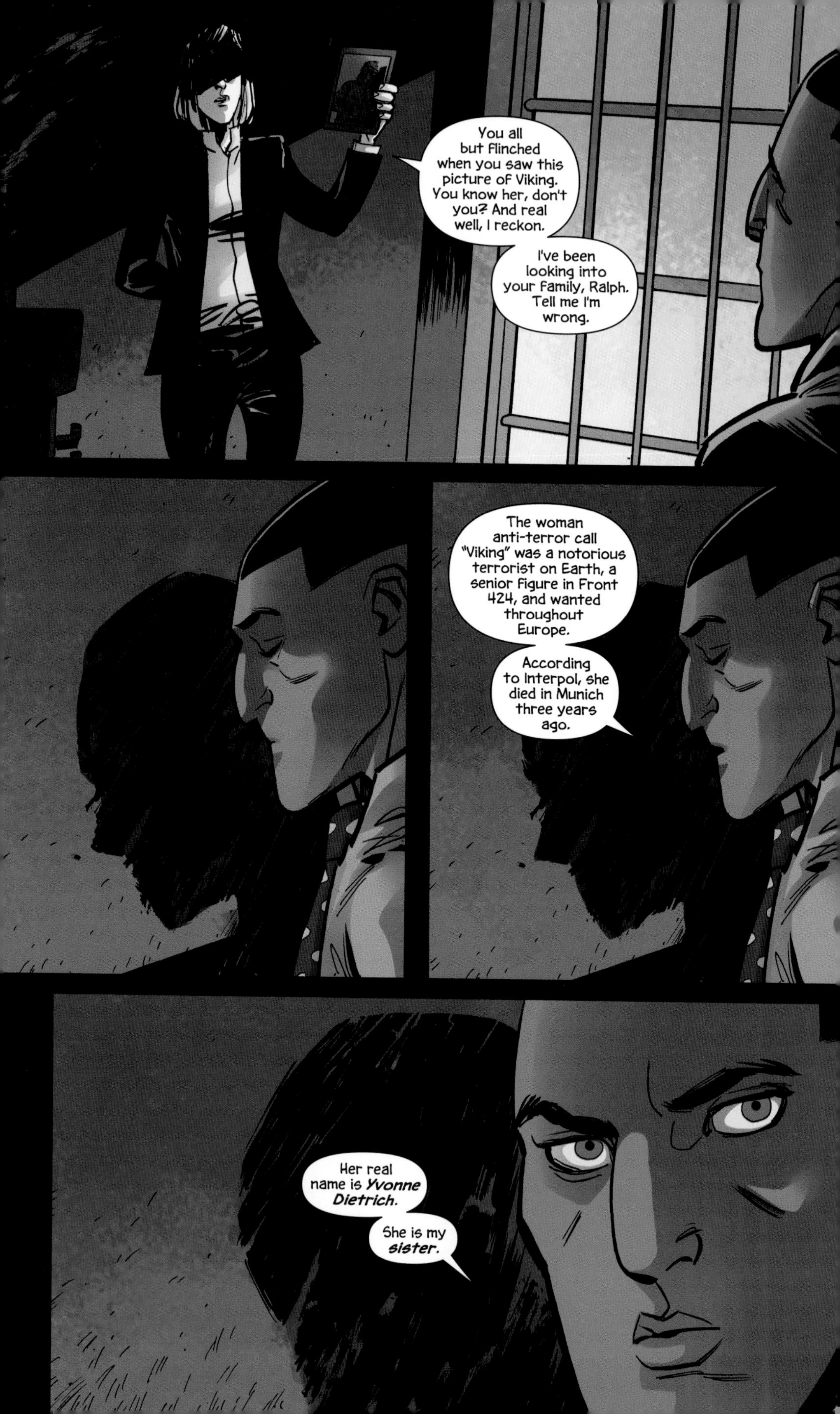

You all but flinched when you saw this picture of Viking. You know her, don't you? And real well, I reckon.
I've been looking into your family, Ralph. Tell me I'm wrong.
The woman anti-terror call "Viking" was a notorious terrorist on Earth, a senior figure in Front 424, and wanted throughout Europe.
According to Interpol, she died in Munich three years ago.
Her real name is *Yvonne Dietrich.*
She is my *sister.*

PART 5

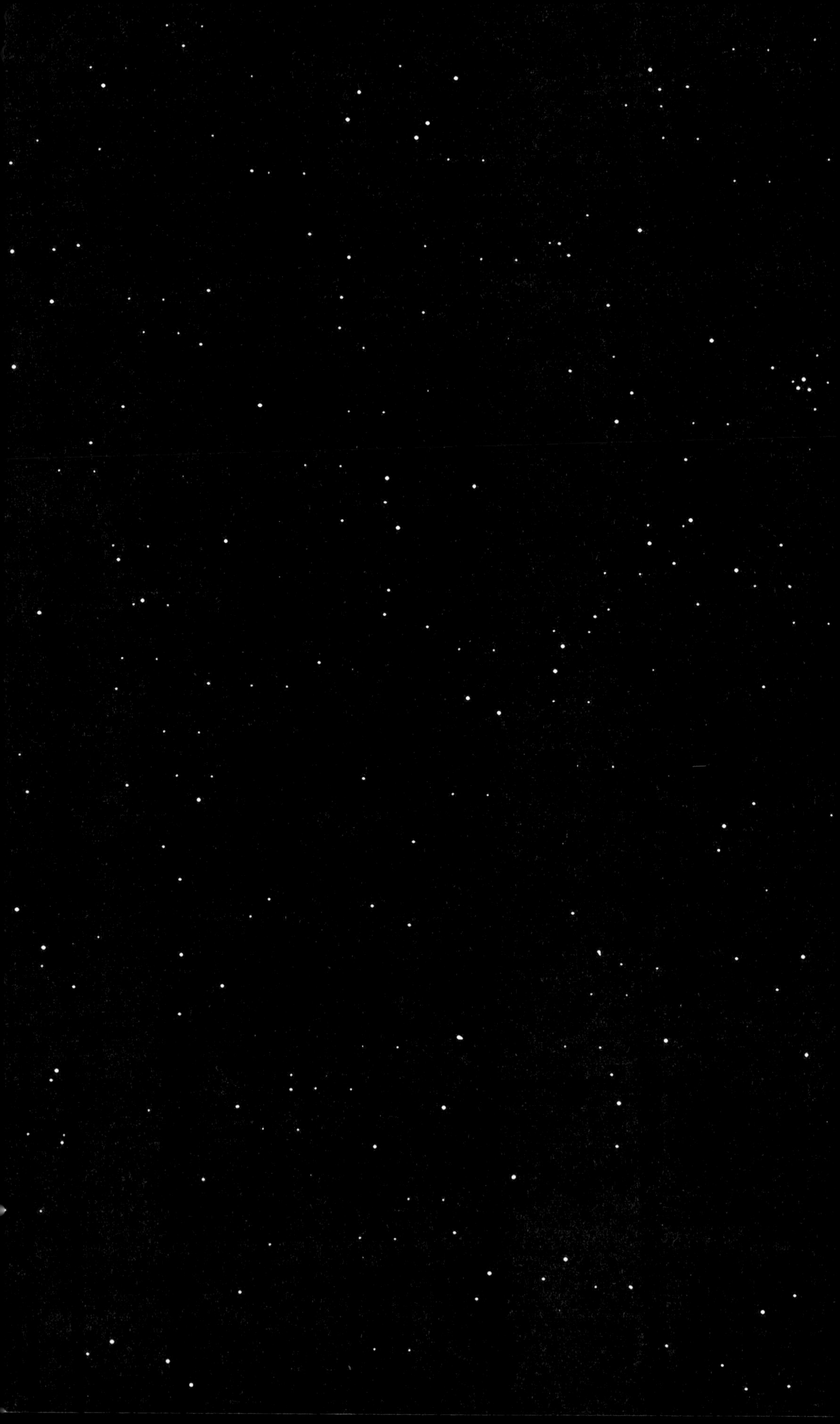

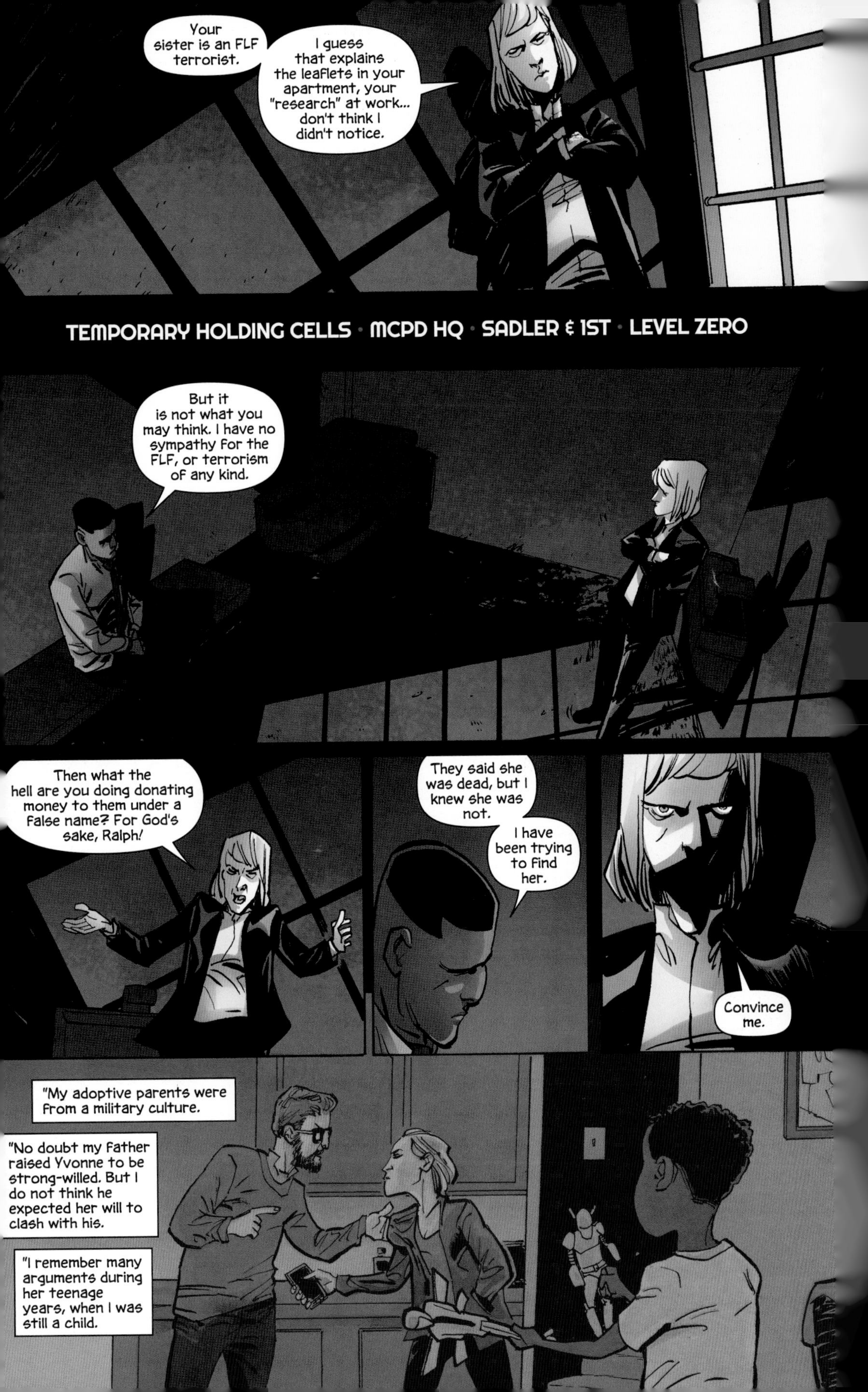

Your sister is an FLF terrorist.
I guess that explains the leaflets in your apartment, your "research" at work... don't think I didn't notice.
TEMPORARY HOLDING CELLS · MCPD HQ · SADLER & 1ST · LEVEL ZERO
But it is not what you may think. I have no sympathy for the FLF, or terrorism of any kind.
Then what the hell are you doing donating money to them under a false name? For God's sake, Ralph!
They said she was dead, but I knew she was not.
I have been trying to find her.
Convince me.
"My adoptive parents were from a military culture.
"No doubt my father raised Yvonne to be strong-willed. But I do not think he expected her will to clash with his.
"I remember many arguments during her teenage years, when I was still a child.

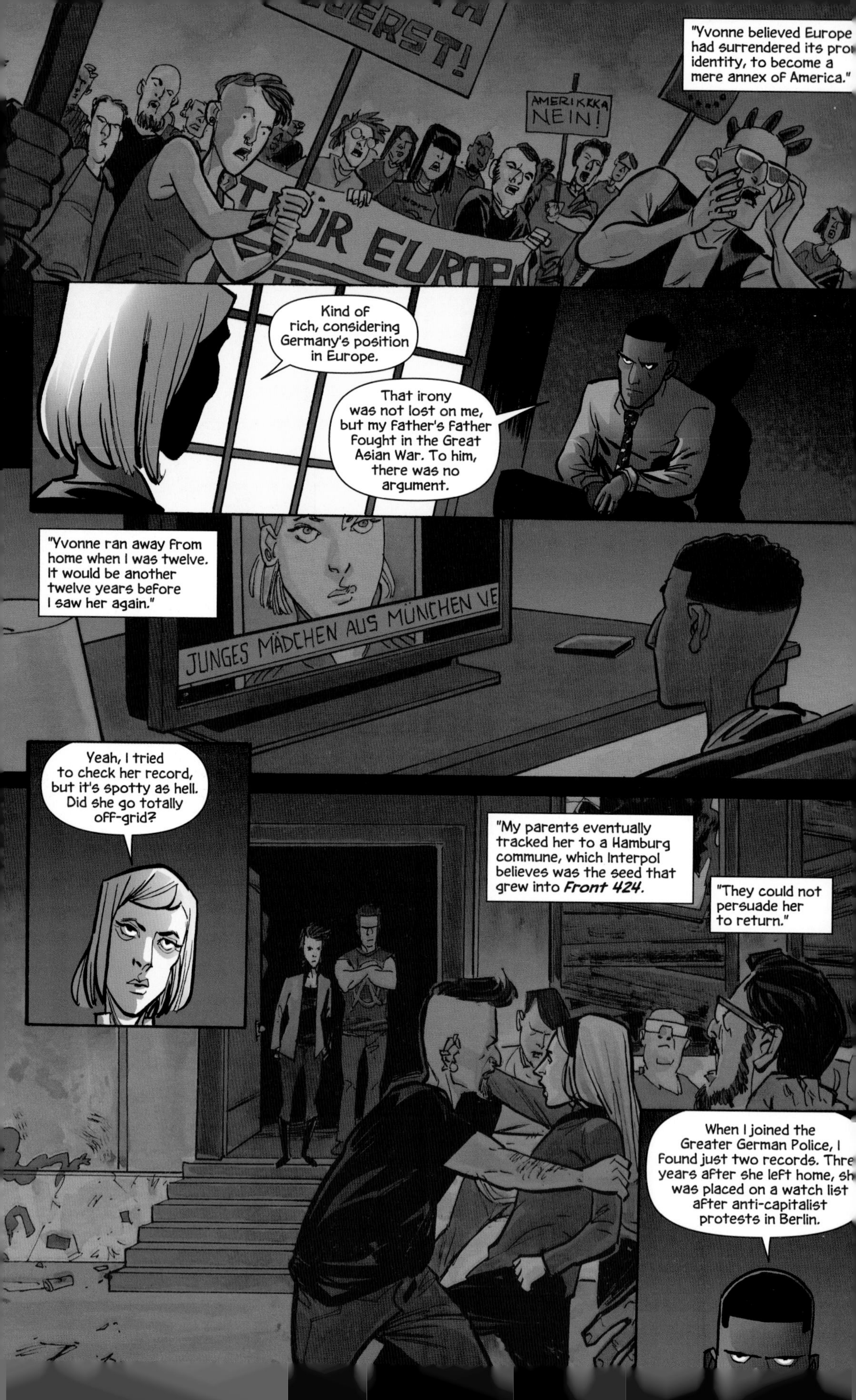
AMERIKKKA NEIN!
"Yvonne believed Europe had surrendered its pro identity, to become a mere annex of America."
Kind of rich, considering Germany's position in Europe.
That irony was not lost on me, but my Father's Father fought in the Great Asian War. To him, there was no argument.
"Yvonne ran away from home when I was twelve. It would be another twelve years before I saw her again."
JUNGES MÄDCHEN AUS MÜNCHEN VE
Yeah, I tried to check her record, but it's spotty as hell. Did she go totally off-grid?
"My parents eventually tracked her to a Hamburg commune, which Interpol believes was the seed that grew into *Front 424*.
"They could not persuade her to return."
When I joined the Greater German Police, I found just two records. Thre years after she left home, sh was placed on a watch list after anti-capitalist protests in Berlin.

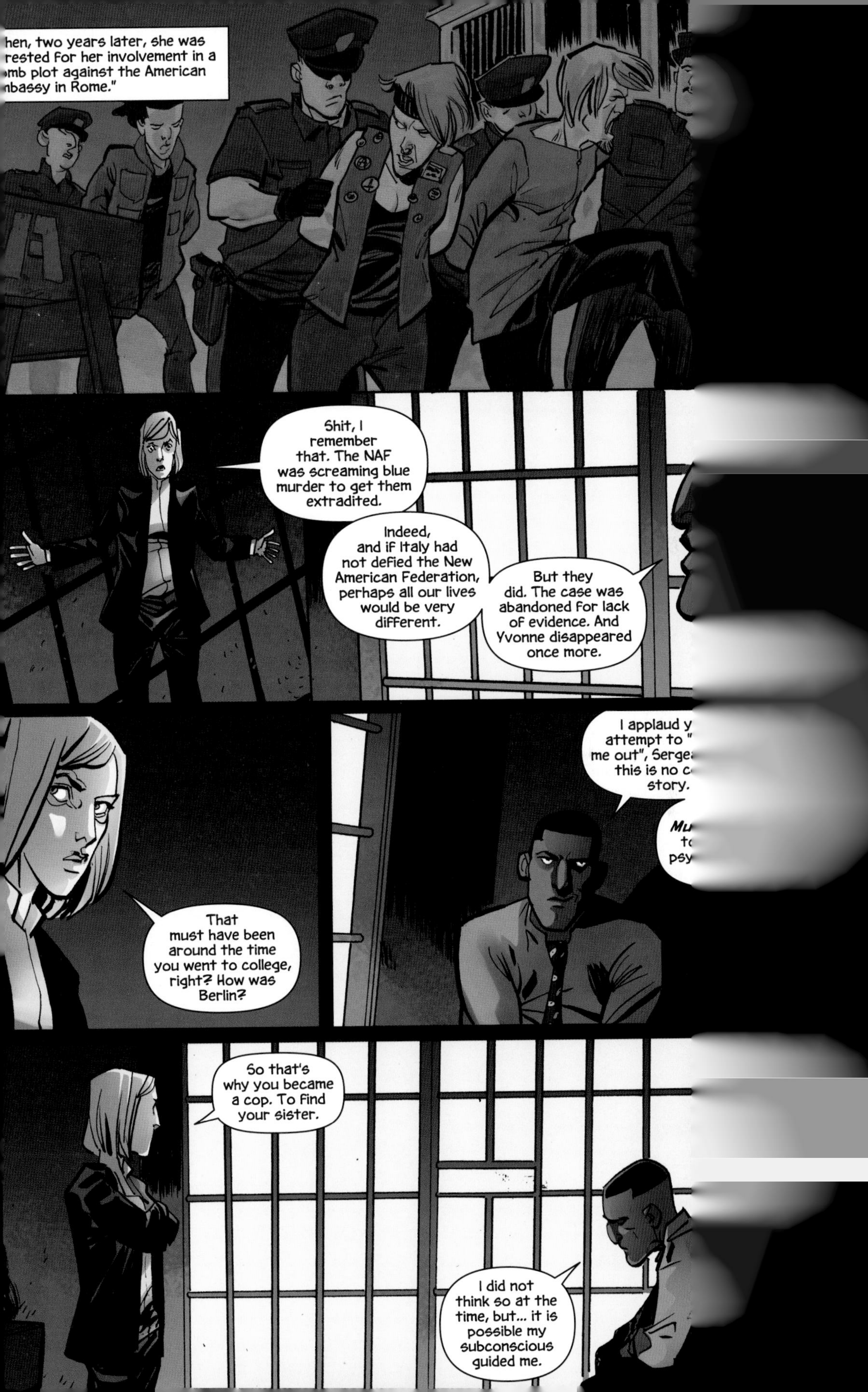
hen, two years later, she was rested for her involvement in a mb plot against the American nbassy in Rome."
Shit, I remember that. The NAF was screaming blue murder to get them extradited.
Indeed, and if Italy had not defied the New American Federation, perhaps all our lives would be very different.
But they did. The case was abandoned for lack of evidence. And Yvonne disappeared once more.
That must have been around the time you went to college, right? How was Berlin?
I applaud y attempt to " me out", Serge this is no c story.
So that's why you became a cop. To find your sister.
I did not think so at the time, but... it is possible my subconscious guided me.

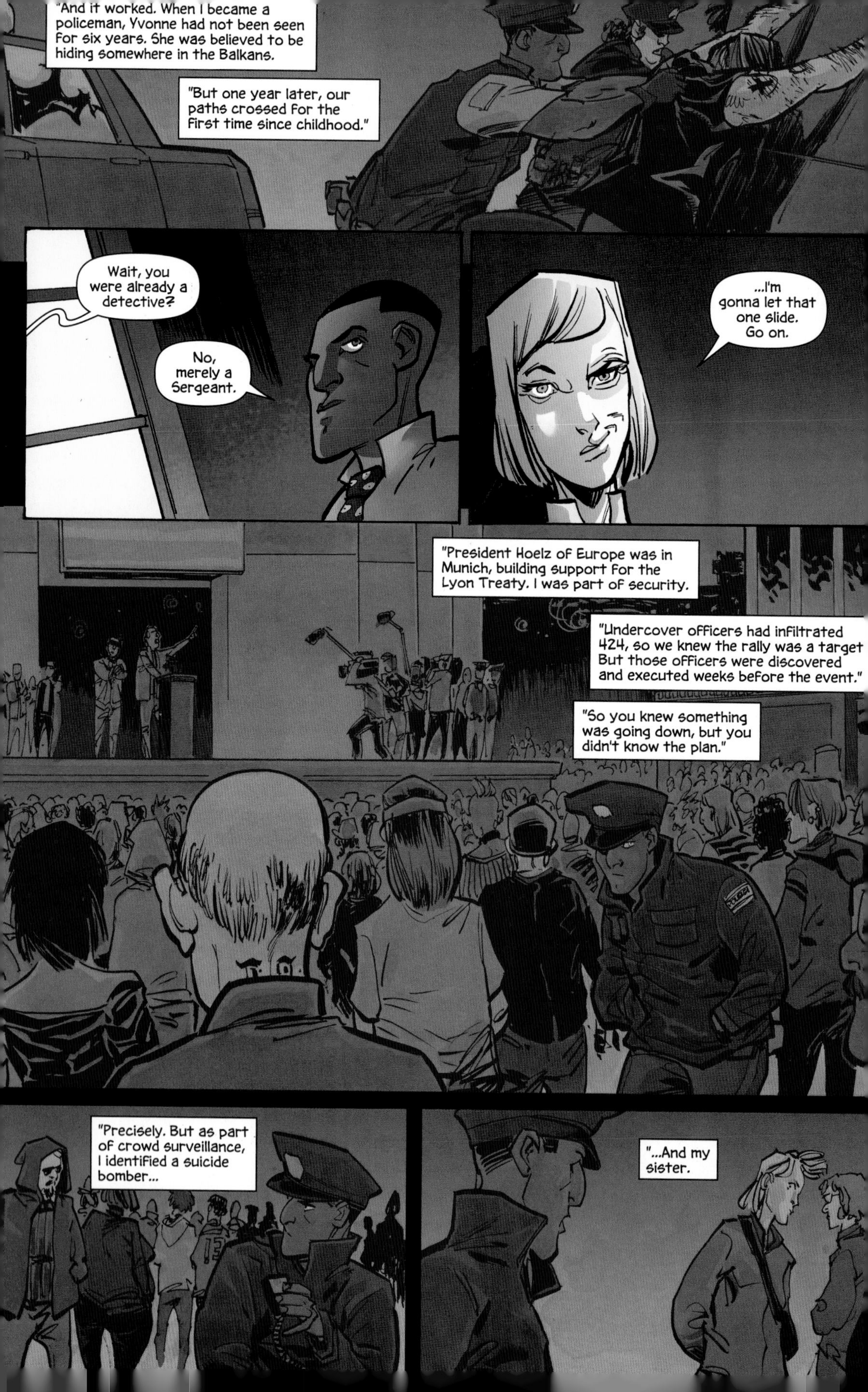
"And it worked. When I became a policeman, Yvonne had not been seen for six years. She was believed to be hiding somewhere in the Balkans.
"But one year later, our paths crossed for the first time since childhood."
Wait, you were already a detective?
No, merely a Sergeant.
...I'm gonna let that one slide. Go on.
"President Hoelz of Europe was in Munich, building support for the Lyon Treaty. I was part of security.
"Undercover officers had infiltrated 424, so we knew the rally was a target But those officers were discovered and executed weeks before the event."
"So you knew something was going down, but you didn't know the plan."
"Precisely. But as part of crowd surveillance, I identified a suicide bomber...
"...And my sister.

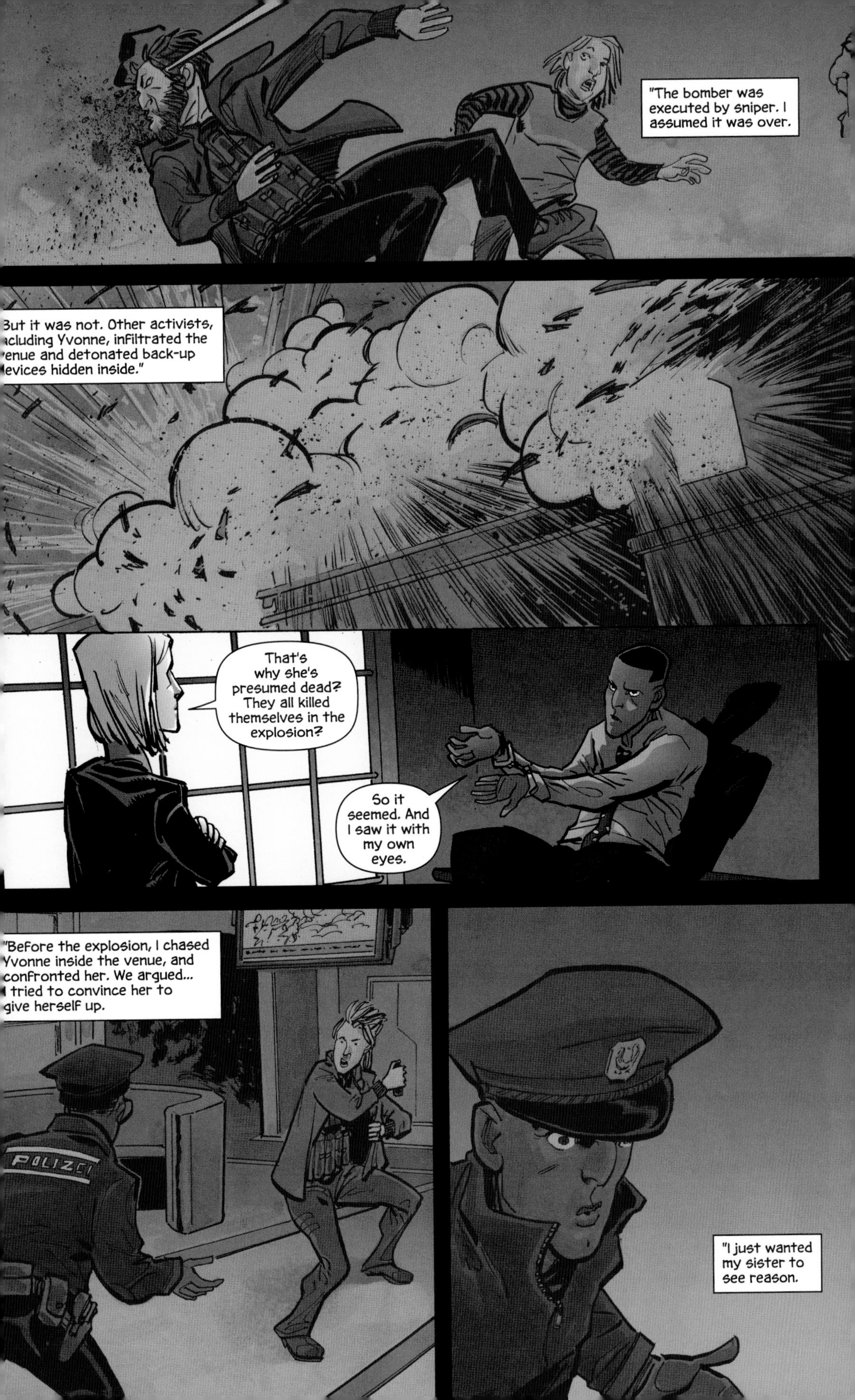
"The bomber was executed by sniper. I assumed it was over.
But it was not. Other activists, including Yvonne, infiltrated the venue and detonated back-up devices hidden inside."
That's why she's presumed dead? They all killed themselves in the explosion?
So it seemed. And I saw it with my own eyes.
"Before the explosion, I chased Yvonne inside the venue, and confronted her. We argued... I tried to convince her to give herself up.
POLIZEI
"I just wanted my sister to see reason.

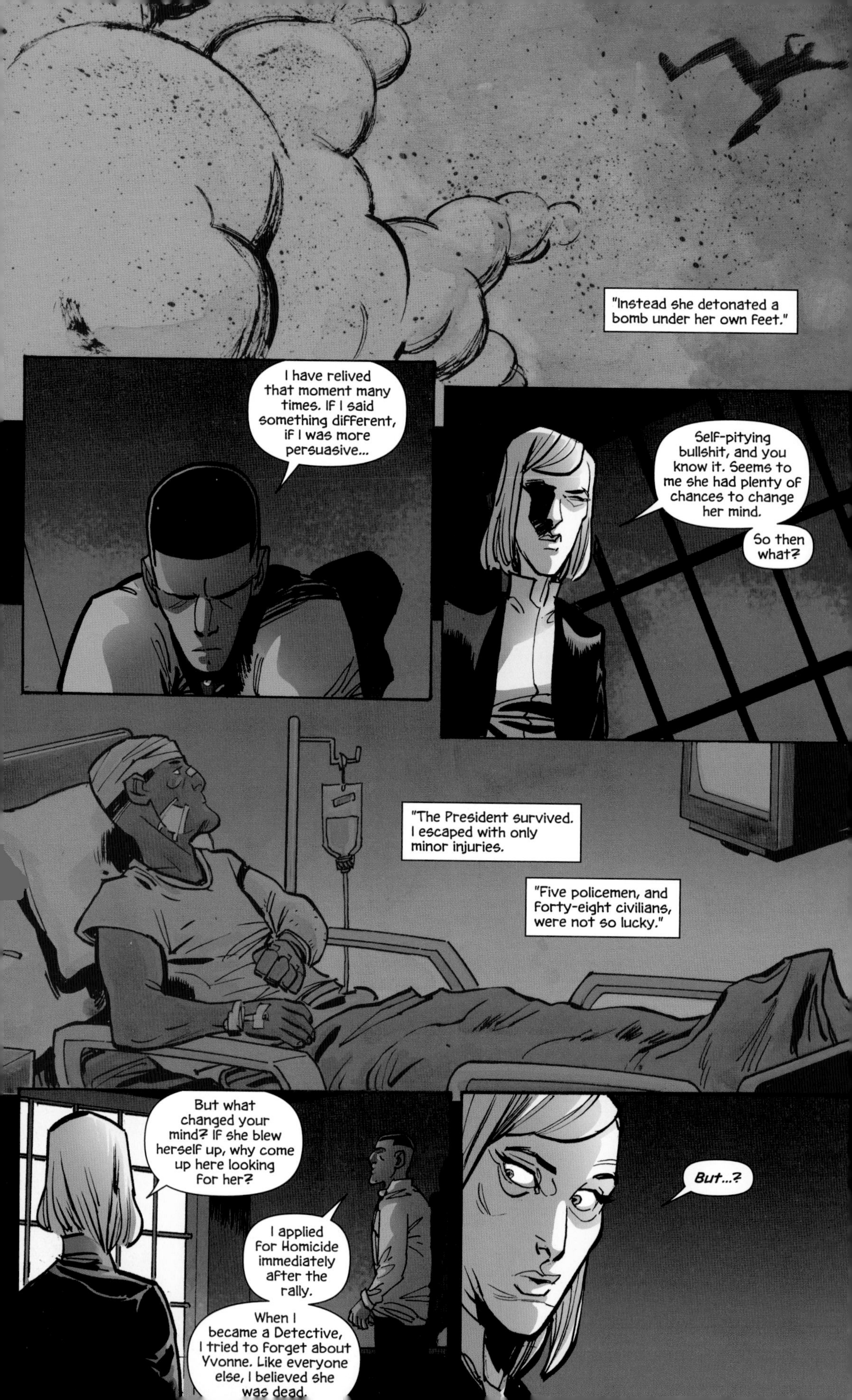
"Instead she detonated a bomb under her own feet."
I have relived that moment many times. If I said something different, if I was more persuasive...
Self-pitying bullshit, and you know it. Seems to me she had plenty of chances to change her mind.
So then what?
"The President survived. I escaped with only minor injuries.
"Five policemen, and forty-eight civilians, were not so lucky."
But what changed your mind? If she blew herself up, why come up here looking for her?
I applied for Homicide immediately after the rally.
When I became a Detective, I tried to forget about Yvonne. Like everyone else, I believed she was dead.
But...?

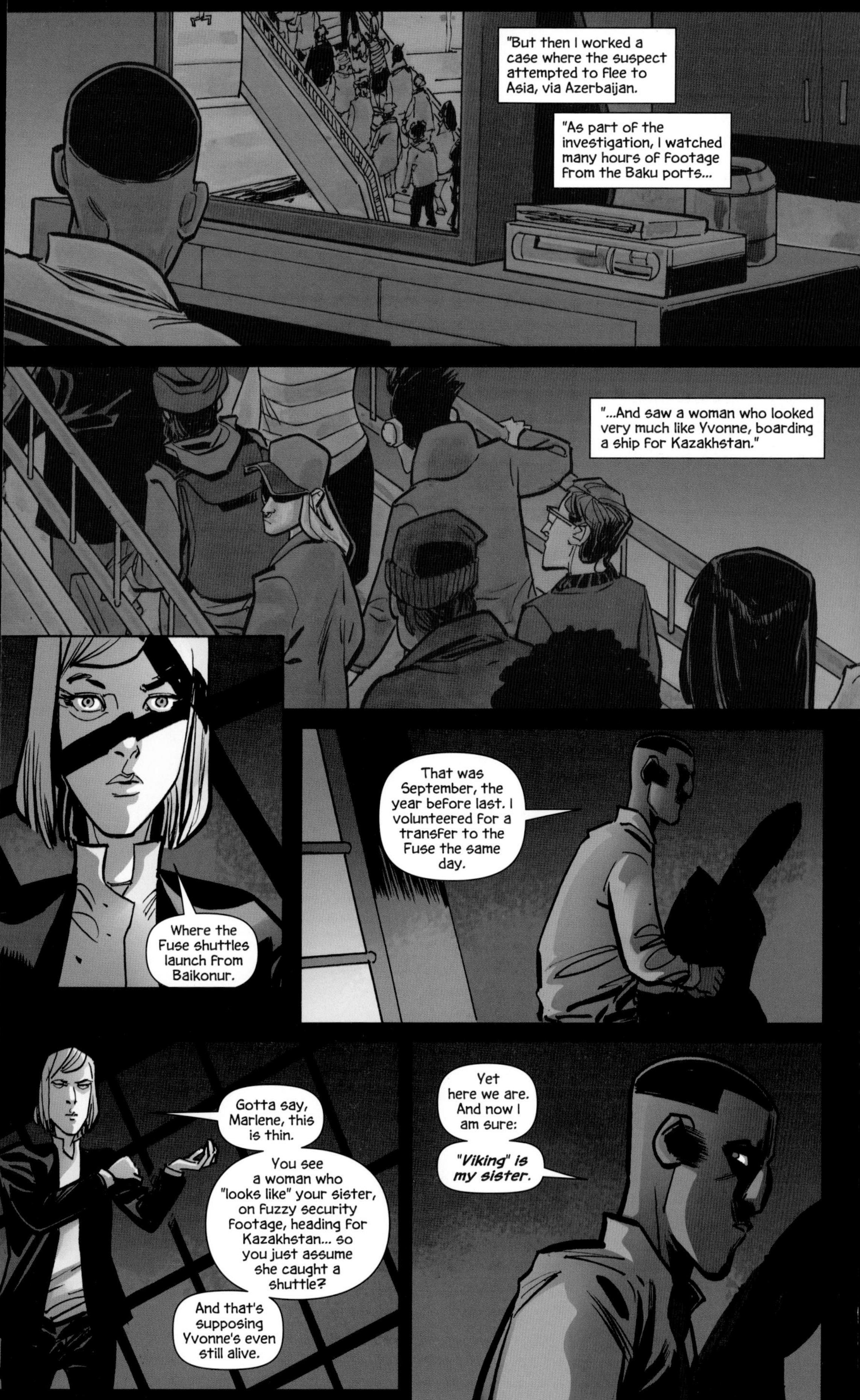
"But then I worked a case where the suspect attempted to flee to Asia, via Azerbaijan.
"As part of the investigation, I watched many hours of footage from the Baku ports...
"...And saw a woman who looked very much like Yvonne, boarding a ship for Kazakhstan."
That was September, the year before last. I volunteered for a transfer to the Fuse the same day.
Where the Fuse shuttles launch from Baikonur.
Gotta say, Marlene, this is thin.
You see a woman who "looks like" your sister, on fuzzy security footage, heading for Kazakhstan... so you just assume she caught a shuttle?
And that's supposing Yvonne's even still alive.
Yet here we are. And now I am sure:
"Viking" is my sister.

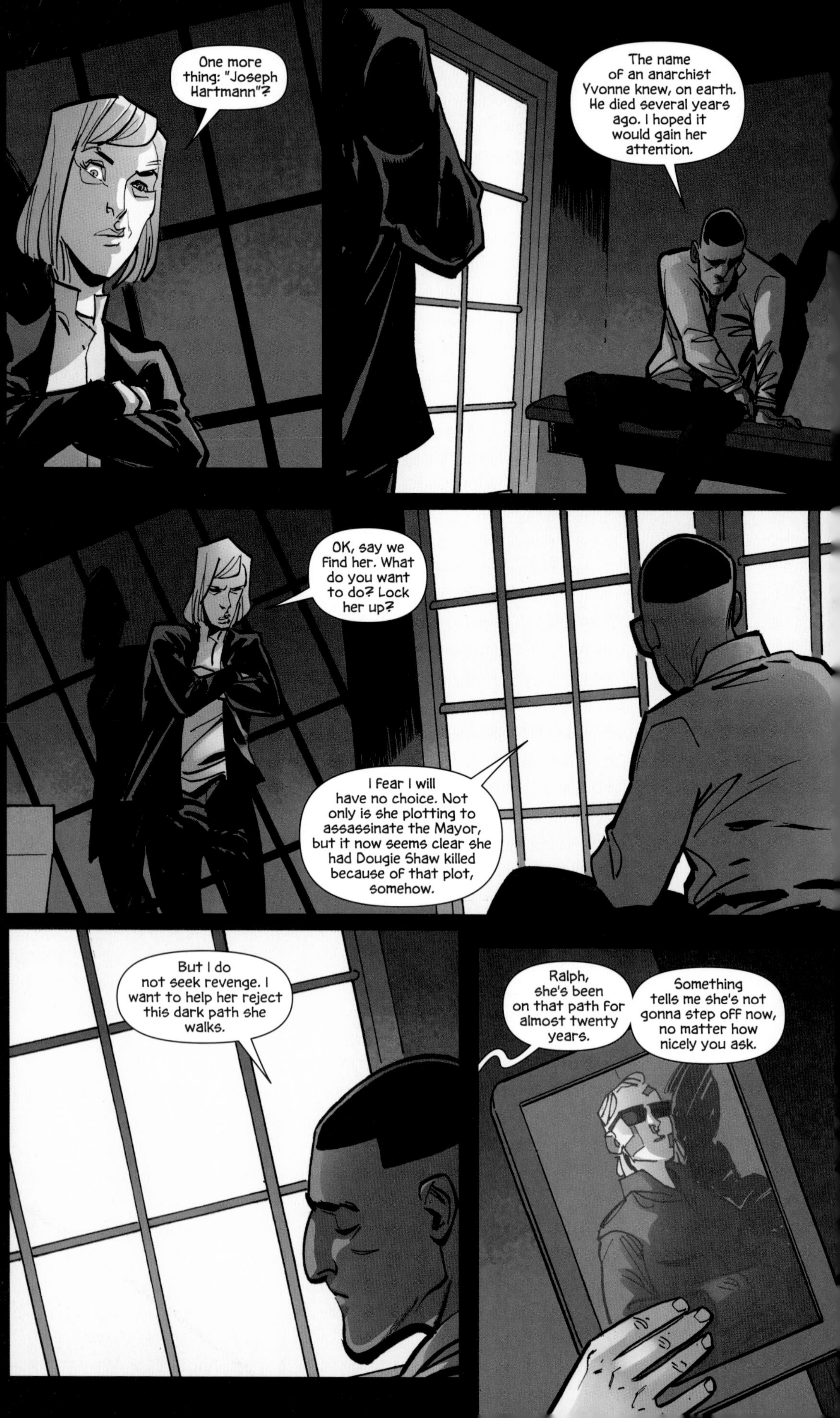
One more thing: "Joseph Hartmann"?
The name of an anarchist Yvonne knew, on earth. He died several years ago. I hoped it would gain her attention.
OK, say we find her. What do you want to do? Lock her up?
I fear I will have no choice. Not only is she plotting to assassinate the Mayor, but it now seems clear she had Dougie Shaw killed because of that plot, somehow.
But I do not seek revenge. I want to help her reject this dark path she walks.
Ralph, she's been on that path for almost twenty years.
Something tells me she's not gonna step off now, no matter how nicely you ask.

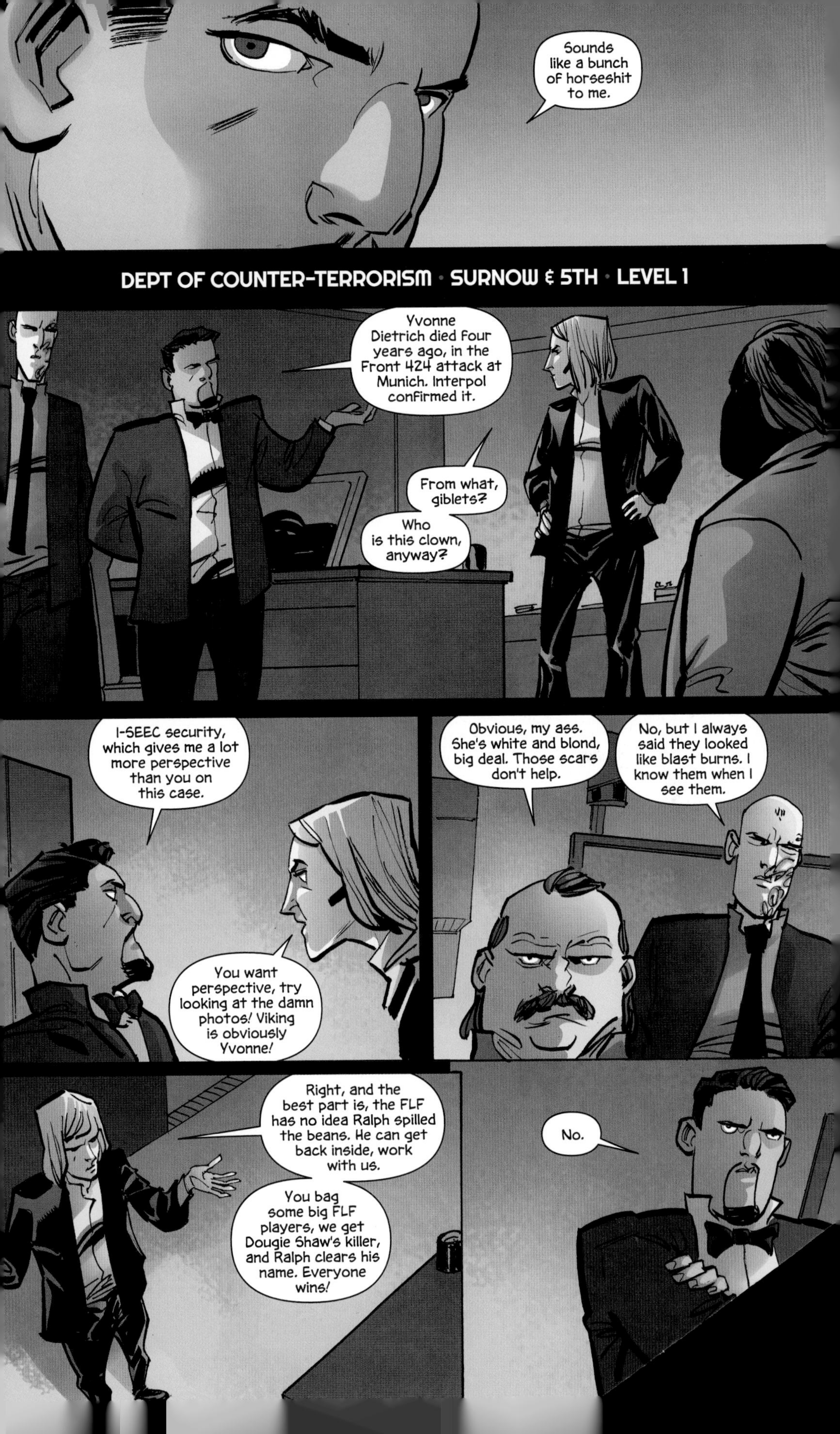
Sounds like a bunch of horseshit to me.
DEPT OF COUNTER-TERRORISM • SURNOW & 5TH • LEVEL 1
Yvonne Dietrich died four years ago, in the Front 424 attack at Munich. Interpol confirmed it.
From what, giblets?
Who is this clown, anyway?
I-SEEC security, which gives me a lot more perspective than you on this case.
You want perspective, try looking at the damn photos! Viking is obviously Yvonne!
Obvious, my ass. She's white and blond, big deal. Those scars don't help.
No, but I always said they looked like blast burns. I know them when I see them.
Right, and the best part is, the FLF has no idea Ralph spilled the beans. He can get back inside, work with us.
You bag some big FLF players, we get Dougie Shaw's killer, and Ralph clears his name. Everyone wins!
No.

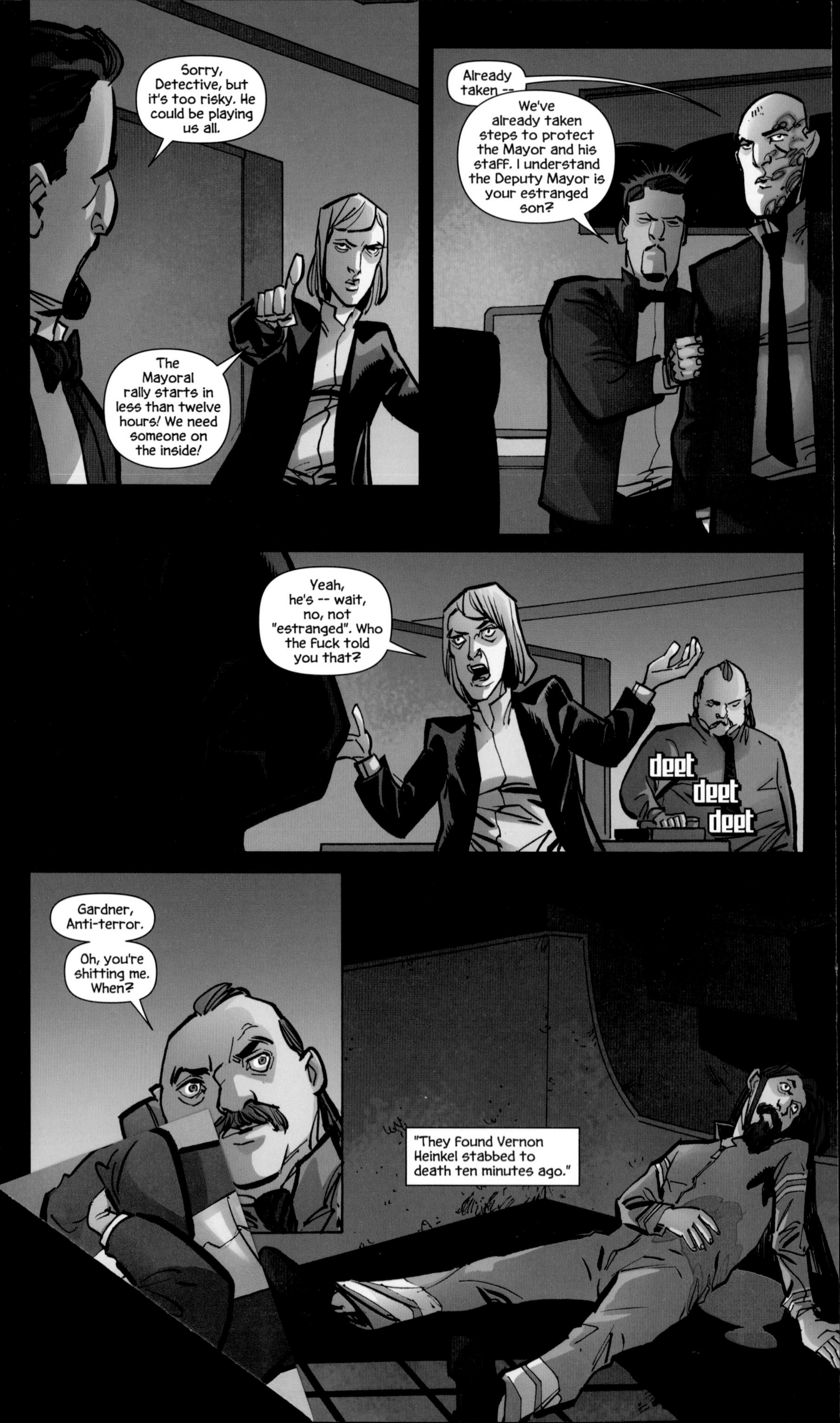
Sorry, Detective, but it's too risky. He could be playing us all.
The Mayoral rally starts in less than twelve hours! We need someone on the inside!
Already taken --
We've already taken steps to protect the Mayor and his staff. I understand the Deputy Mayor is your estranged son?
Yeah, he's -- wait, no, not "estranged". Who the fuck told you that?
deet deet deet
Gardner, Anti-terror.
Oh, you're shitting me. When?
"They found Vernon Heinkel stabbed to death ten minutes ago."

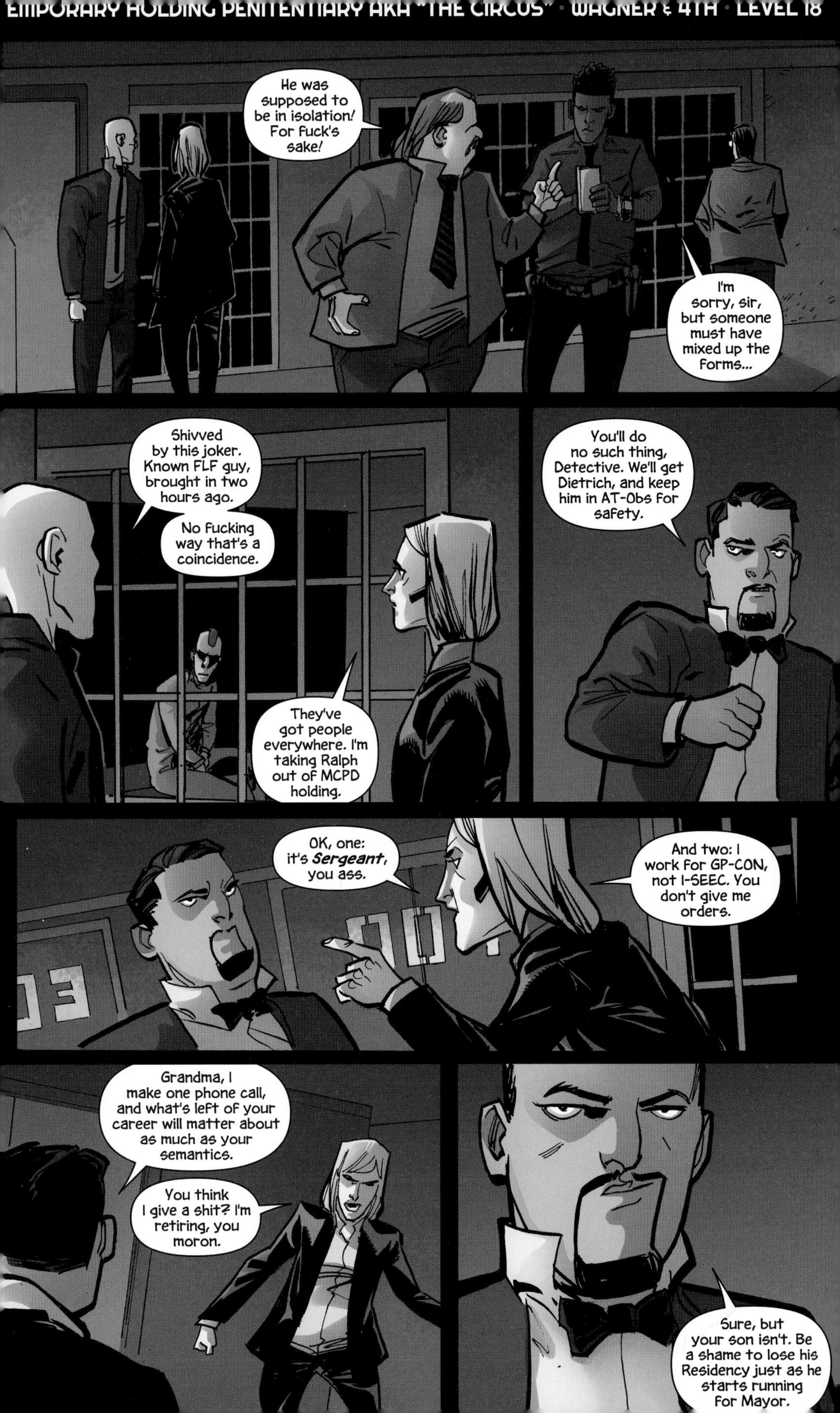
EMPORARY HOLDING PENITENTIARY AKA "THE CIRCUS" • WAGNER & 4TH • LEVEL 18
He was supposed to be in isolation! For fuck's sake!
I'm sorry, sir, but someone must have mixed up the forms...
Shivved by this joker. Known FLF guy, brought in two hours ago.
No fucking way that's a coincidence.
They've got people everywhere. I'm taking Ralph out of MCPD holding.
You'll do no such thing, Detective. We'll get Dietrich, and keep him in AT-Obs for safety.
OK, one: it's *Sergeant*, you ass.
And two: I work for GP-CON, not I-SEEC. You don't give me orders.
Grandma, I make one phone call, and what's left of your career will matter about as much as your semantics.
You think I give a shit? I'm retiring, you moron.
Sure, but your son isn't. Be a shame to lose his Residency just as he starts running for Mayor.

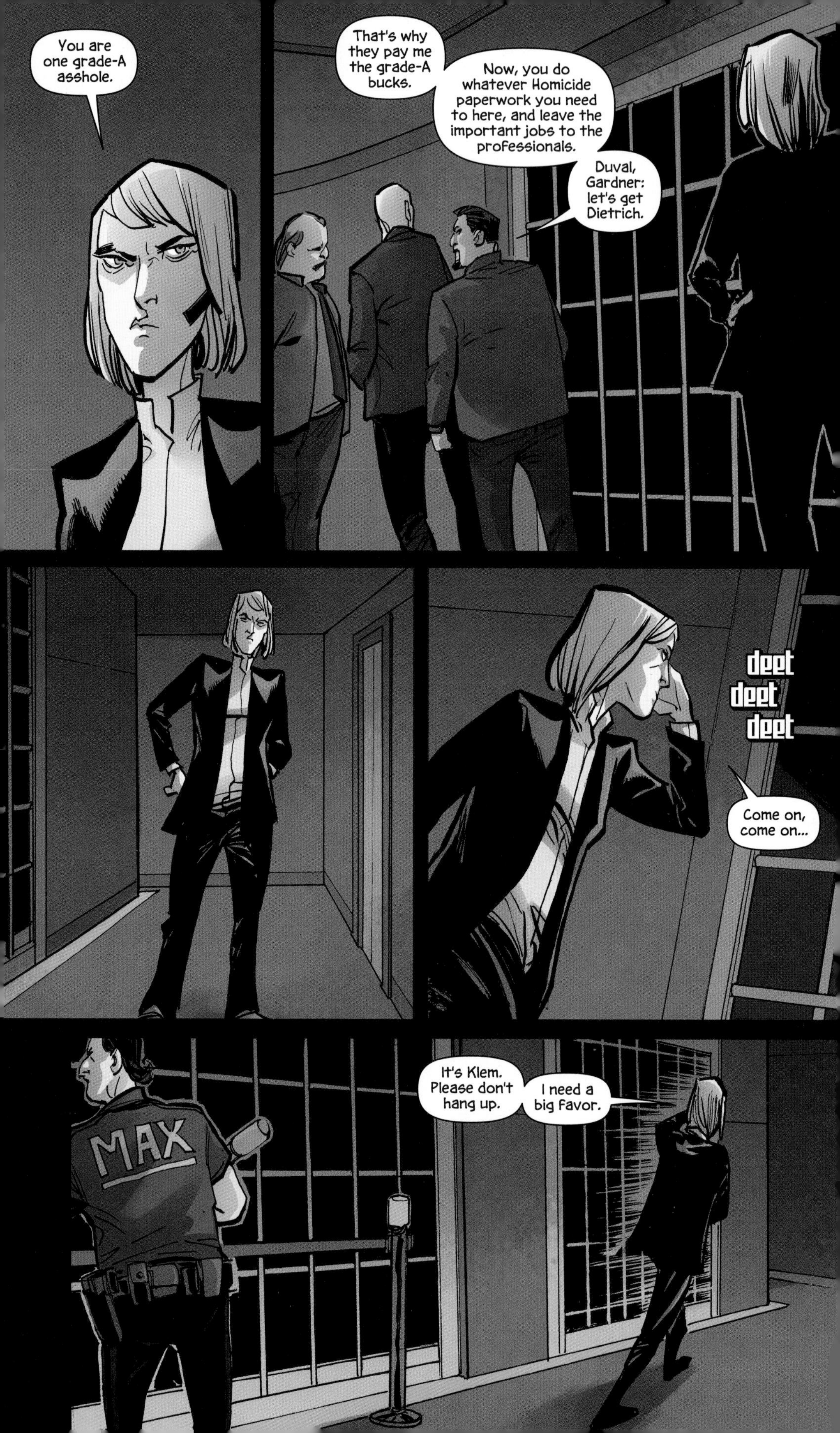
You are one grade-A asshole.
That's why they pay me the grade-A bucks.
Now, you do whatever Homicide paperwork you need to here, and leave the important jobs to the professionals.
Duval, Gardner: let's get Dietrich.
deet deet deet
Come on, come on...
MAX
It's Klem. Please don't hang up.
I need a big favor.

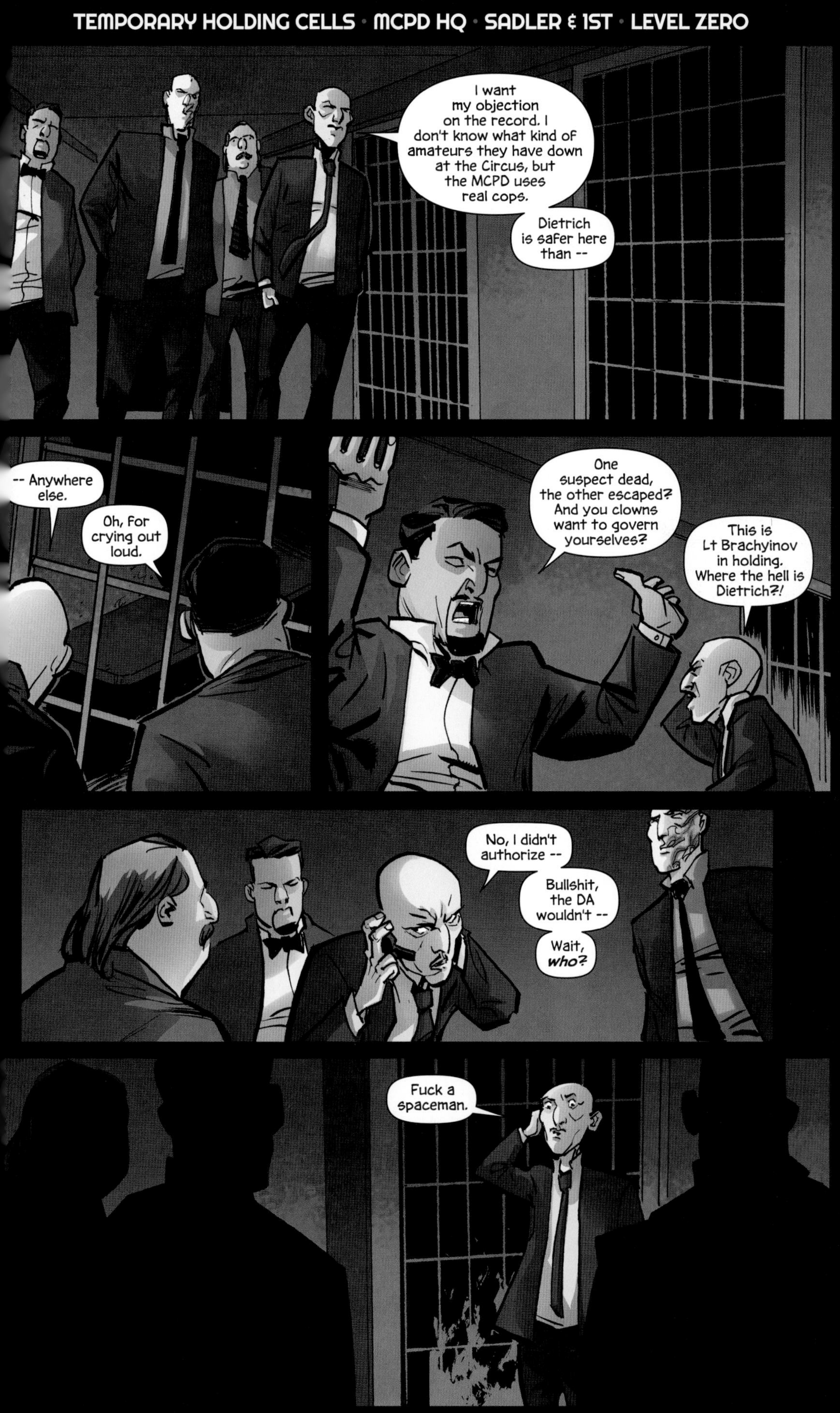
TEMPORARY HOLDING CELLS · MCPD HQ · SADLER & 1ST · LEVEL ZERO
I want my objection on the record. I don't know what kind of amateurs they have down at the Circus, but the MCPD uses real cops.
Dietrich is safer here than --
-- Anywhere else.
Oh, for crying out loud.
One suspect dead, the other escaped? And you clowns want to govern yourselves?
This is Lt Brachyinov in holding. Where the hell is Dietrich?!
No, I didn't authorize --
Bullshit, the DA wouldn't --
Wait, *who?*
Fuck a spaceman.

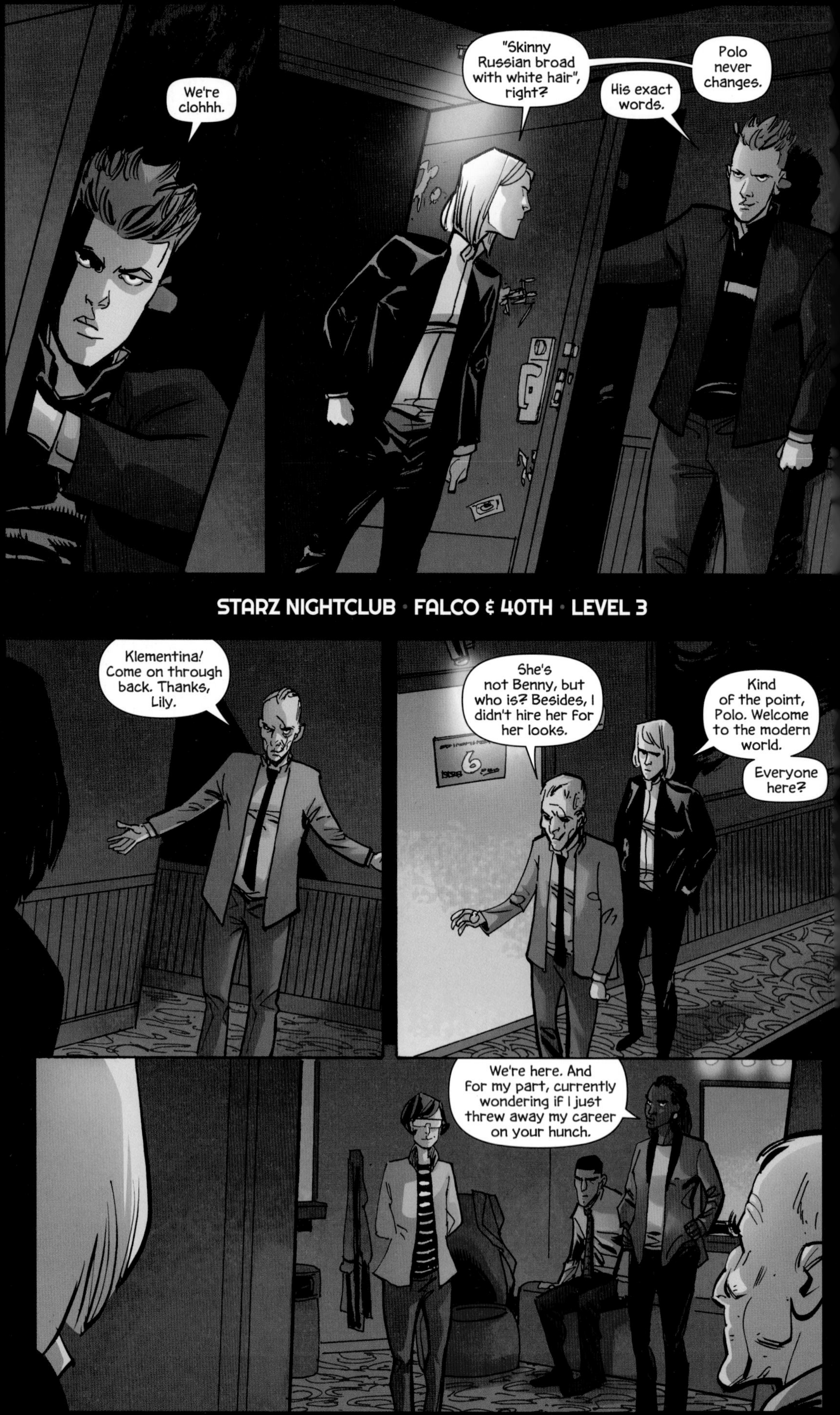

We're clohhh.
"Skinny Russian broad with white hair", right?
His exact words.
Polo never changes.
STARZ NIGHTCLUB · FALCO & 40TH · LEVEL 3
Klementina! Come on through back. Thanks, Lily.
She's not Benny, but who is? Besides, I didn't hire her for her looks.
Kind of the point, Polo. Welcome to the modern world.
Everyone here?
We're here. And for my part, currently wondering if I just threw away my career on your hunch.

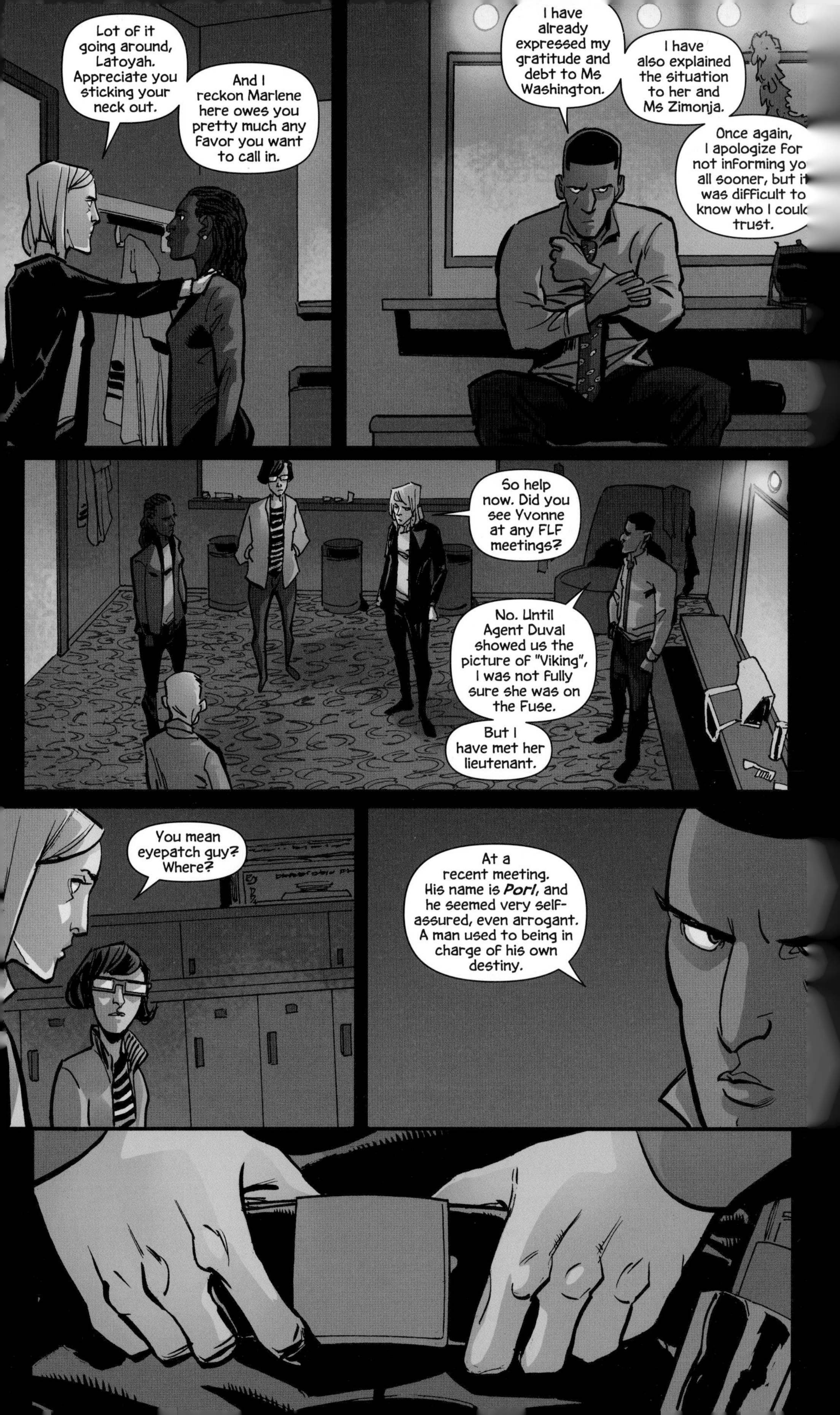
Lot of it going around, Latoyah. Appreciate you sticking your neck out.
And I reckon Marlene here owes you pretty much any favor you want to call in.
I have already expressed my gratitude and debt to Ms Washington.
I have also explained the situation to her and Ms Zimonja.
Once again, I apologize for not informing yo all sooner, but it was difficult to know who I coulc trust.
So help now. Did you see Yvonne at any FLF meetings?
No. Until Agent Duval showed us the picture of "Viking", I was not fully sure she was on the Fuse.
But I have met her lieutenant.
You mean eyepatch guy? Where?
At a recent meeting. His name is *Porl*, and he seemed very self-assured, even arrogant. A man used to being in charge of his own destiny.

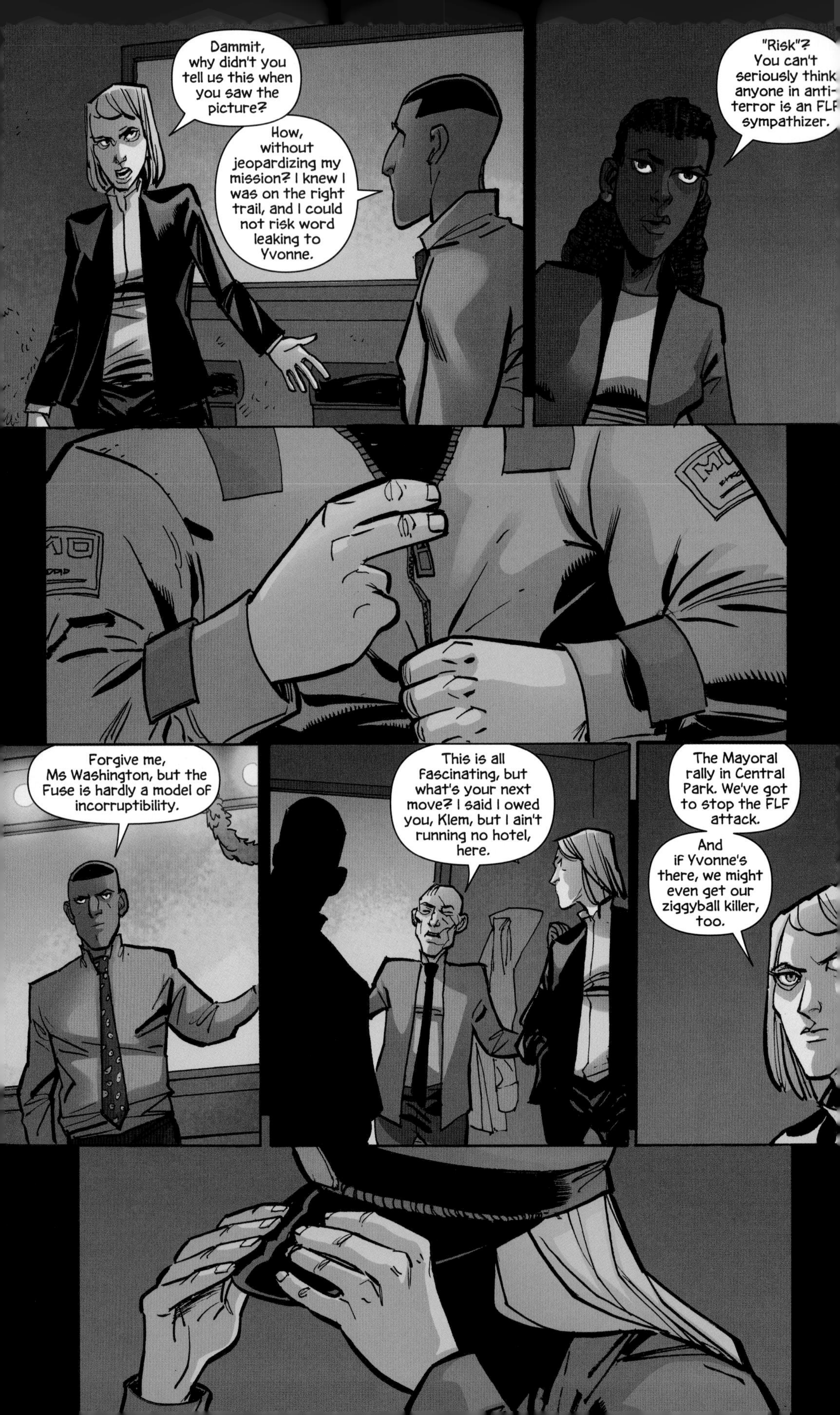
Dammit, why didn't you tell us this when you saw the picture?
How, without jeopardizing my mission? I knew I was on the right trail, and I could not risk word leaking to Yvonne.
"Risk"? You can't seriously think anyone in anti-terror is an FLF sympathizer.
Forgive me, Ms Washington, but the Fuse is hardly a model of incorruptibility.
This is all fascinating, but what's your next move? I said I owed you, Klem, but I ain't running no hotel, here.
The Mayoral rally in Central Park. We've got to stop the FLF attack.
And if Yvonne's there, we might even get our ziggyball killer, too.

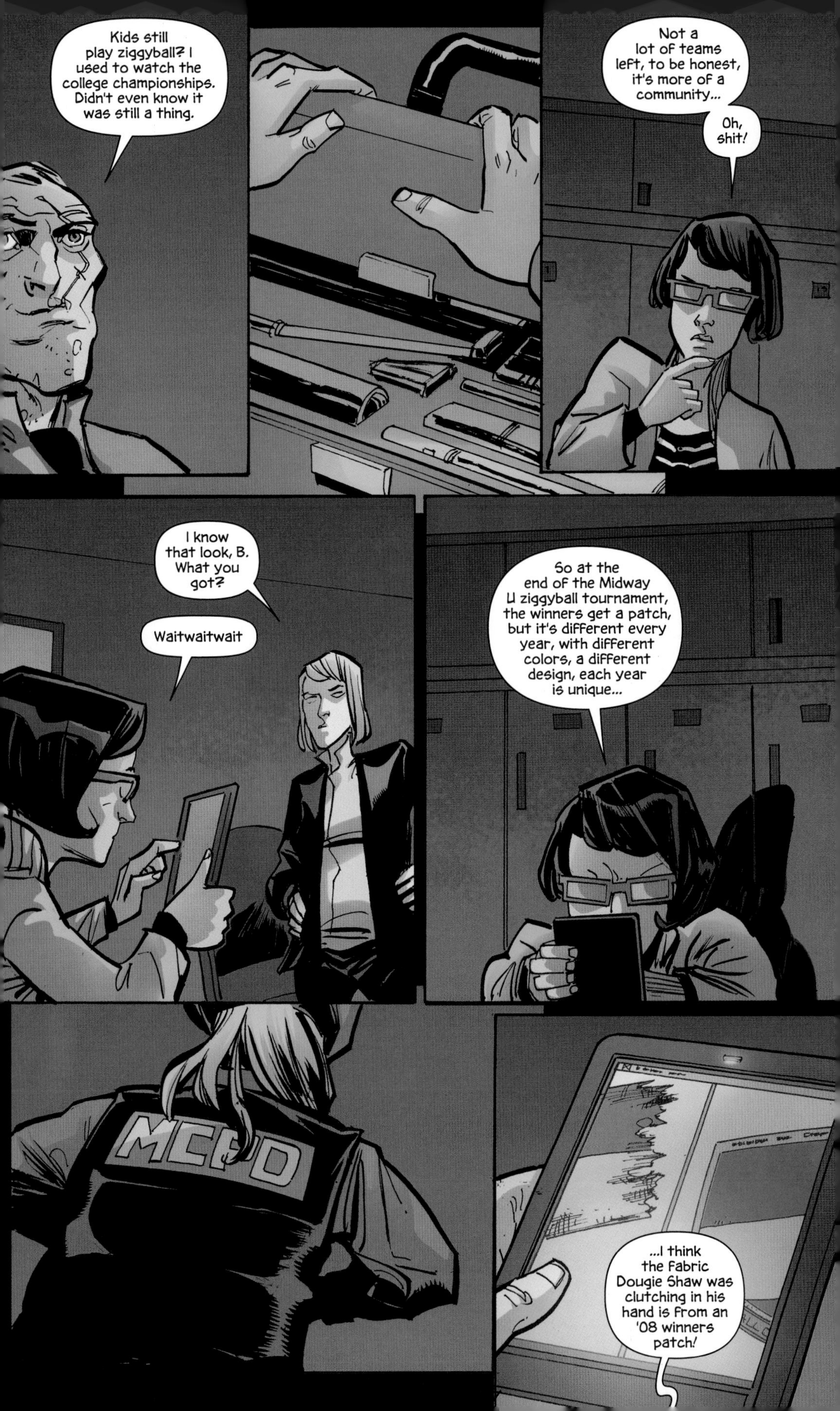
Kids still play ziggyball? I used to watch the college championships. Didn't even know it was still a thing.
Not a lot of teams left, to be honest, it's more of a community...
Oh, shit!
I know that look, B. What you got?
Waitwaitwait
So at the end of the Midway U ziggyball tournament, the winners get a patch, but it's different every year, with different colors, a different design, each year is unique...
MCPD
...I think the fabric Dougie Shaw was clutching in his hand is from an '08 winners patch!

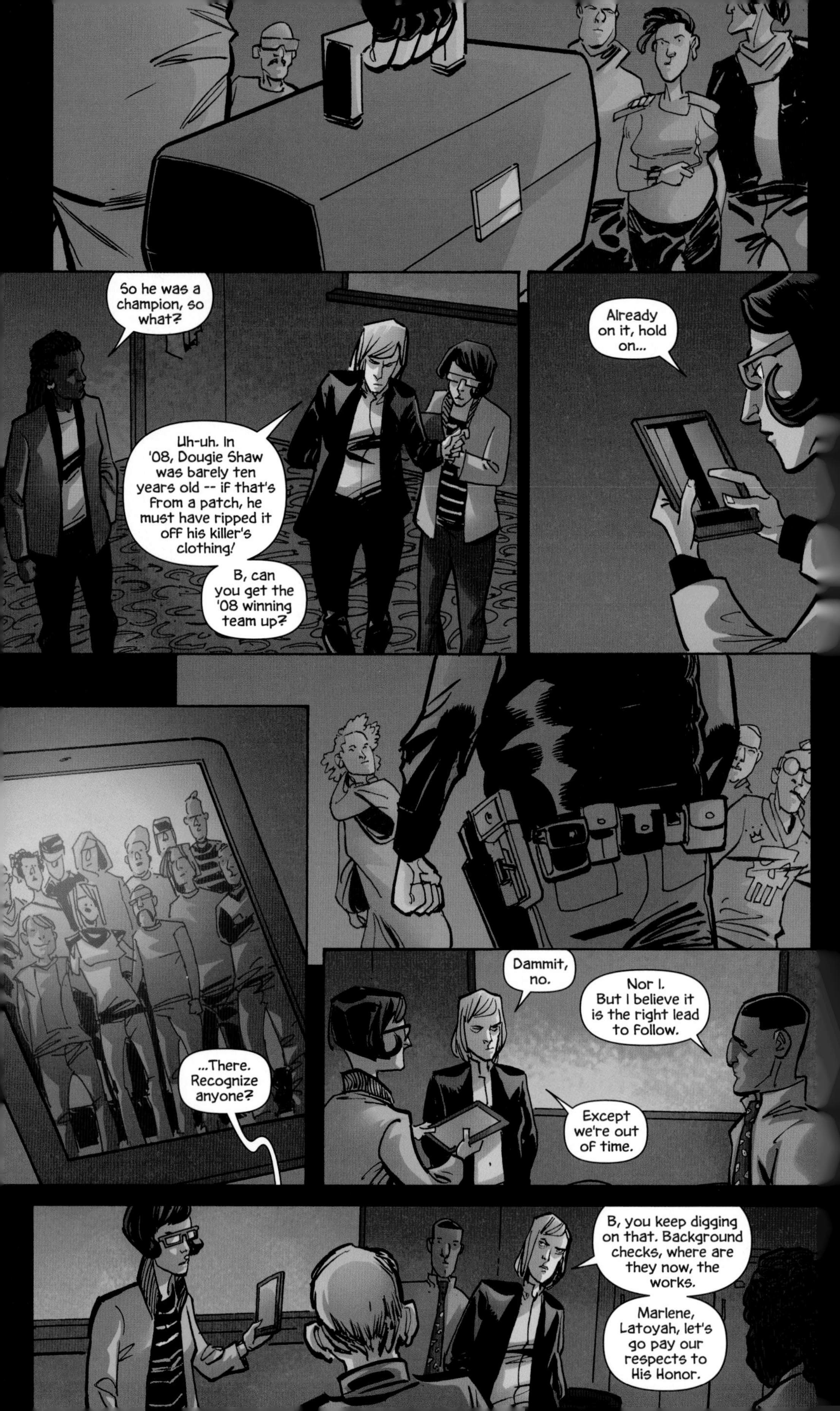
So he was a champion, so what?
Uh-uh. In '08, Dougie Shaw was barely ten years old -- if that's from a patch, he must have ripped it off his killer's clothing!
B, can you get the '08 winning team up?
Already on it, hold on...
...There. Recognize anyone?
Dammit, no.
Nor I. But I believe it is the right lead to follow.
Except we're out of time.
B, you keep digging on that. Background checks, where are they now, the works.
Marlene, Latoyah, let's go pay our respects to His Honor.

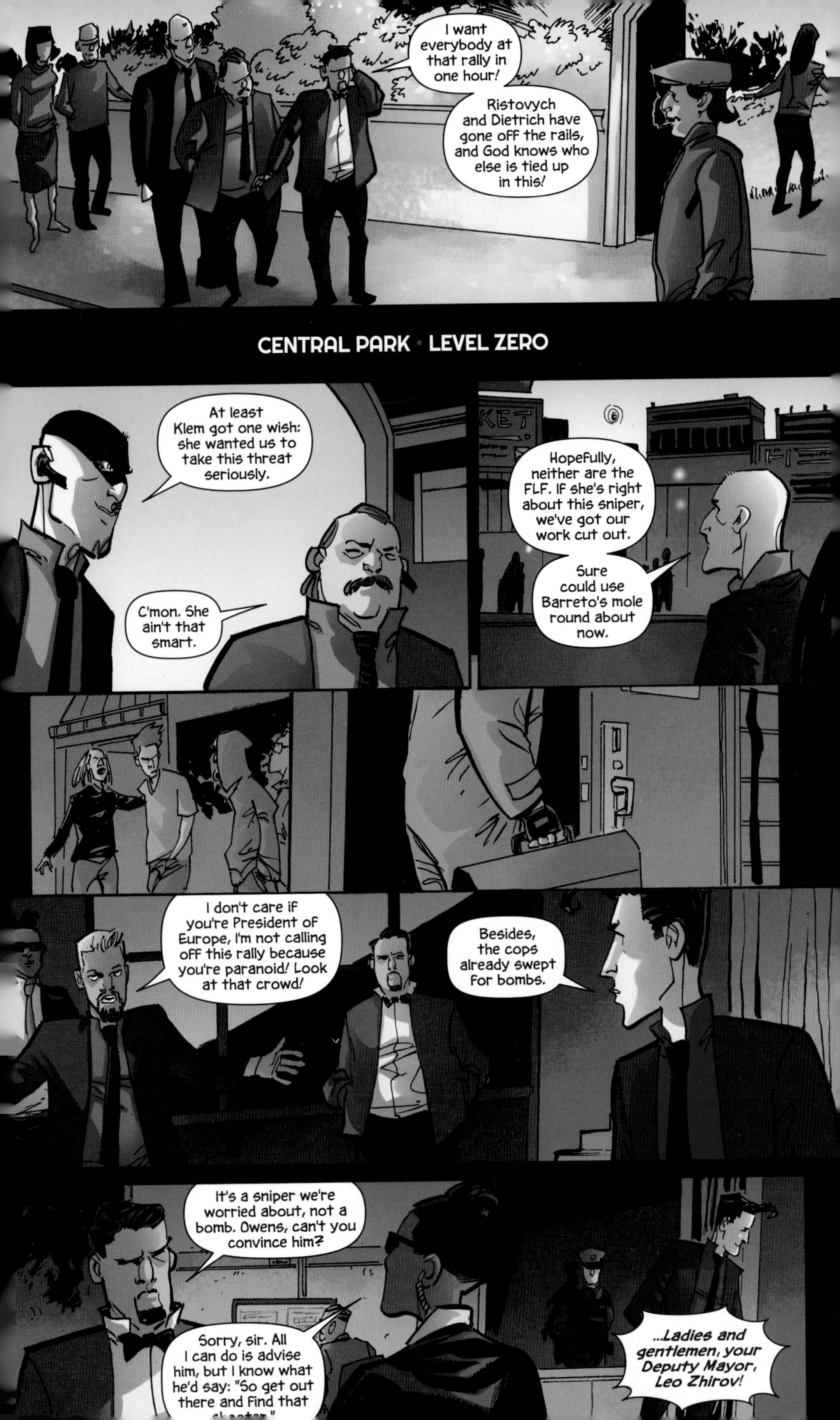

I want everybody at that rally in one hour!
Ristovych and Dietrich have gone off the rails, and God knows who else is tied up in this!
CENTRAL PARK · LEVEL ZERO
At least Klem got one wish: she wanted us to take this threat seriously.
C'mon. She ain't that smart.
Hopefully, neither are the FLF. If she's right about this sniper, we've got our work cut out.
Sure could use Barreto's mole round about now.
I don't care if you're President of Europe, I'm not calling off this rally because you're paranoid! Look at that crowd!
Besides, the cops already swept for bombs.
It's a sniper we're worried about, not a bomb. Owens, can't you convince him?
Sorry, sir. All I can do is advise him, but I know what he'd say: "So get out there and find that
...Ladies and gentlemen, your Deputy Mayor, Leo Zhirov!

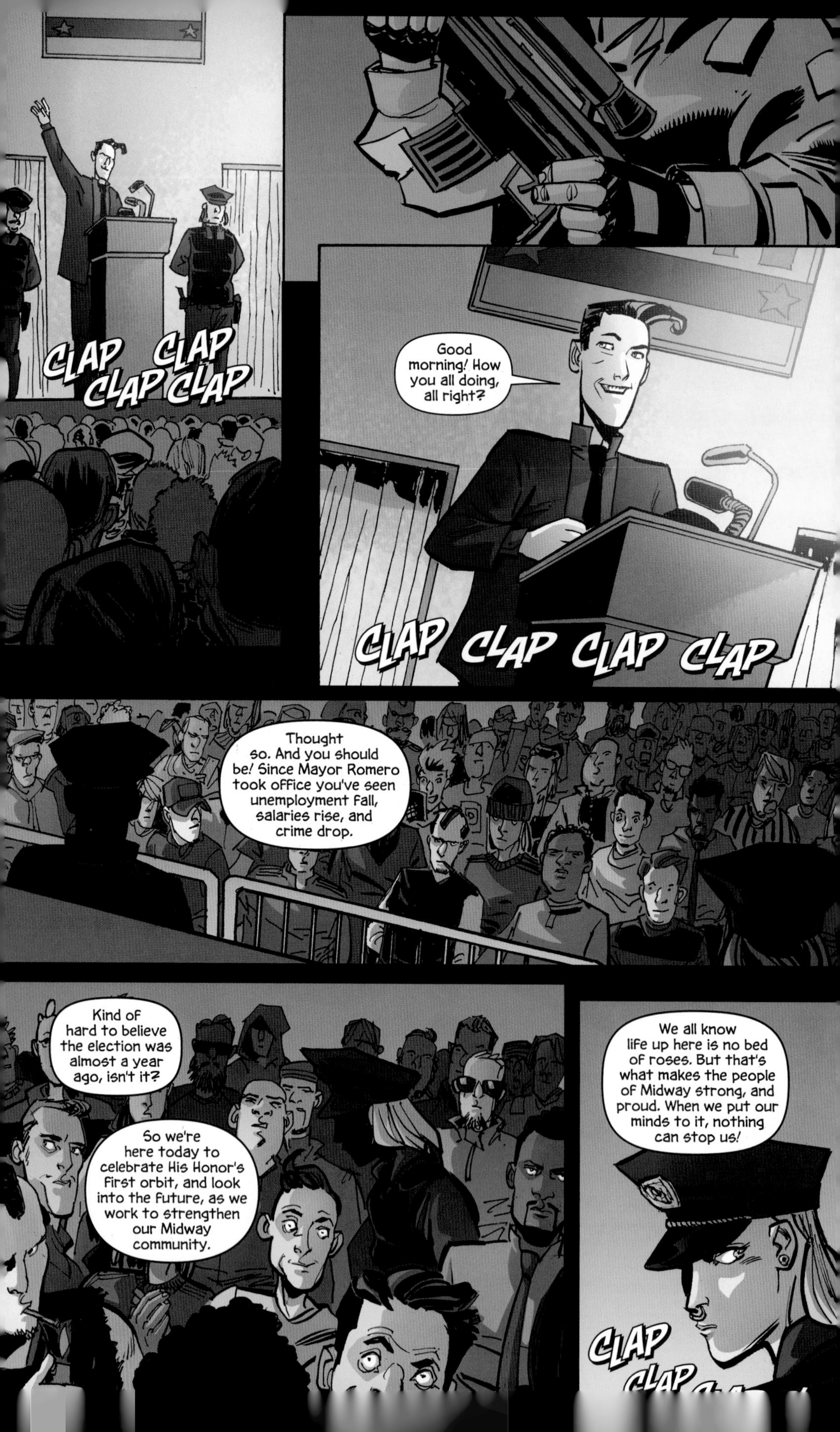
CLAP CLAP
CLAP CLAP
Good morning! How you all doing, all right?
CLAP CLAP CLAP CLAP
Thought so. And you should be! Since Mayor Romero took office you've seen unemployment fall, salaries rise, and crime drop.
Kind of hard to believe the election was almost a year ago, isn't it?
So we're here today to celebrate His Honor's first orbit, and look into the future, as we work to strengthen our Midway community.
We all know life up here is no bed of roses. But that's what makes the people of Midway strong, and proud. When we put our minds to it, nothing can stop us!
CLAP
CLAP

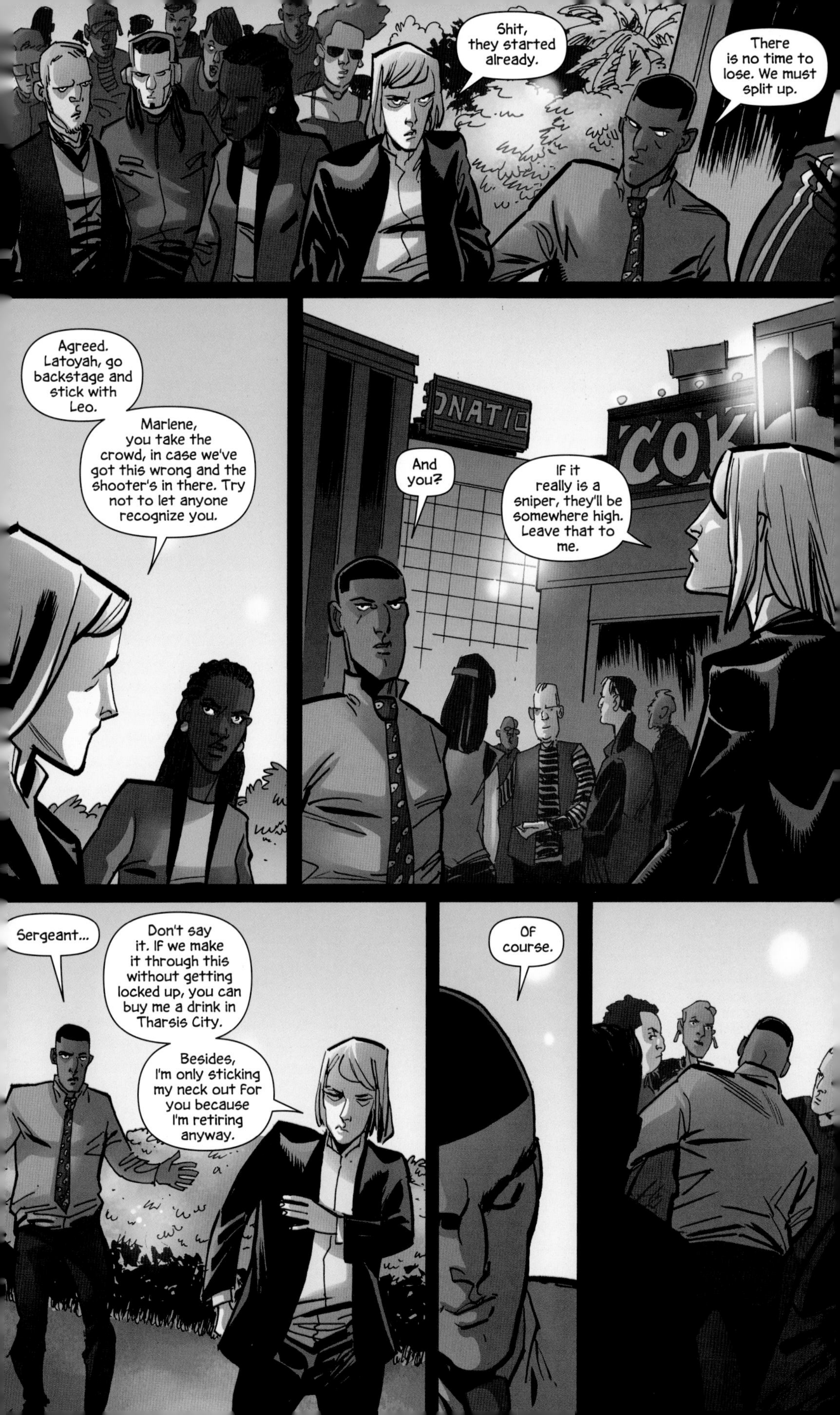
Shit, they started already.
There is no time to lose. We must split up.
Agreed. Latoyah, go backstage and stick with Leo.
Marlene, you take the crowd, in case we've got this wrong and the shooter's in there. Try not to let anyone recognize you.
And you?
If it really is a sniper, they'll be somewhere high. Leave that to me.
Sergeant...
Don't say it. If we make it through this without getting locked up, you can buy me a drink in Tharsis City.
Besides, I'm only sticking my neck out for you because I'm retiring anyway.
Of course.

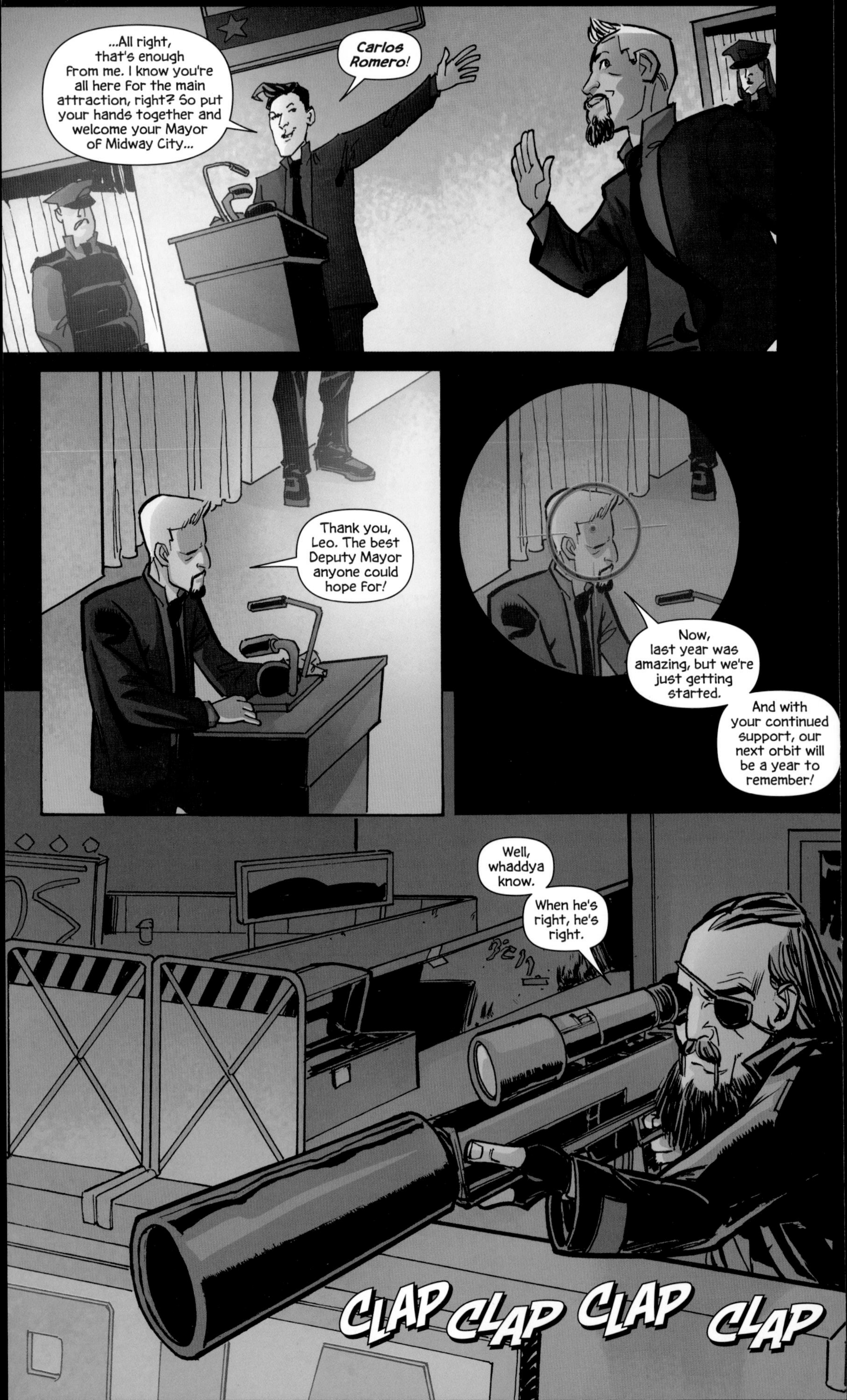
...All right, that's enough from me. I know you're all here for the main attraction, right? So put your hands together and welcome your Mayor of Midway City...
Carlos Romero!
Thank you, Leo. The best Deputy Mayor anyone could hope for!
Now, last year was amazing, but we're just getting started.
And with your continued support, our next orbit will be a year to remember!
Well, whaddya know.
When he's right, he's right.
CLAP CLAP CLAP CLAP

CONCLUSION

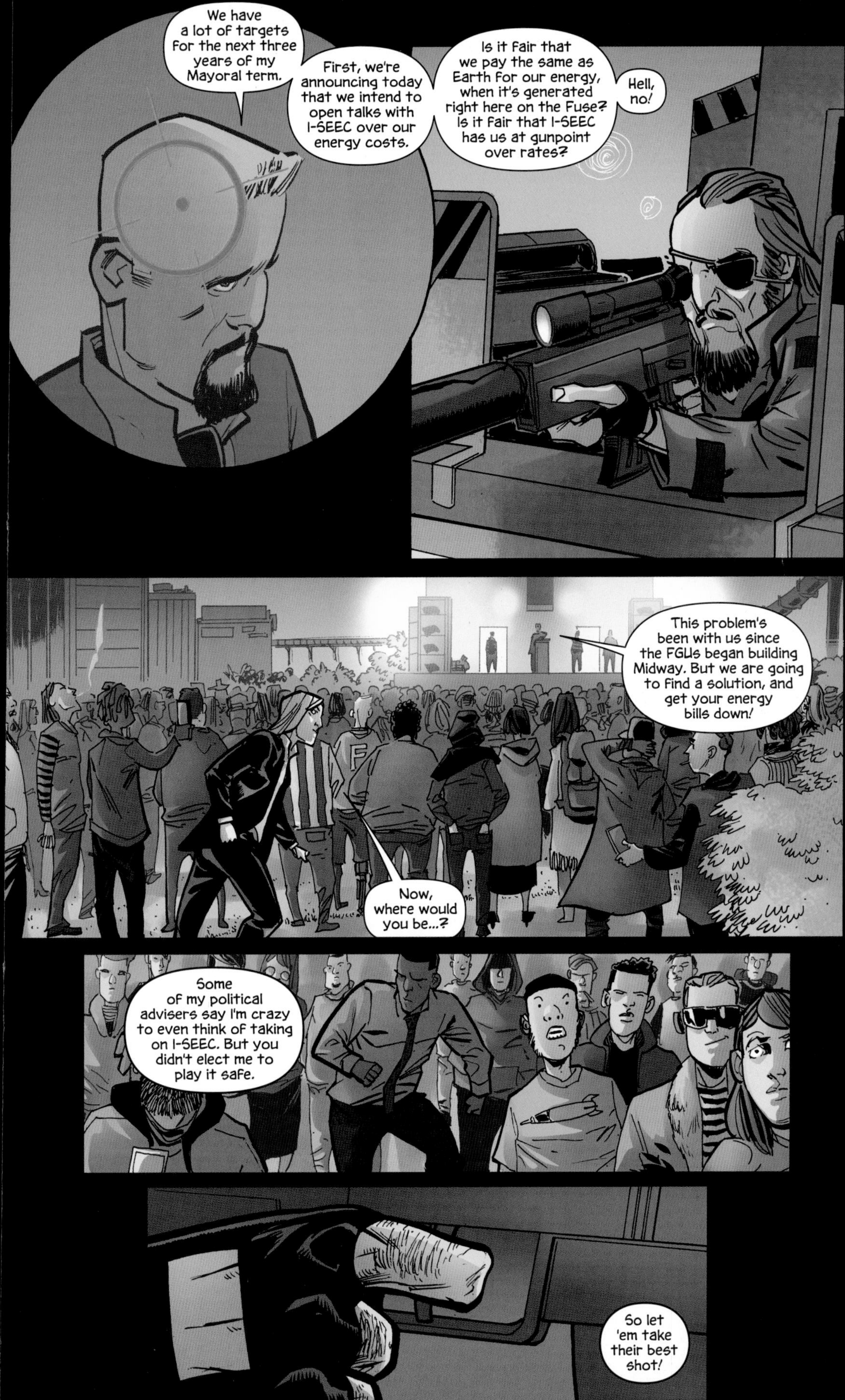
We have a lot of targets for the next three years of my Mayoral term.
First, we're announcing today that we intend to open talks with I-SEEC over our energy costs.
Is it fair that we pay the same as Earth for our energy, when it's generated right here on the Fuse? Is it fair that I-SEEC has us at gunpoint over rates?
Hell, no!
This problem's been with us since the FGUs began building Midway. But we are going to find a solution, and get your energy bills down!
Now, where would you be...?
Some of my political advisers say I'm crazy to even think of taking on I-SEEC. But you didn't elect me to play it safe.
So let 'em take their best shot!

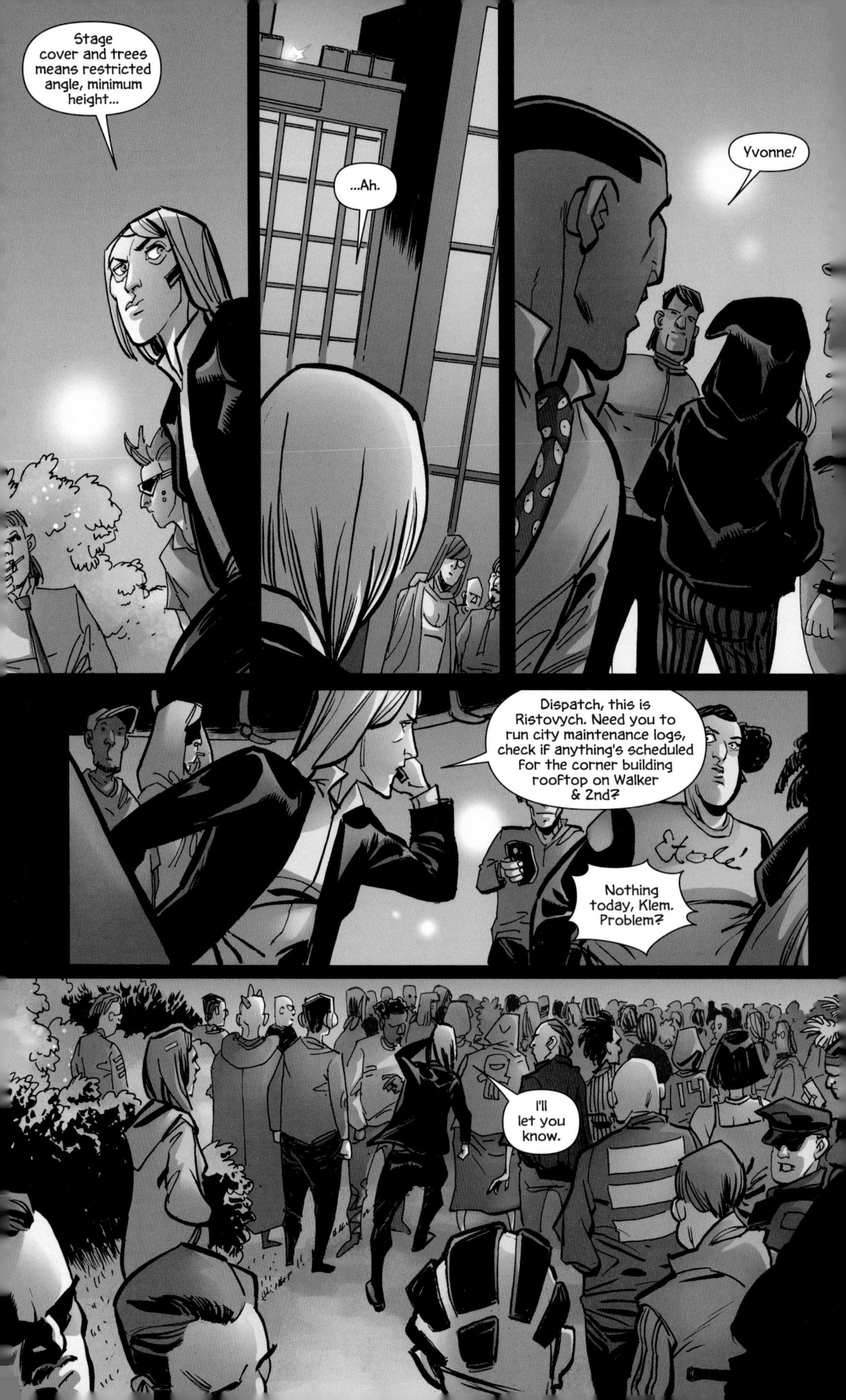
Stage cover and trees means restricted angle, minimum height...
...Ah.
Yvonne!
Dispatch, this is Ristovych. Need you to run city maintenance logs, check if anything's scheduled for the corner building rooftop on Walker & 2nd?
Nothing today, Klem. Problem?
I'll let you know.

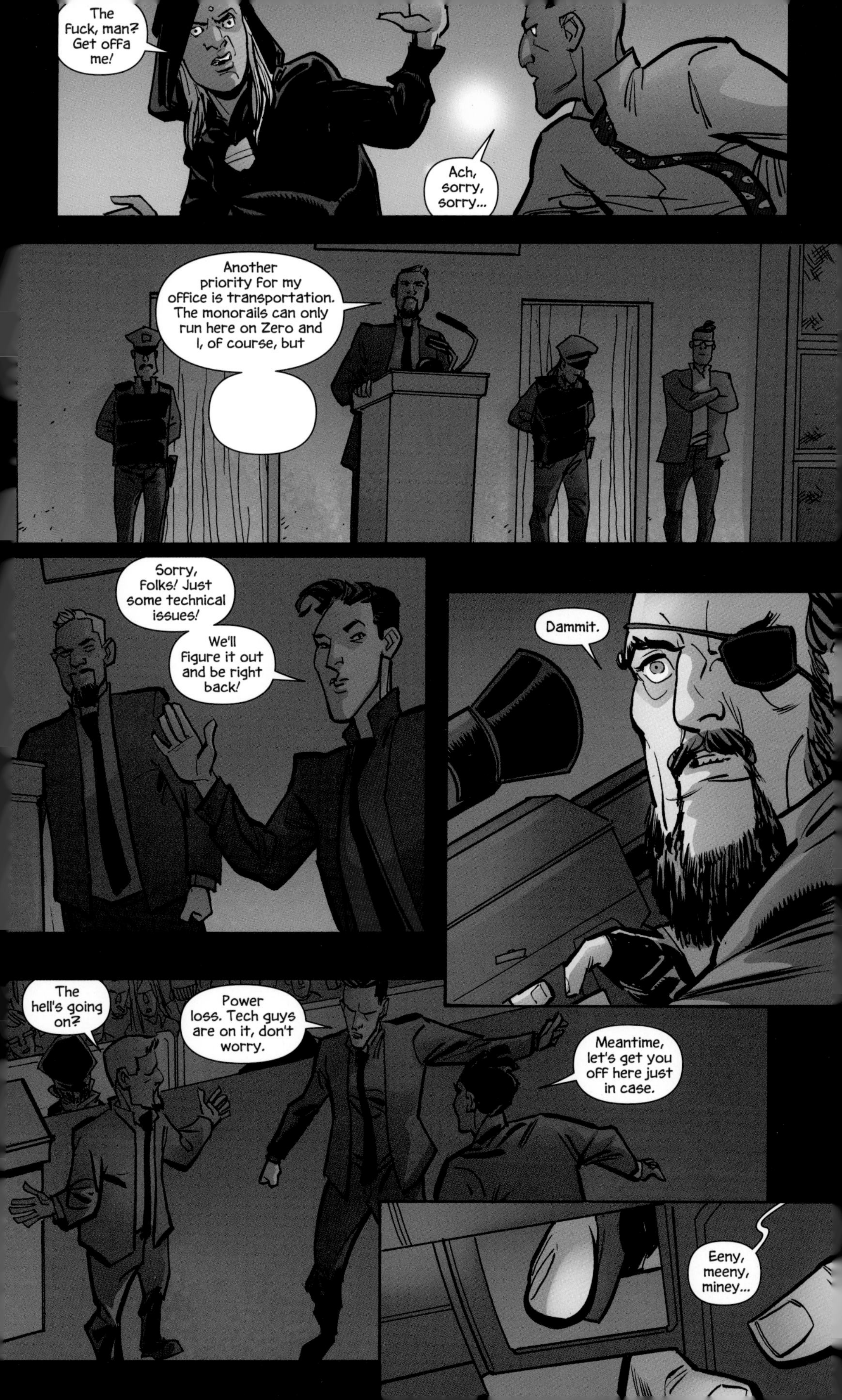
The fuck, man? Get offa me!
Ach, sorry, sorry...
Another priority for my office is transportation. The monorails can only run here on Zero and I, of course, but
Sorry, folks! Just some technical issues!
We'll figure it out and be right back!
Dammit.
The hell's going on?
Power loss. Tech guys are on it, don't worry.
Meantime, let's get you off here just in case.
Eeny, meeny, miney...

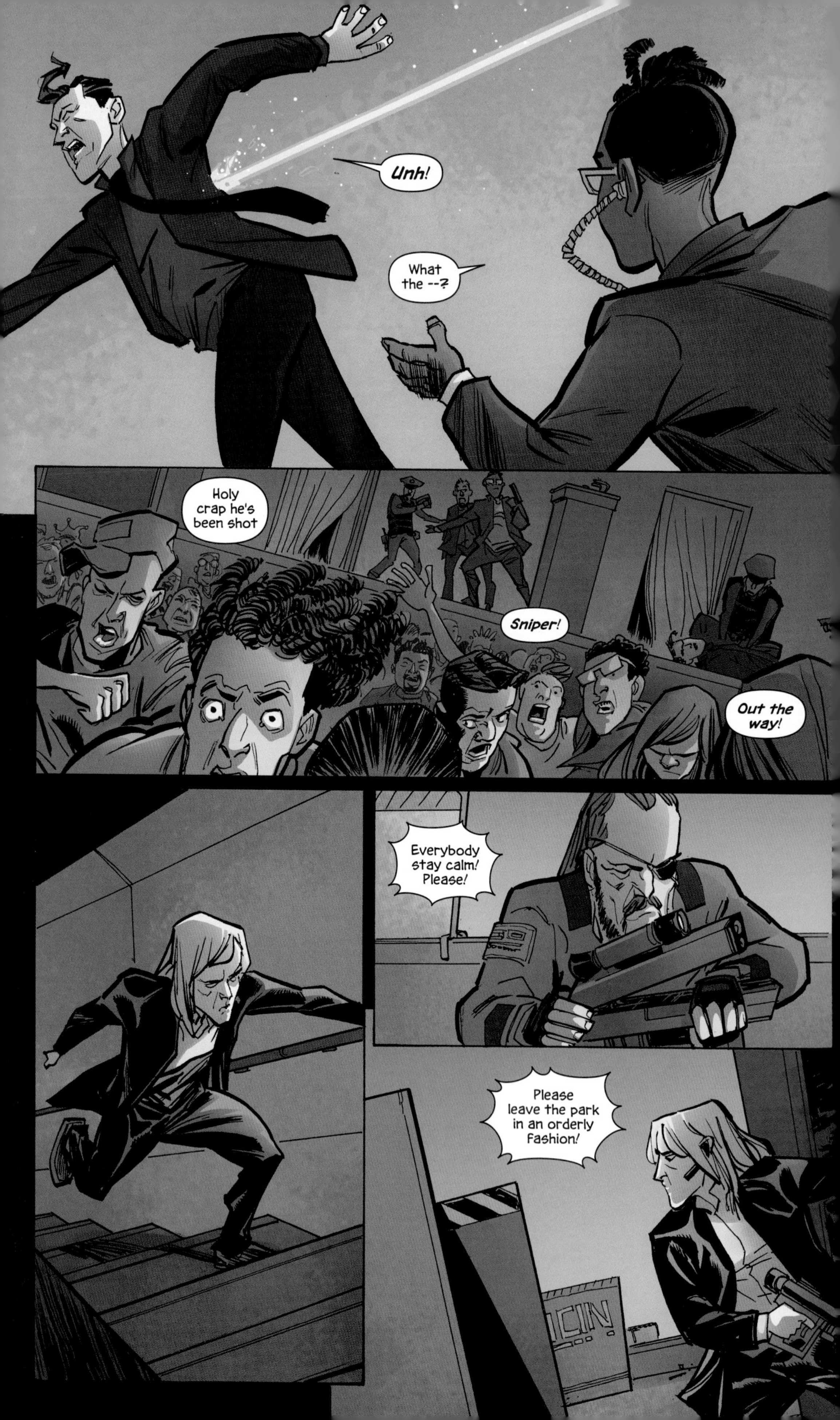
Unh!
What the --?
Holy crap he's been shot
Sniper!
Out the way!
Everybody stay calm! Please!
Please leave the park in an orderly fashion!

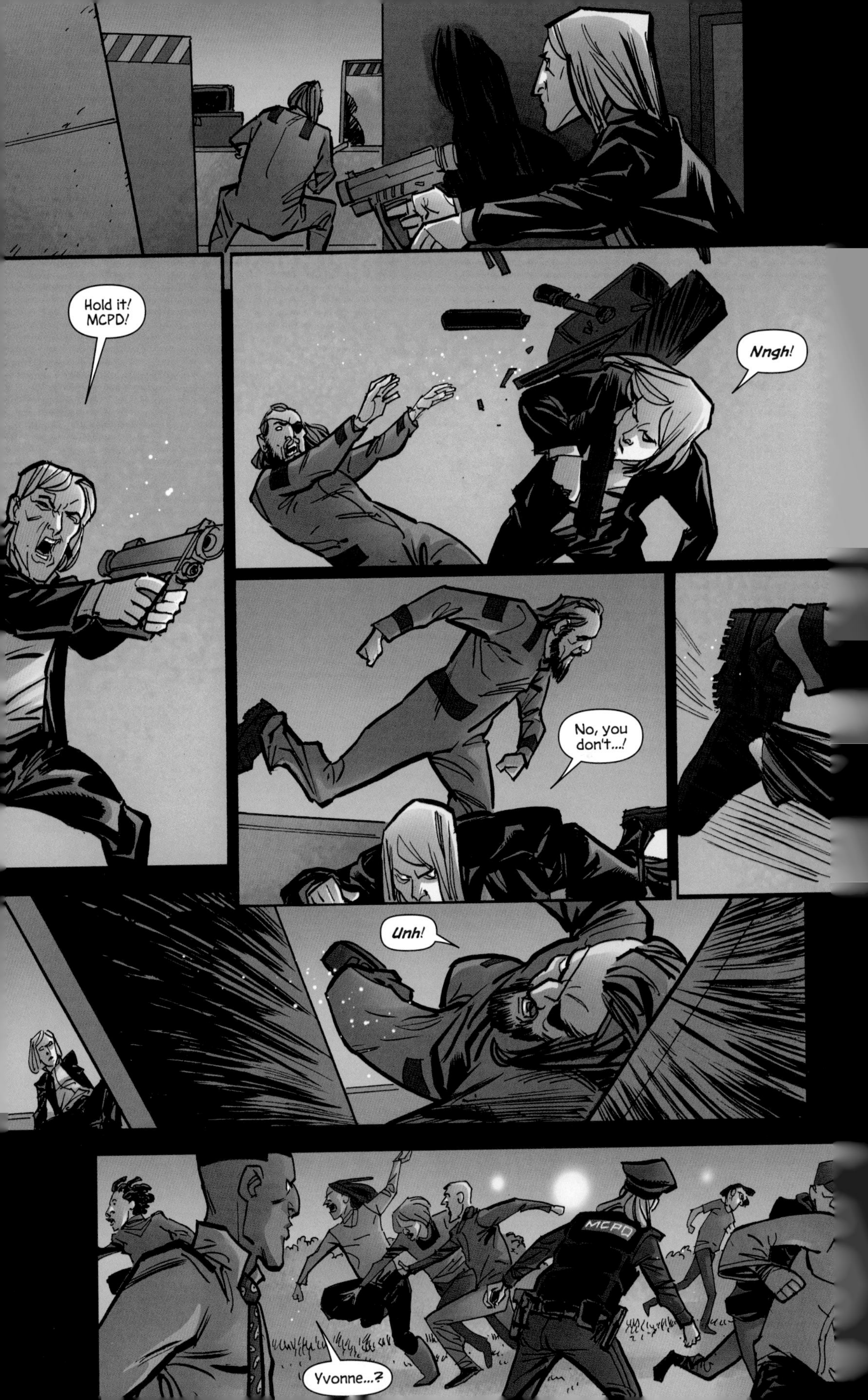
Hold it! MCPD!
Nngh!
No, you don't...!
Unh!
MCPD
Yvonne...?

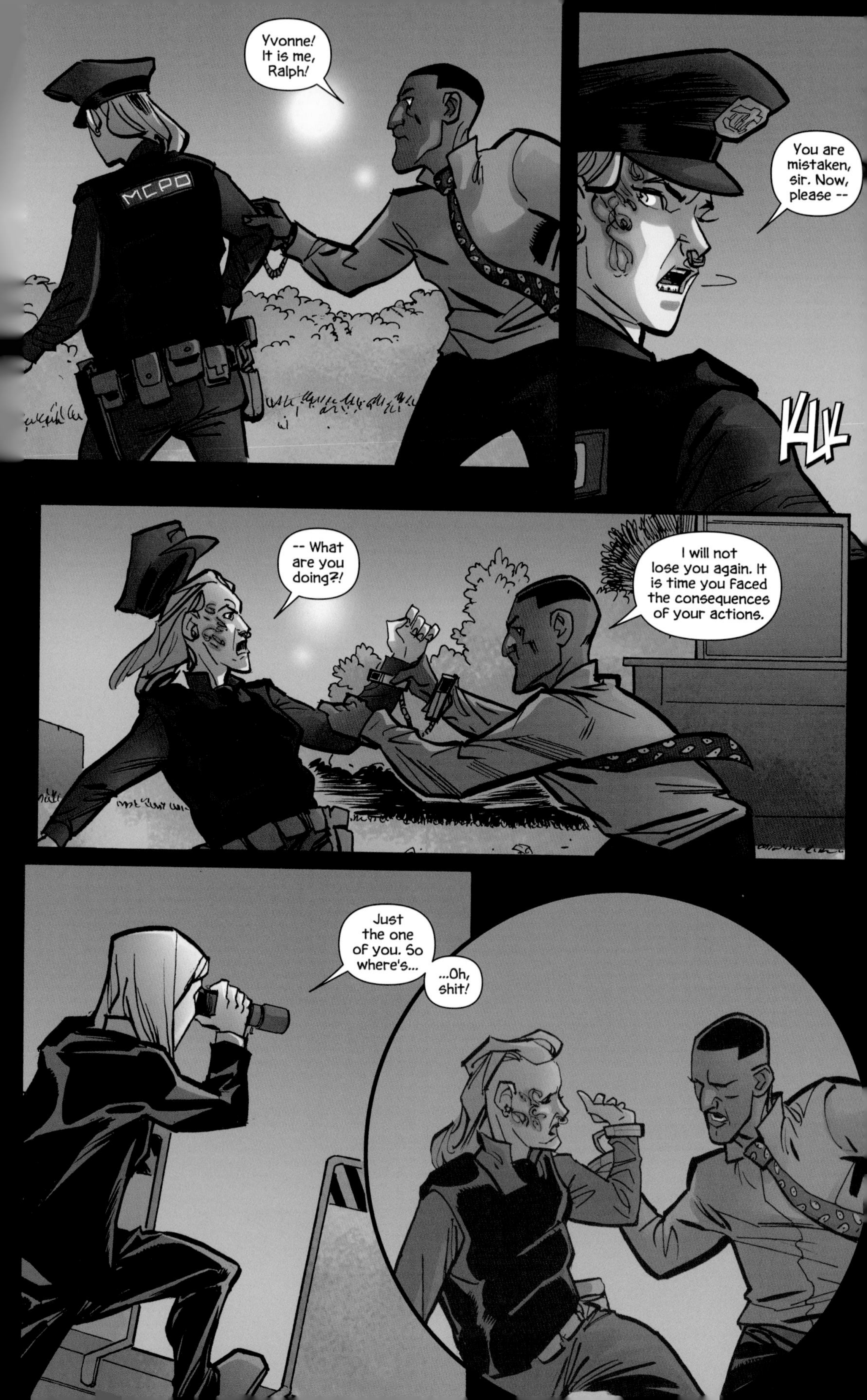
Yvonne! It is me, Ralph!
You are mistaken, sir. Now, please --
KLIK
-- What are you doing?!
I will not lose you again. It is time you faced the consequences of your actions.
Just the one of you. So where's...
...Oh, shit!

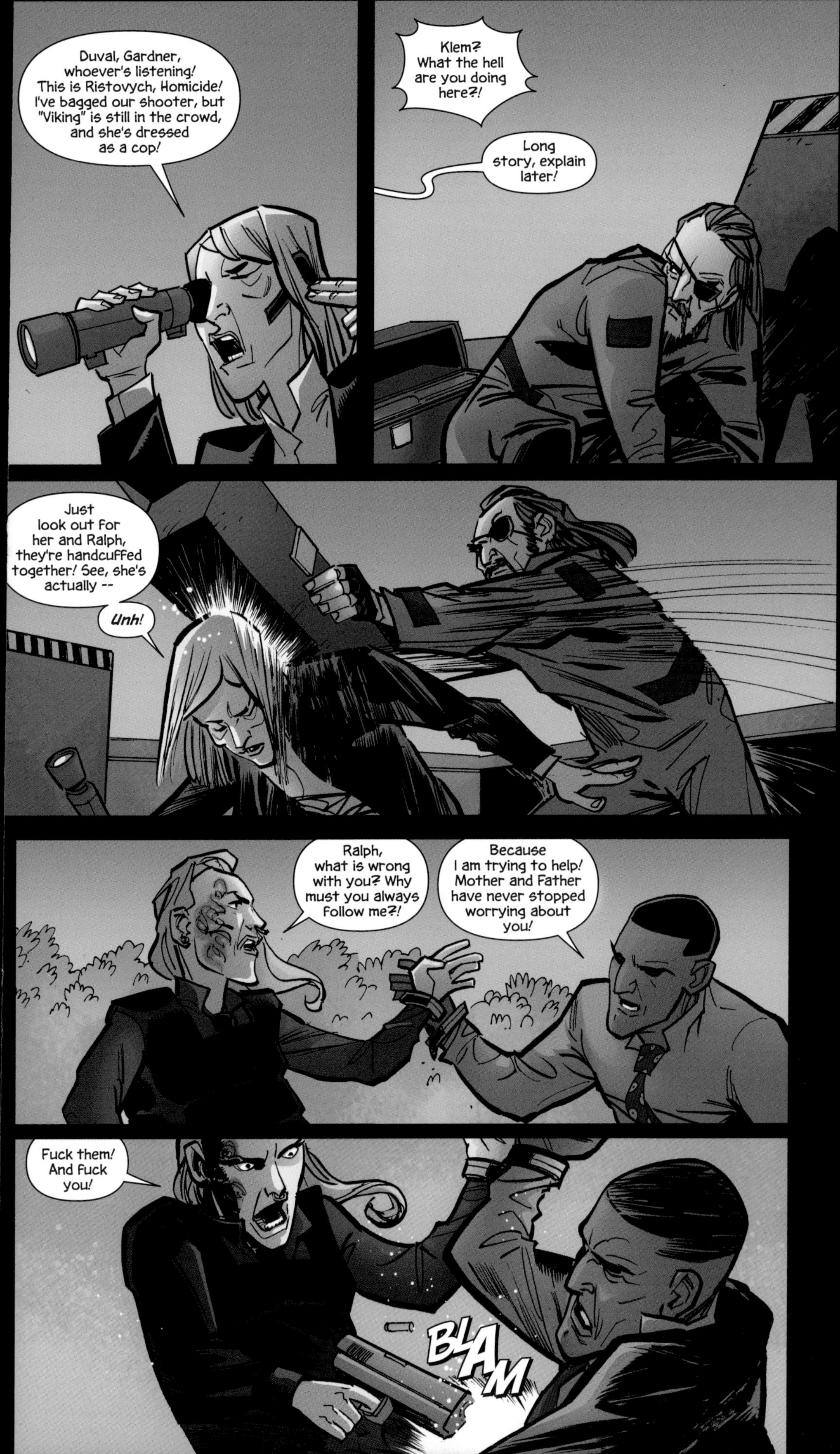
Duval, Gardner, whoever's listening! This is Ristovych, Homicide! I've bagged our shooter, but "Viking" is still in the crowd, and she's dressed as a cop!
Klem?! What the hell are you doing here?!
Long story, explain later!
Just look out for her and Ralph, they're handcuffed together! See, she's actually --
Unh!
Ralph, what is wrong with you? Why must you always follow me?!
Because I am trying to help! Mother and Father have never stopped worrying about you!
Fuck them! And fuck you!
BLAM

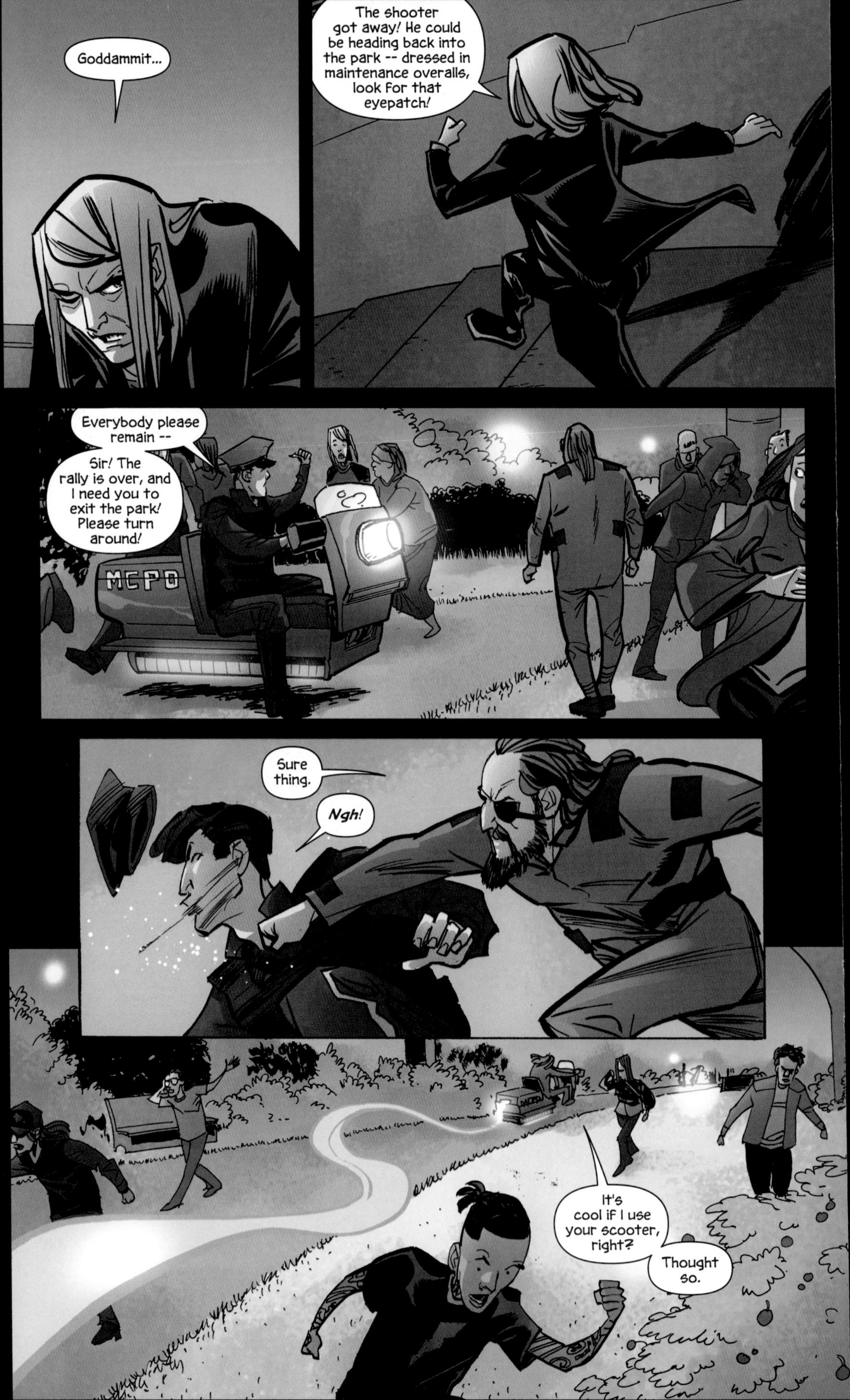
Goddammit...
The shooter got away! He could be heading back into the park -- dressed in maintenance overalls, look for that eyepatch!
Everybody please remain --
Sir! The rally is over, and I need you to exit the park! Please turn around!
MCPD
Sure thing.
Ngh!
It's cool if I use your scooter, right?
Thought so.

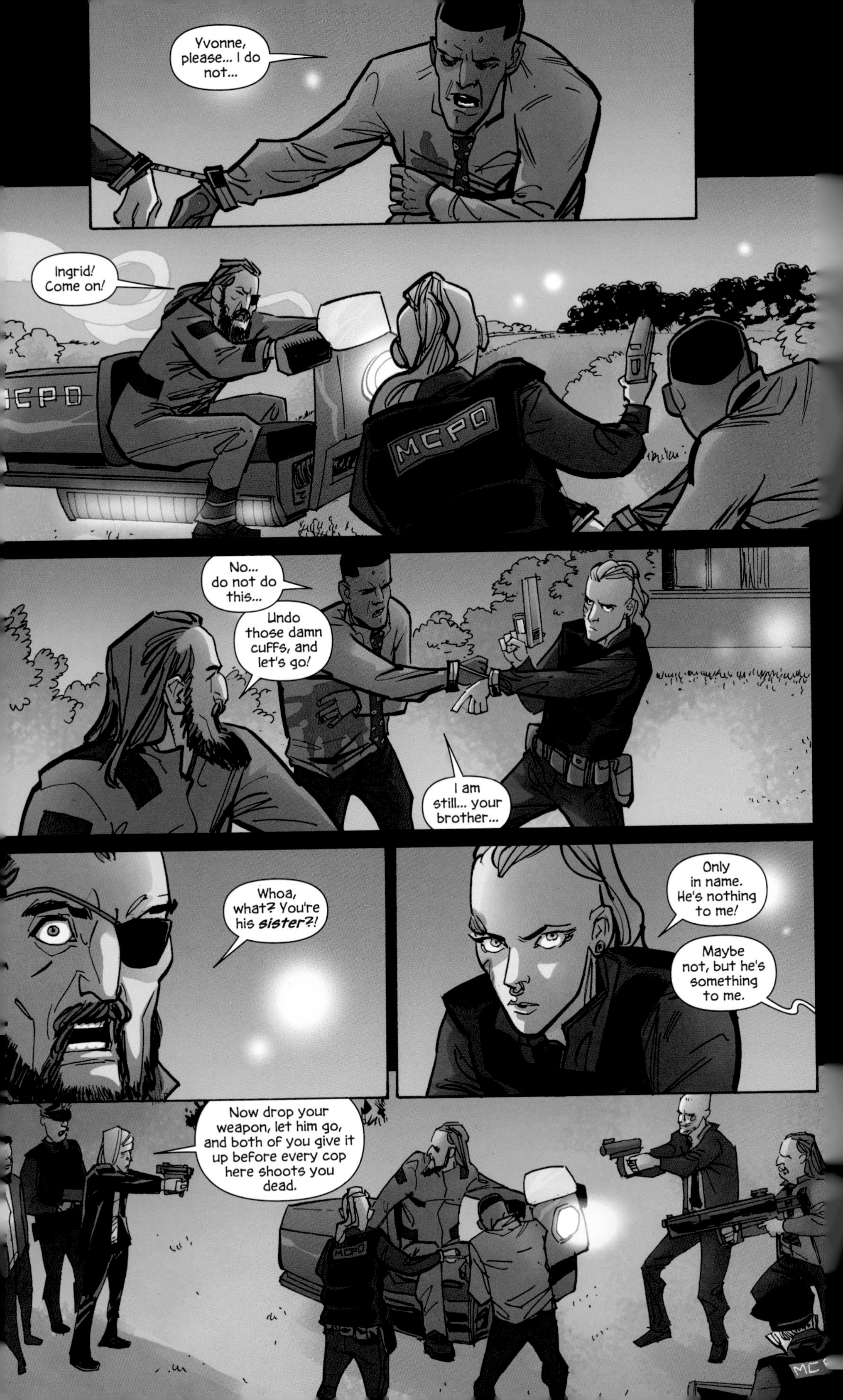
Yvonne, please... I do not...
Ingrid! Come on!
No... do not do this...
Undo those damn cuffs, and let's go!
I am still... your brother...
Whoa, what? You're his *sister*?!
Only in name. He's nothing to me!
Maybe not, but he's something to me.
Now drop your weapon, let him go, and both of you give it up before every cop here shoots you dead.

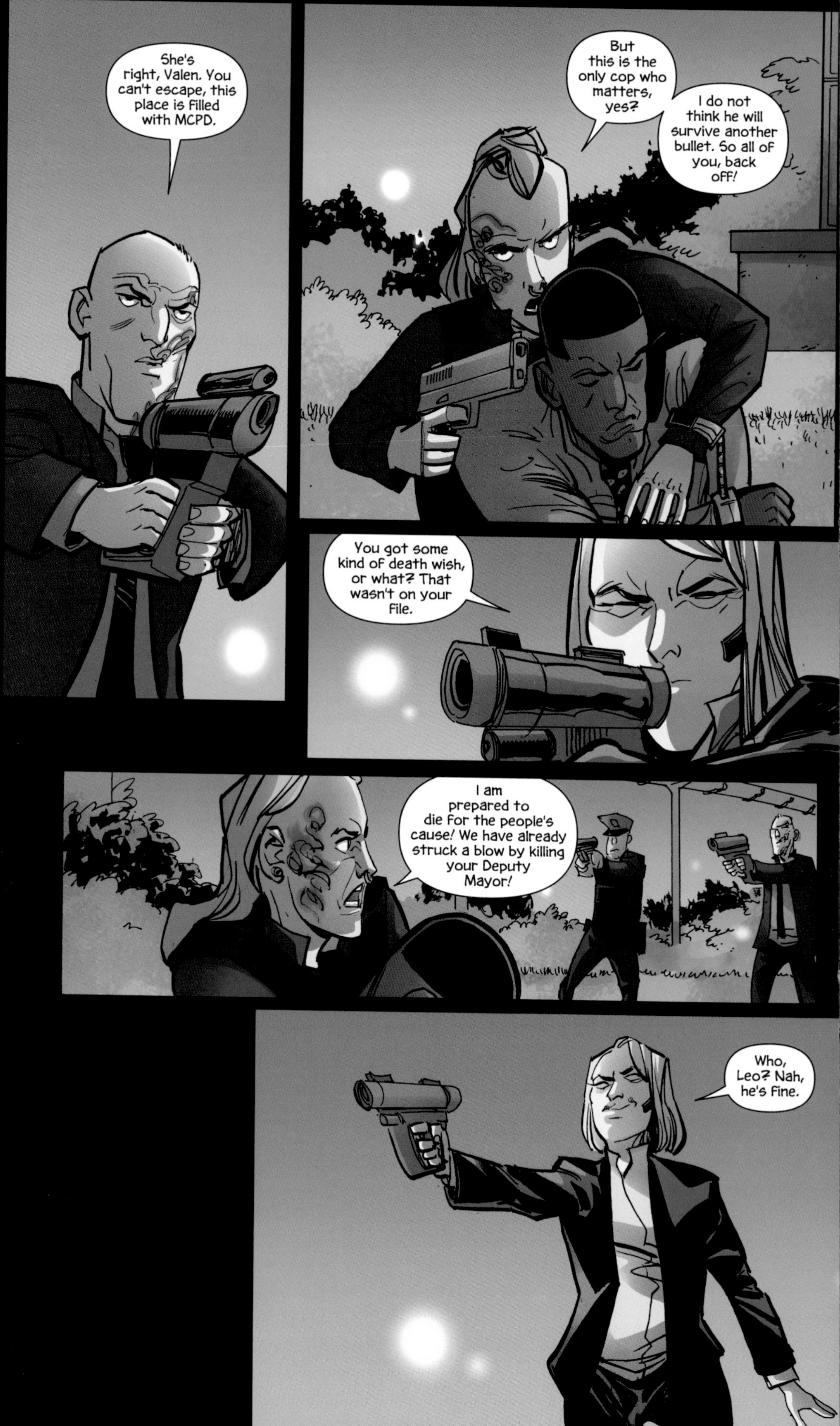
She's right, Valen. You can't escape, this place is filled with MCPD.
But this is the only cop who matters, yes?
I do not think he will survive another bullet. So all of you, back off!
You got some kind of death wish, or what? That wasn't on your file.
I am prepared to die for the people's cause! We have already struck a blow by killing your Deputy Mayor!
Who, Leo? Nah, he's fine.

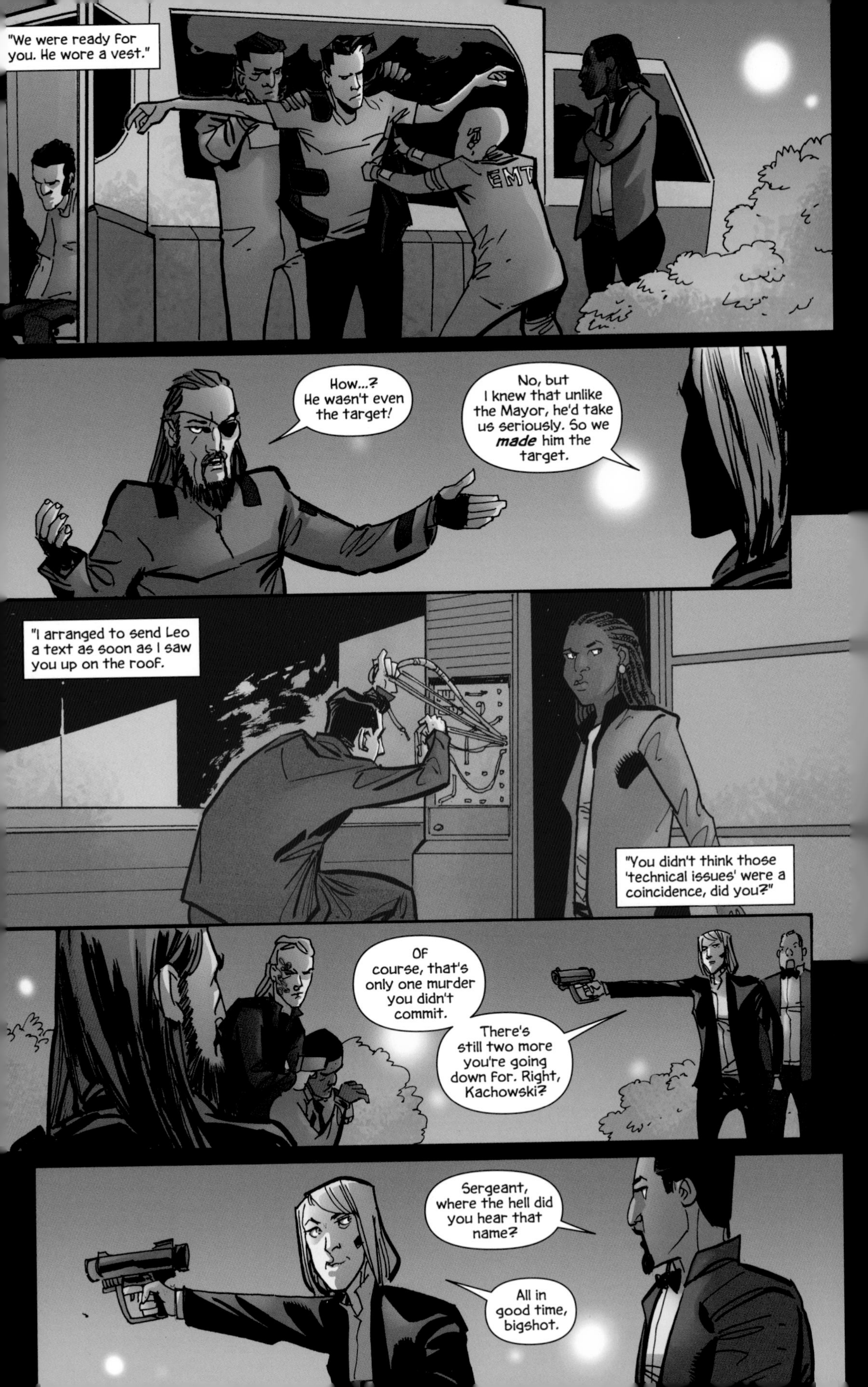
"We were ready for you. He wore a vest."
EMT
How...? He wasn't even the target!
No, but I knew that unlike the Mayor, he'd take us seriously. So we *made* him the target.
"I arranged to send Leo a text as soon as I saw you up on the roof.
"You didn't think those 'technical issues' were a coincidence, did you?"
Of course, that's only one murder you didn't commit.
There's still two more you're going down for. Right, Kachowski?
Sergeant, where the hell did you hear that name?
All in good time, bigshot.

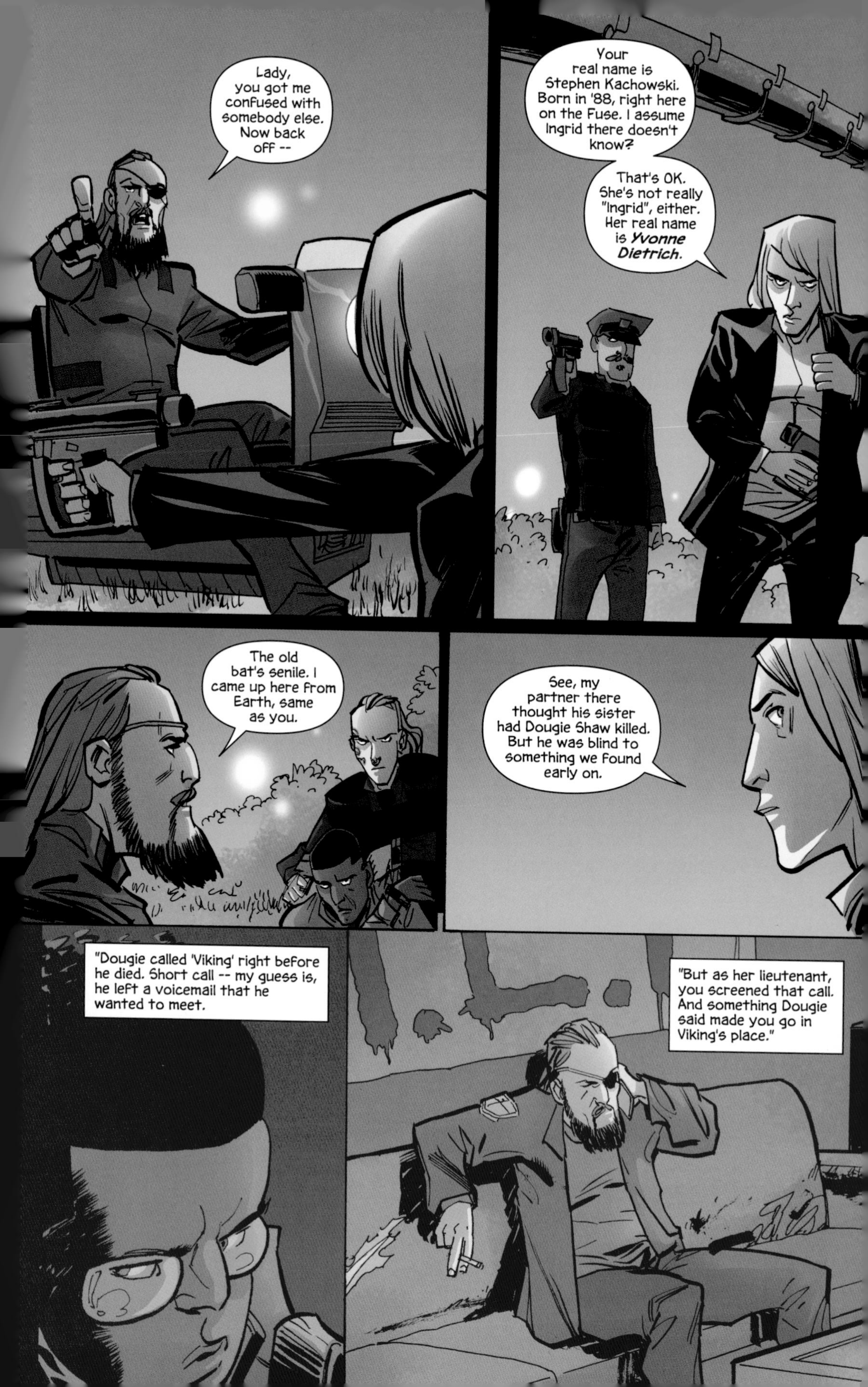
Lady, you got me confused with somebody else. Now back off --
Your real name is Stephen Kachowski. Born in '88, right here on the Fuse. I assume Ingrid there doesn't know?
That's OK. She's not really "Ingrid", either. Her real name is *Yvonne Dietrich*.
The old bat's senile. I came up here from Earth, same as you.
See, my partner there thought his sister had Dougie Shaw killed. But he was blind to something we found early on.
"Dougie called 'Viking' right before he died. Short call -- my guess is, he left a voicemail that he wanted to meet.
"But as her lieutenant, you screened that call. And something Dougie said made you go in Viking's place."

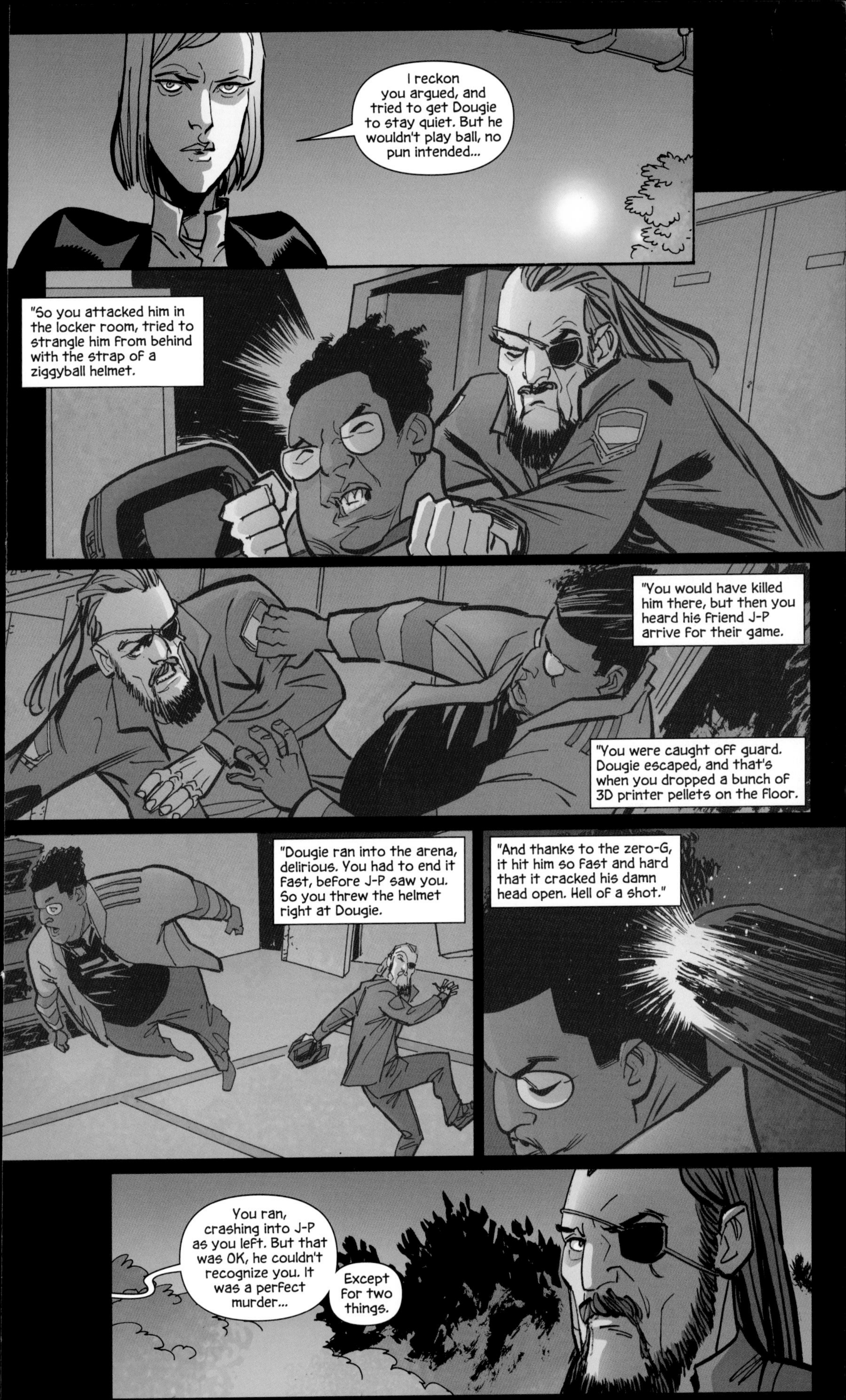

I reckon you argued, and tried to get Dougie to stay quiet. But he wouldn't play ball, no pun intended...
"So you attacked him in the locker room, tried to strangle him from behind with the strap of a ziggyball helmet.
"You would have killed him there, but then you heard his friend J-P arrive for their game.
"You were caught off guard. Dougie escaped, and that's when you dropped a bunch of 3D printer pellets on the floor.
"Dougie ran into the arena, delirious. You had to end it fast, before J-P saw you. So you threw the helmet right at Dougie.
"And thanks to the zero-G, it hit him so fast and hard that it cracked his damn head open. Hell of a shot."
You ran, crashing into J-P as you left. But that was OK, he couldn't recognize you. It was a perfect murder...
Except for two things.

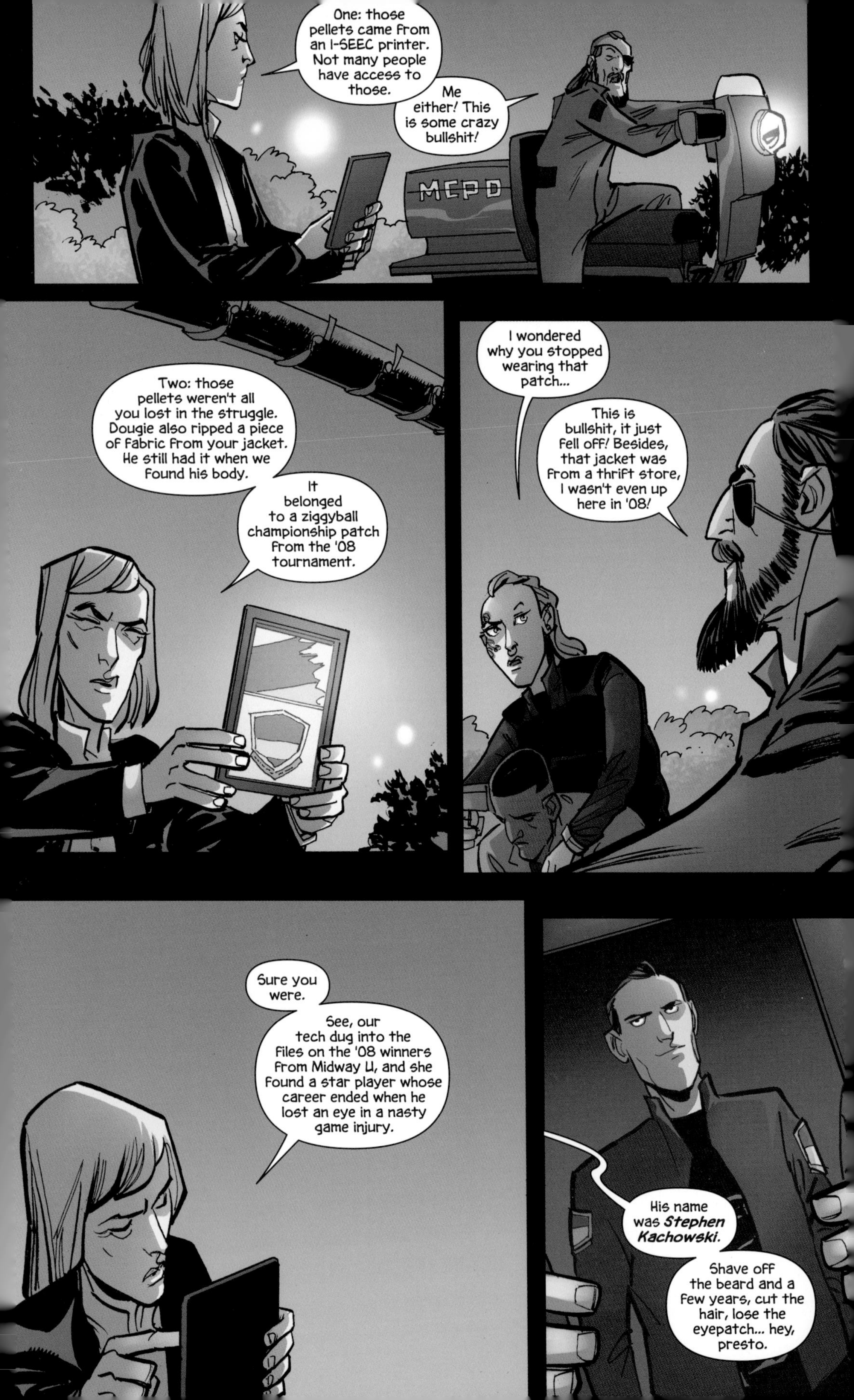
One: those pellets came from an I-SEEC printer. Not many people have access to those.
Me either! This is some crazy bullshit!
Two: those pellets weren't all you lost in the struggle. Dougie also ripped a piece of fabric from your jacket. He still had it when we found his body.
It belonged to a ziggyball championship patch from the '08 tournament.
I wondered why you stopped wearing that patch...
This is bullshit, it just fell off! Besides, that jacket was from a thrift store, I wasn't even up here in '08!
MCPD
Sure you were.
See, our tech dug into the files on the '08 winners from Midway U, and she found a star player whose career ended when he lost an eye in a nasty game injury.
His name was *Stephen Kachowski.*
Shave off the beard and a few years, cut the hair, lose the eyepatch... hey, presto.

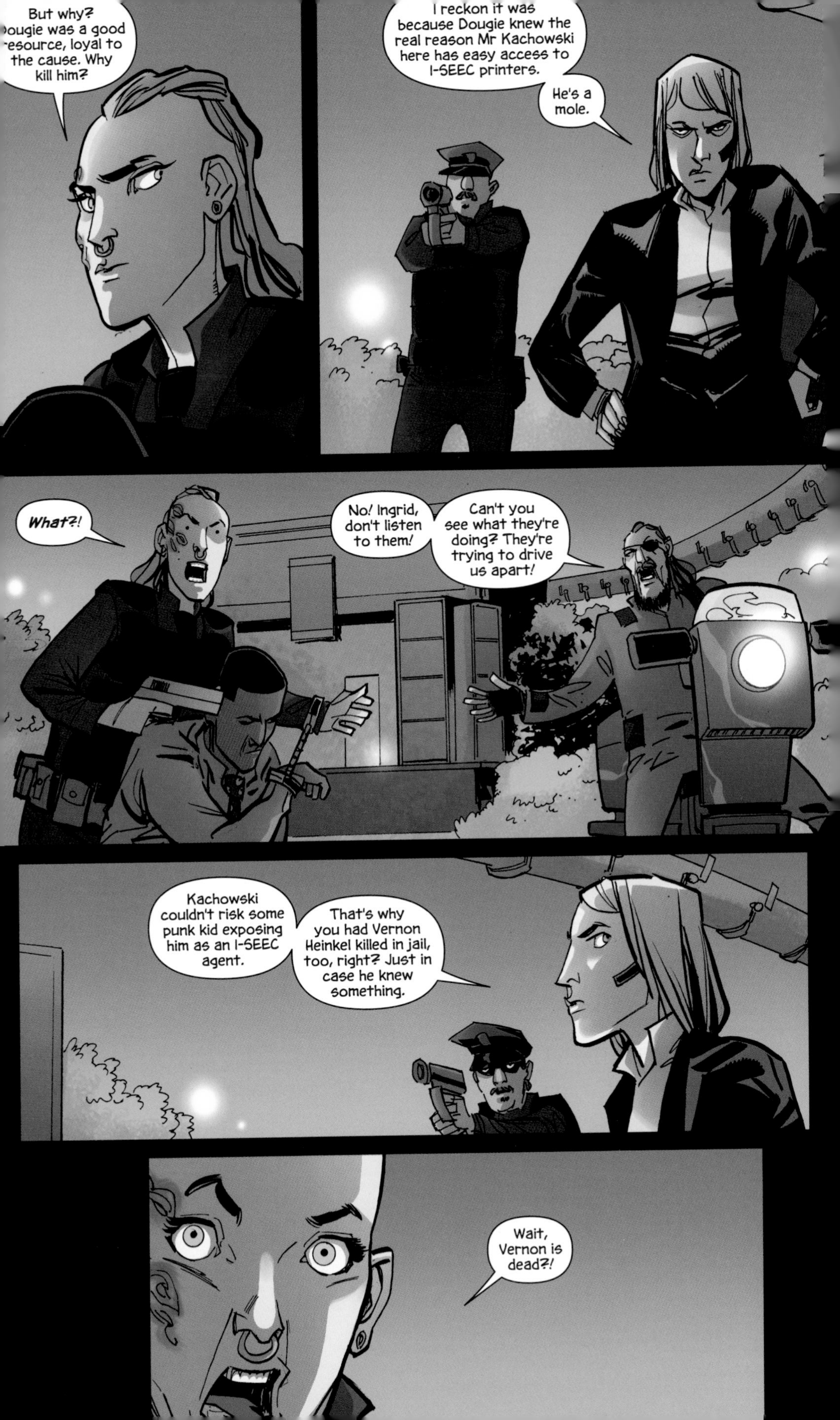
But why? Dougie was a good resource, loyal to the cause. Why kill him?
I reckon it was because Dougie knew the real reason Mr Kachowski here has easy access to I-SEEC printers.
He's a mole.
What?!
No! Ingrid, don't listen to them!
Can't you see what they're doing? They're trying to drive us apart!
Kachowski couldn't risk some punk kid exposing him as an I-SEEC agent.
That's why you had Vernon Heinkel killed in jail, too, right? Just in case he knew something.
Wait, Vernon is dead?!

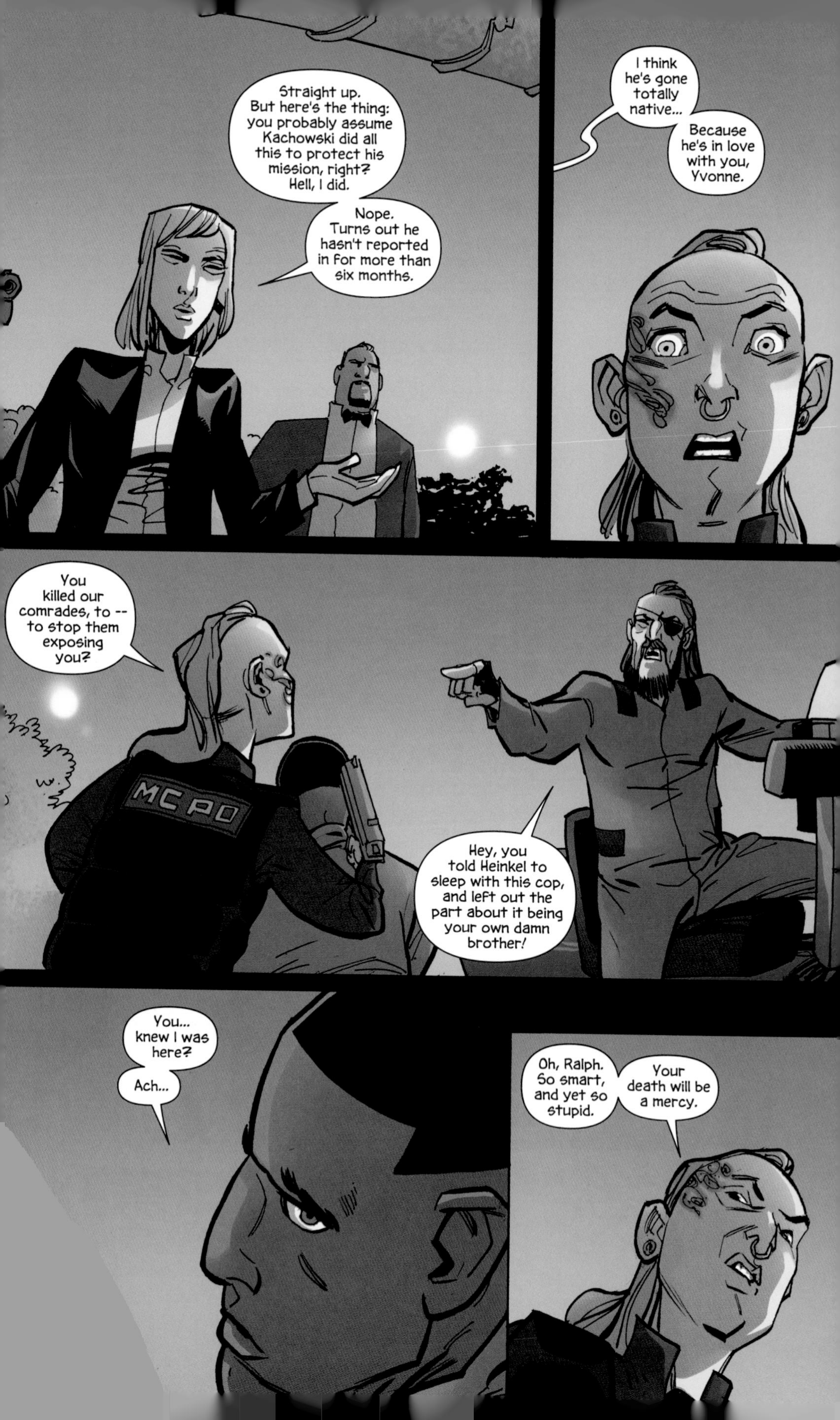
Straight up. But here's the thing: you probably assume Kachowski did all this to protect his mission, right? Hell, I did.
Nope. Turns out he hasn't reported in for more than six months.
I think he's gone totally native...
Because he's in love with you, Yvonne.
You killed our comrades, to -- to stop them exposing you?
MCPD
Hey, you told Heinkel to sleep with this cop, and left out the part about it being your own damn brother!
You... knew I was here?
Ach...
Oh, Ralph. So smart, and yet so stupid.
Your death will be a mercy.

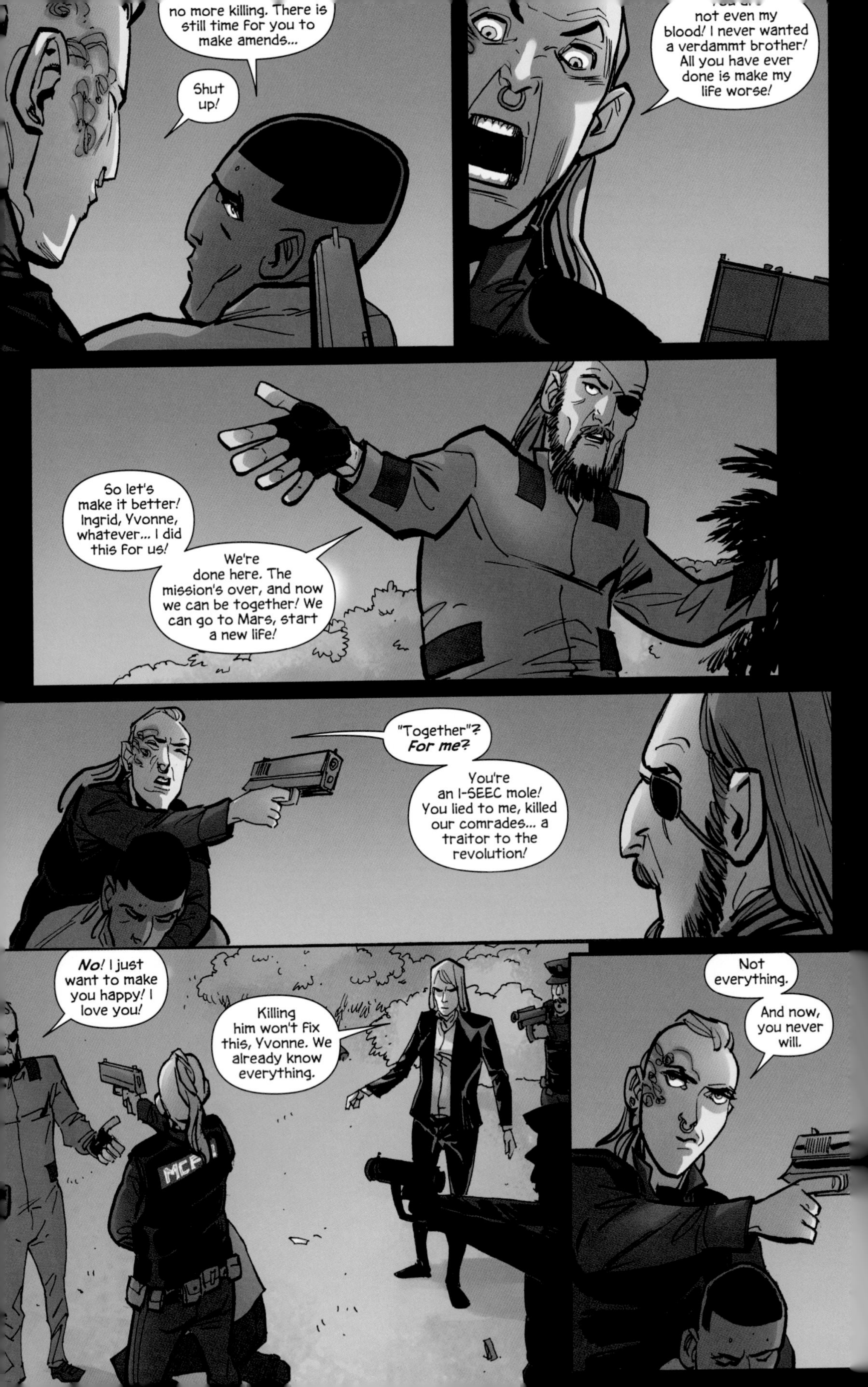
no more killing. There is still time for you to make amends...
Shut up!
not even my blood! I never wanted a verdammt brother! All you have ever done is make my life worse!
So let's make it better! Ingrid, Yvonne, whatever... I did this for us!
We're done here. The mission's over, and now we can be together! We can go to Mars, start a new life!
"Together"? *For me*?
You're an I-SEEC mole! You lied to me, killed our comrades... a traitor to the revolution!
No! I just want to make you happy! I love you!
Killing him won't fix this, Yvonne. We already know everything.
MCF 1
Not everything.
And now, you never will.

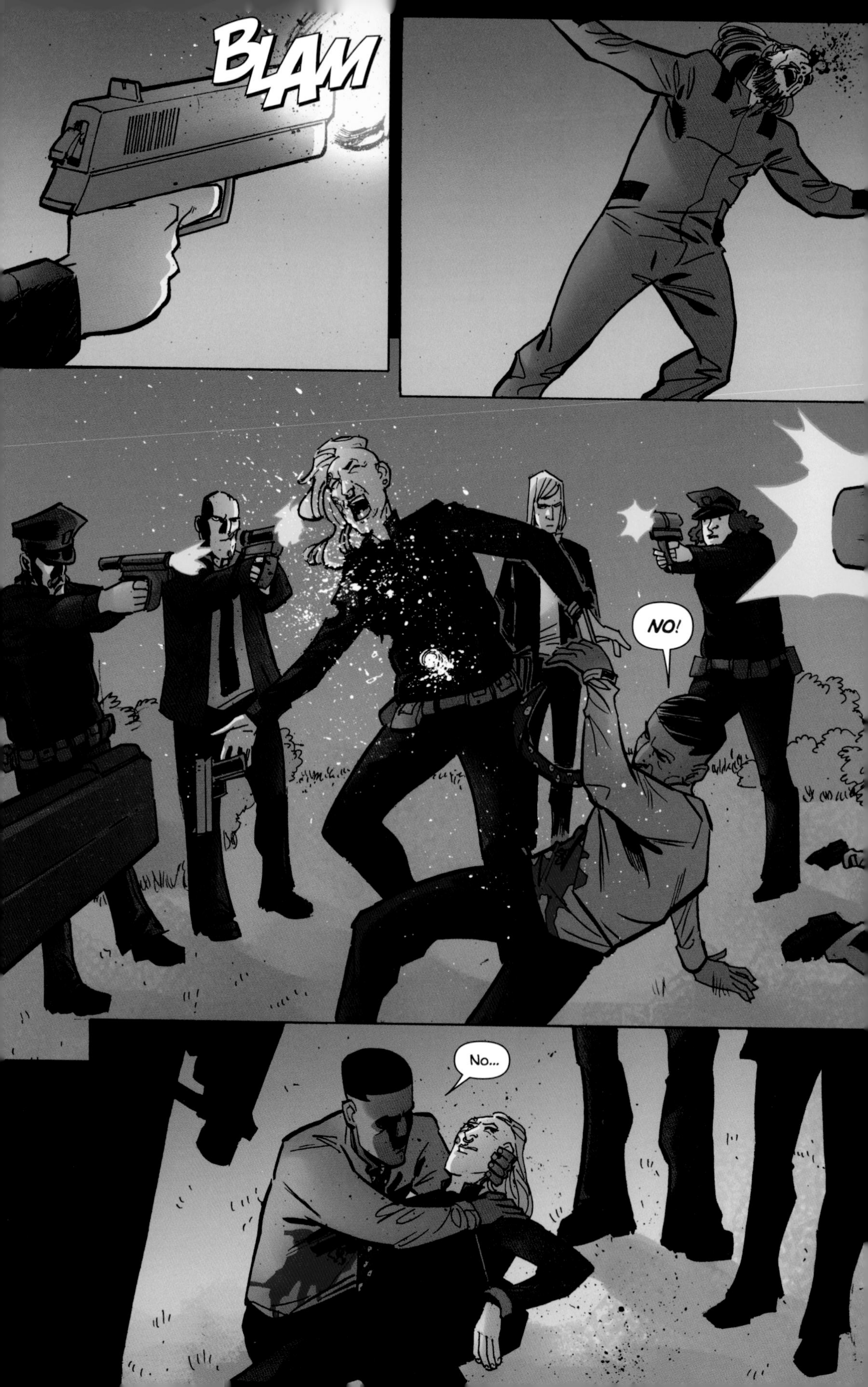
BLAM
NO!
No...

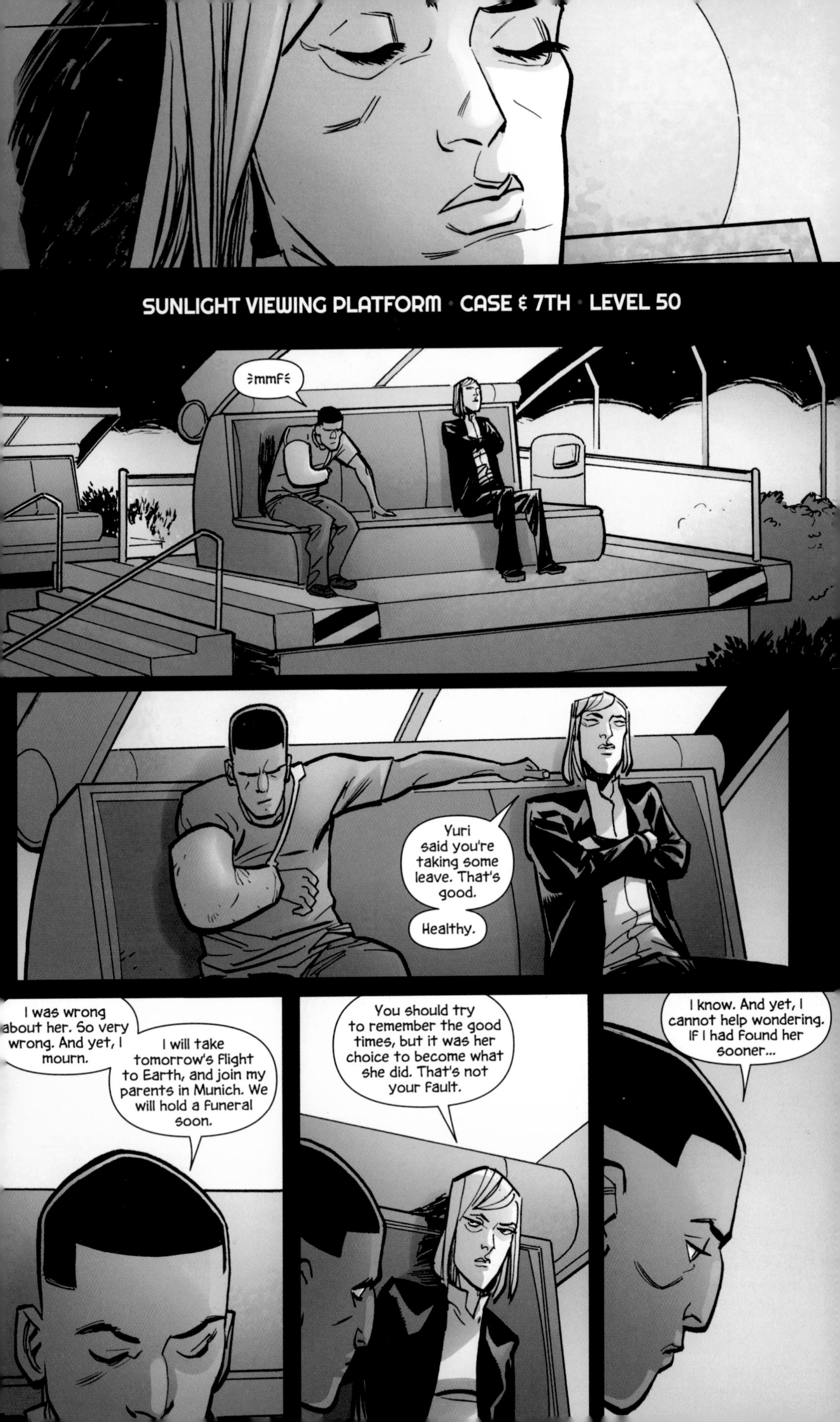
SUNLIGHT VIEWING PLATFORM • CASE & 7TH • LEVEL 50
mmf
Yuri said you're taking some leave. That's good.
Healthy.
I was wrong about her. So very wrong. And yet, I mourn.
I will take tomorrow's flight to Earth, and join my parents in Munich. We will hold a funeral soon.
You should try to remember the good times, but it was her choice to become what she did. That's not your fault.
I know. And yet, I cannot help wondering. If I had found her sooner...

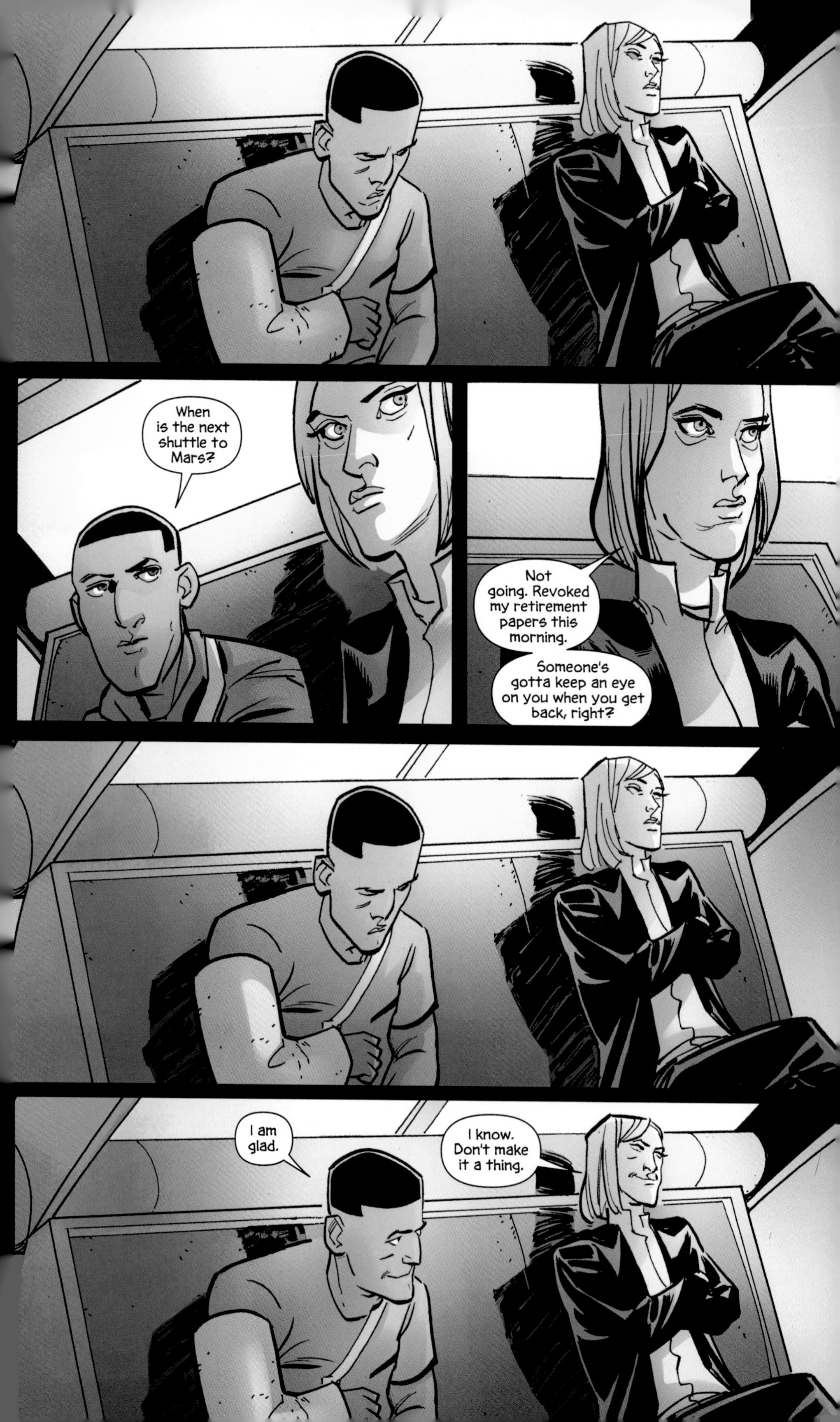
When is the next shuttle to Mars?
Not going. Revoked my retirement papers this morning.
Someone's gotta keep an eye on you when you get back, right?
I am glad.
I know. Don't make it a thing.

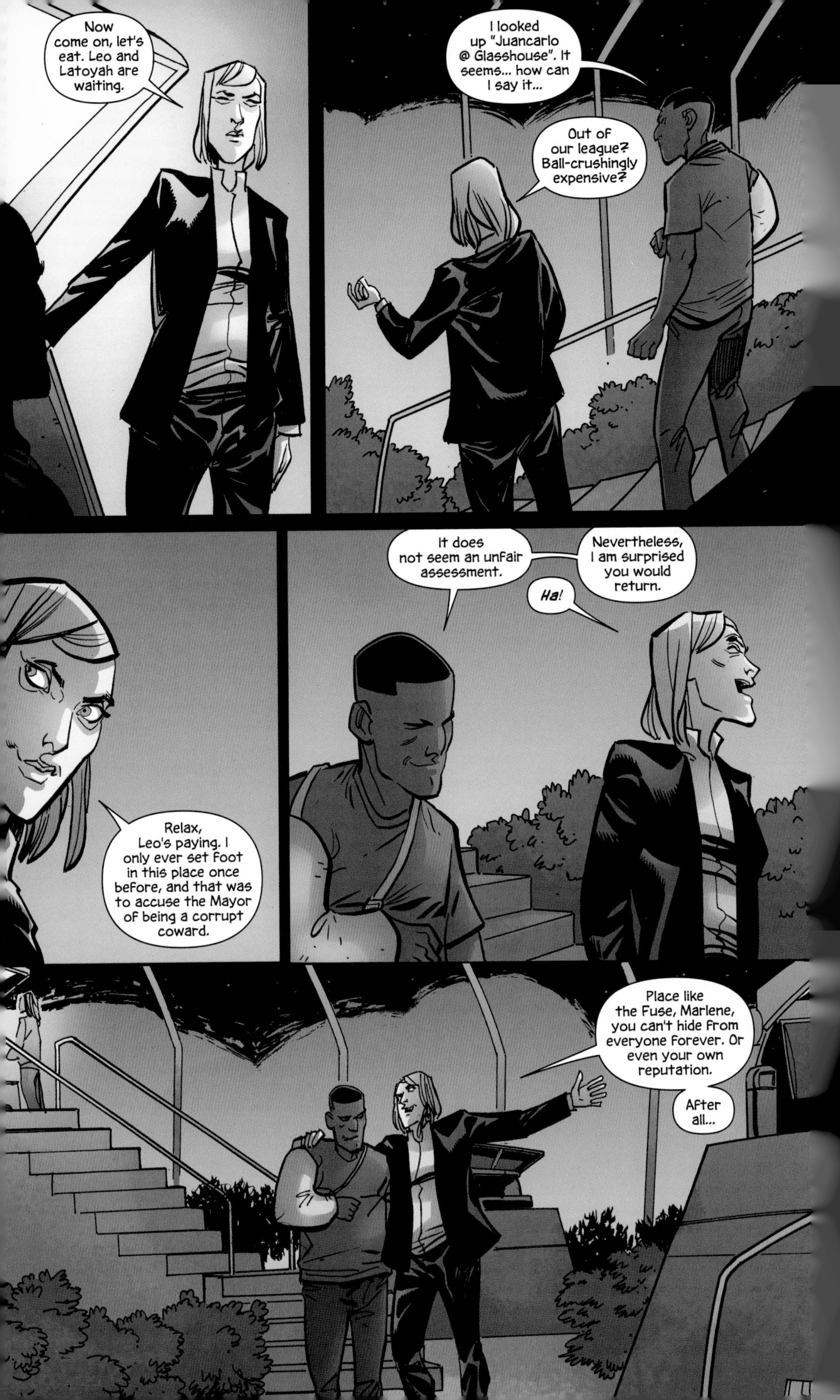

Now come on, let's eat. Leo and Latoyah are waiting.
I looked up "Juancarlo @ Glasshouse". It seems... how can I say it...
Out of our league? Ball-crushingly expensive?
Relax, Leo's paying. I only ever set foot in this place once before, and that was to accuse the Mayor of being a corrupt coward.
It does not seem an unfair assessment.
Ha!
Nevertheless, I am surprised you would return.
Place like the Fuse, Marlene, you can't hide from everyone forever. Or even your own reputation.
After all...

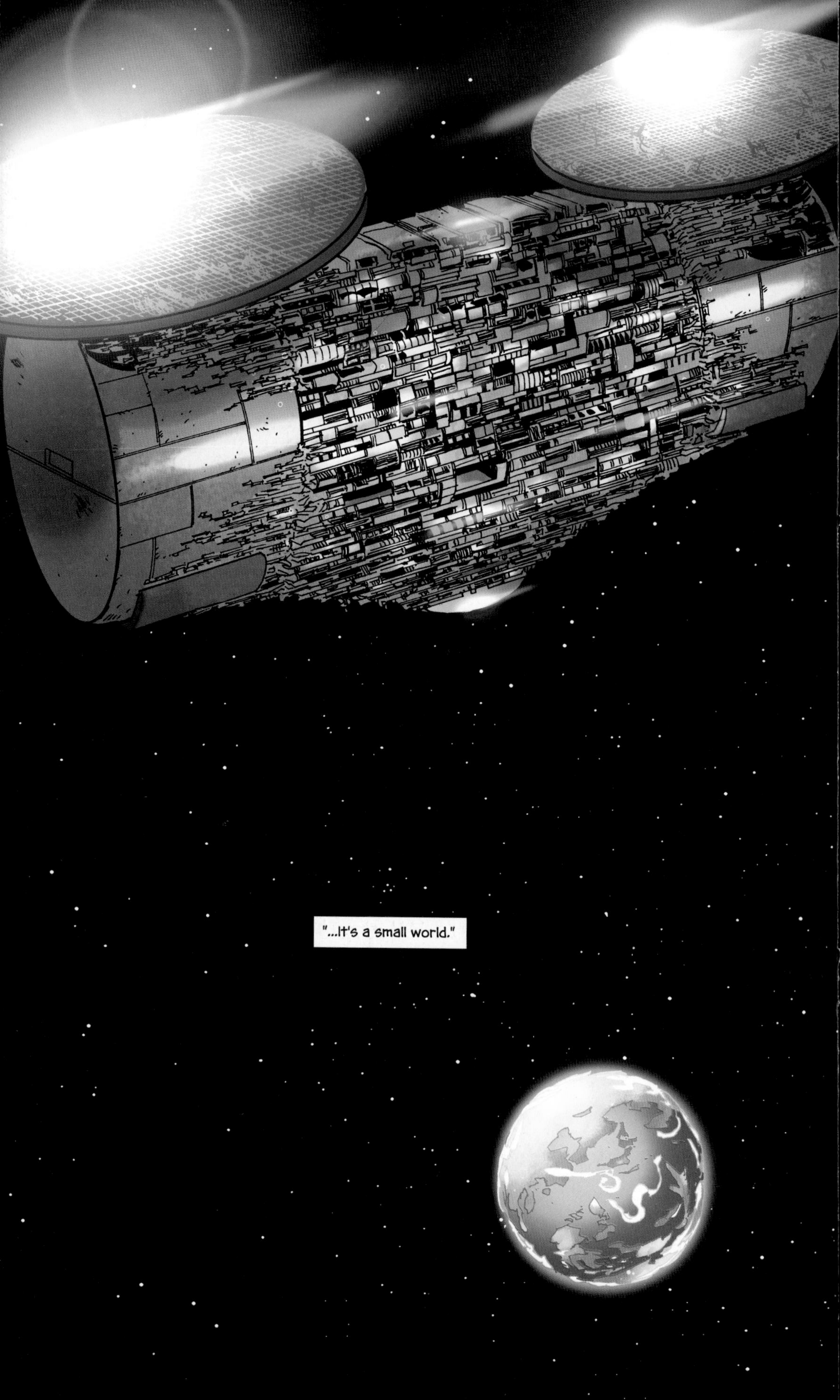
"...It's a small world."

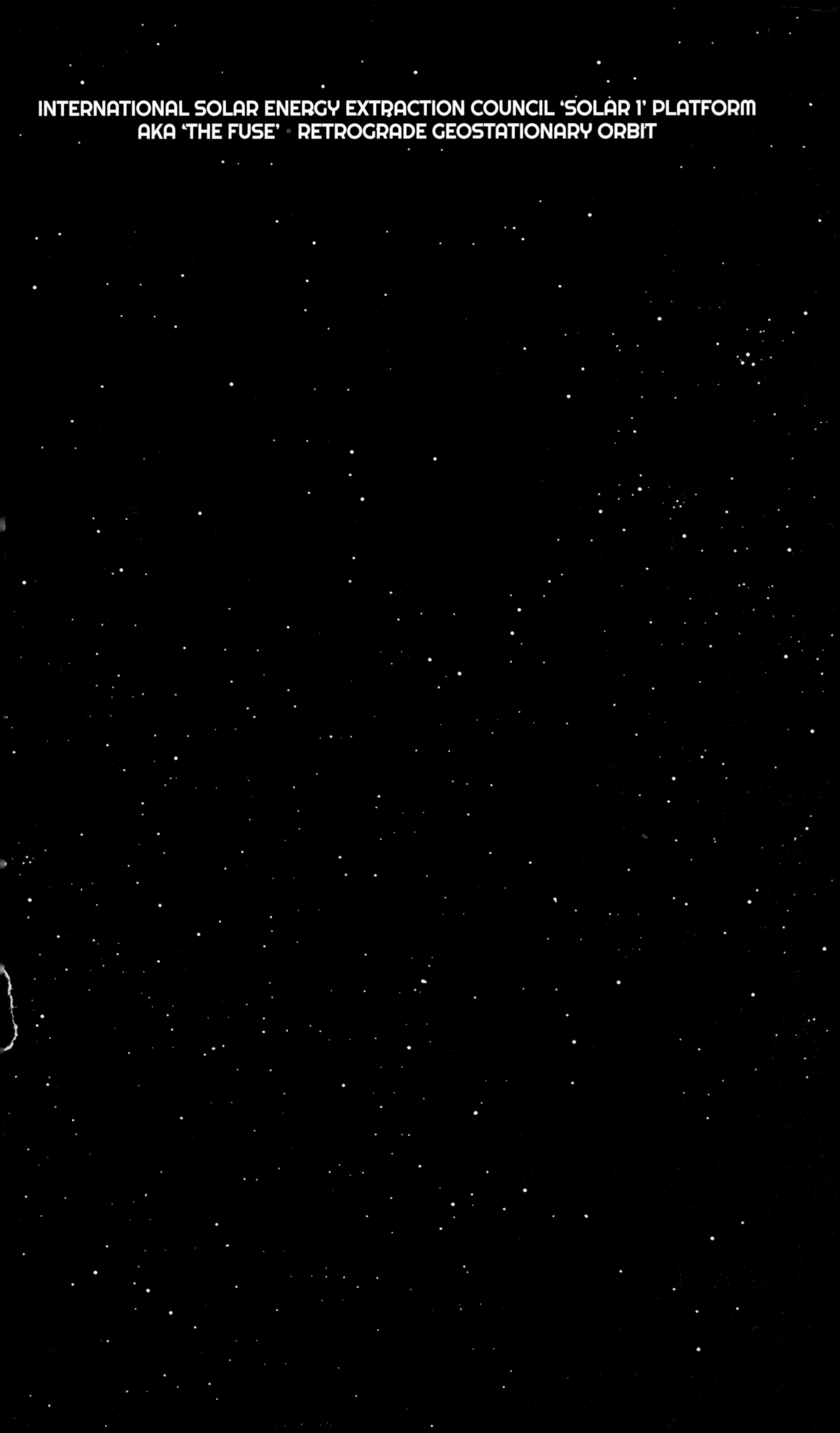
INTERNATIONAL SOLAR ENERGY EXTRACTION COUNCIL 'SOLAR 1' PLATFORM
AKA 'THE FUSE' • RETROGRADE GEOSTATIONARY ORBIT

ANTONY JOHNSTON

Antony is an award-winning, *New York Times* bestselling author of graphic novels, videogames, and books, with titles including *The Coldest City*, *Wasteland*, *Julius*, *Dead Space*, *Shadow of Mordor*, *The Assembly*, and more. He has adapted books by bestselling novelist Anthony Horowitz, collaborated with comics legend Alan Moore, and reinvented Marvel's flagship character *Wolverine* for manga. His titles have been translated throughout the world, and optioned for film and TV. He lives and works in England.

ANTONYJOHNSTON.COM · @ANTONYJOHNSTON

JUSTIN GREENWOOD

Justin is a Bay Area comic artist best known for his work on creator-owned series like *The Fuse*, *Stumptown*, *Stringers*, *Wasteland*, and *Resurrection*. When not drawing, he can be found running around the East Bay with his wife Melissa and their dual wildlings, tracking down unusual produce and the occasional card game with equal vigor.

JUSTINGREENWOODART.COM · @JKGREENWOOD_ART

SHARI CHANKHAMMA

Shari is an artist living in Thailand. Her own works include *The Sisters' Luck*, *The Clarence Principle*, and *Pavlov's Dream*. Her latest project is *Codename Baboushka*, also written by Antony, and her other colorist work includes *Kill Shakespeare* and *Sheltered*. In her spare time she likes to collect games on Steam with no hope of ever finishing them.

SHARII.COM · @SHARIHES

RYAN FERRIER

Ryan is a Canadian comic book letterer and writer. He has lettered comics for Image, Dark Horse, Oni Press, Black Mask, BOOM! Studios, Monkeybrain, Rosy Press, Ghostface Killah, El Rey Network, and many indie/small press creators. His writing credits include *D4VE*, *Curb Stomp*, *Kennel Block Blues*, *Hot Damn*, and *Sons of Anarchy*.

RYANFERRIER.COM · @RYANWRITER